Canada's Playwrights: A Biographical Guide

Edited by Don Rubin
and Alison Cranmer-Byng

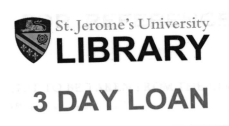
Canadian Theatre Review Publications
Toronto

Design: Martin Obern Graphics; Typesetting: Excalibur Publications; Printing: Garden
City Press.

ISBN 0-920-644-49-X (hardcover), 0-920-644-47-3 (softcover)

Table of Contents

Preface 6

Hrant Alianak 8
Mary Humphrey Baldridge 10
Jean Barbeau 12
Carol Bolt 14
B.A. Cameron (Cam Hubert) 17
Paddy Campbell 19
Roch Carrier 21
Tom Cone 23
Michael Cook 25
John Coulter 30
Robertson Davies 33
James DeFelice 38
Rex Deverell 39
Guy Dufresne 42
Marcel Dubé 45
David Fennario 50
Jacques Ferron 51
Charlotte Fielden 55
Timothy Findley 56
Larry Fineberg 58
David E. Freeman 60
David French 62
Ken Gass 65
Michel Garneau 67
Gratien Gélinas 71
Jean-Claude Germain 73
Joanna Glass 76
Tom Grainger 78
Warren Graves 80
Robert Gurik 83
Herschel Hardin 86
Lezley Havard 88
Tom Hendry 89
Ann Henry 92
John Herbert 94
Michael Hollingsworth 96
Patricia Joudry 98
Betty Lambert 101
Rod Langley 103
Jacques Languirand 105

John Lazarus 107

Roland Lepage 109

Antonine Maillet 111

Des McAnuff 113

Ken Mitchell 115

Mavor Moore 118

Arthur Murphy 122

John Murrell 123

James Nichol 125

Eric Nicol 127

John Palmer 129

Stephen Petch 131

Len Peterson 132

Sharon Pollock 134

Aviva Ravel 137

James Reaney 140

Gwen Pharis Ringwood 144

Erika Ritter 148

Sheldon Rosen 150

Lawrence Russell 152

George Ryga 154

Rick Salutin 158

Brian Shein 160

Beverley Simons 162

Bernard Slade 165

Ben Tarver 167

Yves Thériault 169

Michel Tremblay 172

Herman Voaden 177

Bryan Wade 181

George F. Walker 183

Jack Winter 185

Betty Jane Wylie 188

Larry Zacharko 190

Preface

This book is a starting point—and only a starting point—for information about Canada's playwrights. For too long, those in the theatre, those in education, those in the media, those who were simply curious suffered from what often seemed to be a plot to keep everyone in almost total ignorance about our writers. The most basic information on Canada's most significant playwrights was simply not available. With the publication of this book, that situation will hopefully start to change.

This project therefore began at *CTR* simply out of need. In each issue of the *Canadian Theatre Review,* a play was published and it seemed appropriate to include some background on the playwrights themselves. It was at that point we realized how little was available. In time, we began gathering material, though, and published biographical profiles. These proved to be both popular and useful. *CTR,* however, only publishes four plays a year and such information on only four playwrights a year didn't even begin to answer the need.

So—following the style we had already established in the journal —we set out to put together in book form a collection of this biographical-bibliographical material. Our initial estimate was to include 30 or so playwrights. Surely, we thought, there couldn't be more than 30 Canadian playwrights of significance. Surely there couldn't be more than 30 Canadian playwrights being produced across the country. A cursory look through some of our *Yearbooks,* however, showed us that there were indeed more—well over 150 playwrights in Canada whose work was being produced somewhere. How then to bring the number down, to select 30 for this book?

We discussed this problem with representatives of Canada's two major playwriting organizations—the Guild of Canadian Playwrights and Playwrights Canada (formerly the Playwrights Co-op). Each suggested that we simply include all their members. That brought the number down somewhat but we were still dealing with over a hundred writers. We realized as well that there were also a small number of important writers who were not members of either organization. And what of the Quebec writers working in French? Very few of them belonged to the Guild or the Co-op. We spoke with the editors of *Jeu,* Quebec's theatre journal and we spoke with officials of Montreal's *Centre d'essai des auteurs dramatiques* and they too provided us with names of writers who simply *had* to be included. By a process of elimination (advice, discussion, debate, common-sense, general knowledge and a fair amount of subjectivity) the list was finally brought down to 70 names. Some readers may, of course, quarrel about a few of the names included; others may question why certain names were left out. We can say simply that all the dramatists included are living as of this writing and have been or still are being produced in Canada.

As for gathering the information, it was, to say the least, time-consuming—three years. Our approach? Questionnaires, letters to each of the writers, phone calls, searches through books, magazines and newspaper articles, reconciliation of contradictory material, checks and doublechecks. As much as possible we were in touch with the writers themselves. Many of them seemed pleased that the material was being collected. Others were unable to provide anything beyond titles and approximate dates. Even there, some said, they were themselves guessing. A few provided us with nothing at all—some apologizing for lack of time; others expressing a distinct lack of interest in what we were doing. Nevertheless, our staff, researchers and student assistants plugged on. Hopefully, the results will have justified the long and often frustrating effort.

For all that, it *is* just a beginning. The information does have to be expanded and updated. There are other writers who should also be included. There are gaps in information even among those listed here. Though we believe this book to be the most comprehensive compilation of material on Canada's playwrights yet to reach print, we are painfully aware of how much more still needs to be done. It is inevitable as well that despite our best efforts some mistakes— either of omission or commission—have been made. We trust that such errors will be brought to our attention so that corrections can be made for future editions.

Finally, some words of thanks. First to those playwrights who did help us with time and material. Without their support and help this book would never have survived the research stages. Second, a special thanks to those in and around *CTR* who worked on this project for extended periods of time—Therese Beaupre, Ann-Marie Wierzbicki, Pete Boucher, Chris Blackburn, Mimi Mekler and my co-editor, Alison Cranmer-Byng. Surely none of them believed that we would ever reach the end. And now that we have reached it, it's clear that they were right. The need for information never does end. It just keeps beginning all over again.

Don Rubin
December 1980

Hrant Alianak

Born February 5, 1950 in Khartoum,
Sudan, of Armenian parents. Father in
sales business. Childhood and adolescence
spent in Khartoum. Excels in school,
completing high school requirements in
less time than usual. At the age of 15,
enrols in University of Khartoum to study
Business Administration for one year. In
1967 family moves to Montreal so that
Alianak can continue his studies at
McGill University. Spends one year in an
Economics program. Already fluent in
Arabic, English, and Armenian, gains
proficiency in French language. Family
moves to Toronto in 1968, and he enrols
in York University's night school as an
English major. In the next four years
holds various positions during the day
including mail delivery, factory and office
jobs. At this time he also develops an
interest in the theatre which leads to
technical and acting work with several
small theatre groups. Because his
experience in theatre is limited at this
point, he decides to study acting with Eli
Rill. After two years of training, he works
briefly in the professional theatre,
including a role in Theatre Passe
Muraille's production of *Dog in The
Manger*. Realizing that the hectic pace and
insecurity of an actor's life is not for him,
he tries his hand at playwriting. A
professional production of *Tantrums*, the
first play he writes, convinces him to
pursue writing as a career. After *Tantrums*
in 1972, Alianak decides that he would
like to direct all his own plays. As an
entry into the field, he directs five of his
short plays — *Western, The Violinist and
the Flower Girl, Mathematics, Brandy,* and
Christmas — at various small theatres in
the city, on a production budget of $10
per play. In 1973 he becomes a Canadian
citizen. In 1974, a volume of his plays is
published, and interest in his work is
shown in other parts of the country. In
1976, his play *The Blues* is produced in
Petrolia, Ottawa, and Vancouver. A
movie fan for most of his life, he begins
to describe his plays as "shorts" or "full-

length features." Single, he currently
makes his home in Toronto.

Stage Writing

Tantrums: full-length; written in 1972;
first published by the Playwrights Co-op
(Toronto) in 1972 and subsequently by
Fineglow Plays (Toronto) as part of a
collection of five plays by Alianak,
entitled *Return of The Big Five*, 1974; first
produced by Theatre Passe Muraille
(Toronto) under the direction of Louis
Del Grande, 1972.

Western: a short; written in 1972; first
published by the Playwrights Co-op
(Toronto) in 1973 and subsequently
included in a collection, *Now in Paperback
— Canadian Playwrights of the 1970's,*
published by the Playwrights Co-op
(Toronto) 1973; also included in *Return of
The Big Five* published by Fineglow Plays
(Toronto) in 1974; first produced by
Theatre Passe Muraille in September,
1972, under the direction of the author;
later that year the play is also produced
by Factory Theatre Lab (Toronto)
directed by the author.

The Violinist and the Flower Girl: a short; written in 1972; unpublished; first produced at Theatre Passe Muraille in 1972 under the direction of the author.

Mathematics: a short; written in 1972; first published by the Playwrights Co-op (Toronto) in 1973; subsequently published in four collections: *Now in Paperback — Canadian Playwrights of the 1970's,* Playwrights Co-op (Toronto), 1973; *Return of The Big Five,* Fineglow Plays (Toronto), 1974; *The Director in a Changing Theatre,* Mayfield Publishing Company (Palo Alto, California), 1976; *Transition I: Short Plays,* Commcept Publishing Ltd. (Vancouver), 1978; first produced by the Factory Theatre Lab in 1972 under the direction of the author.

Brandy: a short; written in 1973; first published by the Playwrights Co-op (Toronto) in 1973, and subsequently included in the collection, *Return of The Big Five,* published by Fineglow Plays (Toronto) in 1974; first produced by Theatre Passe Muraille in 1973, under the direction of the author.

Noah's Kiosk: full-length; written in 1973; unpublished; first produced by Theatre Passe Muraille, 1973, under the direction of the author.

Christmas: a short; written in 1973; first published by Fineglow Plays (Toronto) in the collection *Return of the Big Five*, 1974; first produced by Theatre Passe Muraille, 1973, and subsequently by Factory Theatre Lab, 1974, both productions under the direction of the author.

Mousetown: a short; written in 1974; unpublished; first produced at the Factory Theatre Lab, 1974, under the direction of the author.

Night: full-length feature; written in 1975; unpublished; first produced by Theatre Passe Muraille, 1975, under the direction of the author; remounted by Theatre Passe Muraille, 1979, also under the direction of the author.

Passion And Sin: a full-length feature; written in 1976; first published by the *Canadian Theatre Review*, 1978, (*CTR* 19); first produced by Toronto Free Theatre, 1976, under the direction of the author.

The Blues: full-length; written in 1976; unpublished; first produced at Theatre Passe Muraille in June 1976, later that year subsequent productions at Victoria Playhouse (Petrolia), and National Arts Centre (Ottawa); in 1977 produced at Vancouver Playhouse; all productions directed by the author.

Lucky Strike: full-length; written in 1978; unpublished; first produced by Factory Theatre Lab, 1978 under the direction of the author; subsequently presented by Factory at the Theatre of the Americas Festival, Washington D.C. and New York, 1979.

Stage Directing

Rail Tales (by Ray Canale, Rod Langley, and Aar-al-dean) — three short plays produced at Theatre Passe Muraille, 1974.

The Dumb Waiter (Harold Pinter) — 1974 production by Toronto Centre For The Arts.

Tony's Woman (Michael Sesito) — produced by Theatre Passe Muraille, 1975.

Four Little Girls (Pablo Picasso) — adapted by Hrant Alianak; produced at New Theatre (Toronto) in 1975.

The Ballad of Jack O'Diamonds (Phil Schreibman) — produced by the Victoria Playhouse (Petrolia), 1975.

Titus Andronicus (Shakespeare) — adapted by Hrant Alianak; produced at Theatre Passe Muraille (1975).

No! No! No! (Sharon Pollock) — produced at Theatre Passe Muraille, 1977.

I Love You, Baby Blue 2 (Paul Kelman and Hrant Alianak, based on an original idea by Paul Thompson) — produced by Theatre Passe Muraille, 1977.

Miscellaneous Writing

Kiss: a television "Microdrama"; produced with four other short plays under the collective title *Paranoid Fractions* by CBC Television in 1975; all five pieces directed by Hrant Alianak.

Lady In The Night: an opera; libretto by Hrant Alianak, music by Norm Symonds; unpublished; produced by Co-Opera Theatre and Toronto Free Theatre in 1977 written, directed, and produced by Hrant Alianak; 1978.

The Sacrifice: a short demonstration film, written, directed, and produced by Hrant Alianak; 1978

Secondary Sources

A short essay by Alianak included in *Transitions I: Short Plays*, Commcept 1978, pp. 243-244.

Mary Humphrey Baldridge

Born on March 6, 1937, in Edmonton, Alberta. Father a mechanic; mother a teacher. She attends the Banff School of Fine Arts for two years as an actress and two years as a writer, all four years on scholarships. Majoring in English at the University of Alberta, she has some of her poetry published in *The Fiddlehead* and also sells her first radio drama to CFAC Radio in Calgary while still in school. In 1958, she graduates with a B.A. and marries director Harold Baldridge. They move to New York City and spend the next 14 years in the United States. While there, she writes poetry and short stories, some of the latter being sold to CBC Radio and *The Montrealer*. In 1969, her first poetry collection, *Slide-Images*, is published.

She later tries her hand at writing short plays. One of her first, a one-act entitled, *Is This A Friendly Visit,* wins an Alberta Culture Award. She does not begin to concentrate on playwriting until her return to Alberta in 1974 when her husband becomes artistic director of Theatre Calgary. During that same year, she completes her first full-length play, *The Photographic Moment,* "while driving back and forth between Calgary and Banff." Over the next five years she writes several full-length short plays which are professionally produced

Vic LaVica

and/or published. During 1975, she helps to found Lunchbox Theatre and co-authors its first show. In addition, she continues writing poetry. In 1978, her second collection, *the loneliness of the poet housewife*, is published. She teaches playwriting at Mt. Royal College in Calgary where she currently makes her home. She is the mother of two children.

Stage Writing

The Photographic Moment: two acts; written in 1973-74; first published by Playwrights Co-op, 1975, now in its third printing; first produced by Theatre 3, Edmonton, 1974, under the direction of Mark Schoenberg; subsequently produced by Persephone Theatre (Saskatoon), 1978, under the direction of Howard Dallin; produced by Vancouver Community College in 1978 and the Firehall Theatre, Medicine Hat, in 1979; adapted for radio and broadcast nationally by CBC, Calgary, 1975; adapted for film (unproduced), 1976; produced on Australian radio, 1979.

Bride of the Gorilla: one act; written in 1974; first published by Playwrights Co-op, 1974; first produced by Factory Lab West (Calgary), 1974, under the direction of Brian Torpe.

Cry Wolf, Harry: one act; written in 1974; unpublished; first produced in workshop at the Banff Centre, 1976, directed by Shirley Tooke.

Harry and Friends: one-act monologue; written in 1975; unpublished; first produced in workshop at the Banff Centre in 1975 under the direction of Mel Tuck.

How the West Was Won or...: one-act melodrama "based on the discovery of the Banff Hot Springs"; written in 1975; unpublished; first produced by Bishop Carroll High School, Calgary, 1979, under the direction of Elizabeth Ripley.

The Lunchbox Revue: (co-author); one act; unpublished; written for and first produced by Calgary's Lunchbox Theatre to inaugurate its opening in 1975, under the direction of Bartley Bard.

Tonight at Calgary Theatre Hall!: two acts; written in 1975; unpublished; commission-ed and first produced by Theatre Calgary, 1975, in honour of Calgary's Centennial year, under the direction of Judy Armstrong; the production tours southern Alberta before playing at Theatre Calgary.

Canadian Skittish: one act; written in 1976; first published by Playwrights Co-op under the title **The Suicide Meet** in 1977; first produced by City Stage, Vancouver, 1977, under the direction of Ray Michal; subsequently produced at Lunchbox Theatre, Calgary, in 1977, under the direction of Bartley Bard; produced by Theatre 2000, Ottawa, in 1979, under the direction of Rick McNair.

The Mary Shelley Play: two acts; first published by Playwrights Co-op, 1979; first produced in workshop at Theatre 3, Edmonton (1977), under the direction of Mark Schoenberg; subsequently produced by Ryerson Polytechnical Institute, Toronto, in 1978; first full staging by Theatre Calgary, 1978, under the direction of Rick McNair.

An Act of War: long one act; written in 1978; unpublished; first produced in workshop at Northern Light Theatre, Edmonton, 1978, under the direction of Harold Baldridge.

The Old Colette: one act; one-woman show based on the life of Colette; written in 1978; unpublished; unproduced.

Miscellaneous

Slide-Images: a poetry collection; first published, 1969, by Retort Press, Woodstock, New York.

The Man Who Wanted To Be Like Nijinsky: 60-minute radio play; written in 1978; unpublished; unproduced.

the loneliness of the poet/housewife: poetry collection; first published by Fiddlehead Poetry Books, Fredericton, in 1978.

Jean Barbeau

Born February 10, 1945 in St. Romuald near Quebec City. He studies classics at the Seminary of Levis where he writes his first plays, *Cain et Babel* and *La Geôle*, which are produced by the seminary's drama group. He enrols as a student of literature and Spanish at Université de Laval. Although he leaves in 1968, he remains a member of Laval's Troupe de Treize until 1970 when he and his friends — Dorothy Berryman, Marc Legault, Claude Septembre and Claude Fleury — found Théâtre Quotidien in Montreal. That year the company produces several of his plays including *Le Chemin de Lacroix, Manon-Lastcall, Tripez-vous vous* and *Joualez-moi d'amour*. Between 1969 and 1970, he receives grants from the Canada Council which allow him to continue writing. During this time, he works in radio and writes short scripts for the Radio-Canada series *Atelier*. In 1972, he moves to Amos Abitibi where he writes *Une Brosse* which is produced by Théâtre du Trident in 1975 and in English at the Banff Centre the same year. Although living in relative isolation in the countryside, he remains interested in the political and cultural situation in the province. For him, living outside the cities means "that I have a perspective now which allows me to write about Quebec society in a much more integrated way." He continues to make his home today in Amos Abitibi living there with his wife, Monique (a teacher) and their son, François.

Stage Writing

Cain et Babel: one-act; written in 1965; unpublished; first produced by Levis Seminary drama group.

La Geôle: one-act; written in 1967; unpublished; first produced by Levis Seminary drama group.

Et cetera: one-act; written in 1968; unpublished; first produced by Troupe de Treize de l'Université Laval, 1968.

Les Temps tranquilles: one-act; written in 1968; unpublished; first produced by Troupe de Treize de l'Université Laval, 1968.

Le Frame all-dress: one-act; written in 1969; unpublished; first produced by Troupe de Treize de l'Université Laval, 1969.

Ben-Ur ou La Vie inquietante de Joseph Benoit Urbain Theberge: full-length; written in 1970; first published by Leméac, Montreal, 1971; first produced by Théâtre Populaire du Québec, Montreal, 1970, under the direction of Albert Millaire.

Manon Lastcall: one-act; written in 1970; original version unpublished; first produced at the Conservatoire de Montréal under the direction of Yvon Thiboutot; adapted for radio by Michel Gariepy; subsequently produced on television by Radio-Canada in an adaptation by Andre Dionne and Yvon Thiboutot; subsequent adaptation by Jean Barbeau; published by Leméac, 1972, in same volume as *Joualez-moi d'amour*.

Joualez-moi d'amour: one-act; written in 1970; first published by Leméac, 1972, in same edition as *Manon Lastcall*; first produced by Théâtre Quotidien, 1970.

Goglu: one-act; written in 1970; first published by Leméac, 1971, in same volume as *Le Chemin de Lacroix*; subsequently published in English in *Canadian Theatre Review*, summer 1976 (*CTR* 11), in a translation by John Van Burek; first produced by Théâtre Quotidien, 1970; subsequently produced in English with *Solange* by Pleiade Theatre Company at St. Nicholas Street Theatre, Toronto, 1976, under the direction of John Van Burek.

Le Chemin de Lacroix: two-acts; written in 1971; first published by Leméac 1971, in same volume as *Goglu*; subsequently published in English by Playwrights Co-op, 1972, under the title *The Street of Lacross,* first produced by Théâtre Quotidien, 1970, under the direction of the author; subsequently produced in English at the Poor Alex Theatre, Toronto, 1972.

0-71: full-length; written in 1971; unpublished; first produced by Théâtre du Trident, Quebec City, 1971, under the direction of Jean-Guy Solange.

L'Herbe: full-length; written in 1971; unpublished; first produced by Théâtre Quotidien, 1971, under the direction of the author; subsequent production by Théâtre de la Maintenance, 1973.

Le Chant du sink: two-act comedy; written in 1971; first published by Leméac, 1973; first produced by Théâtre Populaire du Québec, Montreal, 1972, under the direction of Jean-Guy Sabourin, Jean-Louis Martel and Fernand Quirion.

La Coupe stainless: two parts; written in 1972; first published by Leméac, 1974, in the same volume as *Solange*; first produced by Polygone, 1973, under the direction of Pierre Fortin.

Solange: a monologue; written in 1972; first published by Leméac, 1974, in the same volume as *La Coupe stainless;* subsequently published in English with *Goglu* in *Canadian Theatre Review*, summer 1976 (*CTR* 11), in a translation by John Van Burek; first produced at Théâtre Chântaueuil, 1971; subsequently produced in English with *Goglu* by Pleiade Theatre Company, Toronto, 1976, under the direction of John Van Burek.

Citrouille: two acts; written in 1973; first published by Leméac, 1974; first produced by Théâtre du Nouveau Monde, Montreal, under the direction of Jean-Louis Roux.

Une Brosse: two acts; written in 1974; first published by Leméac, 1975; subsequently published in English under the title *A Binge*, with translation by John Van Burek; first produced by Théâtre du Trident, 1975, under the direction of Jean-Pierre Ronfard.

Dites-le avec des fleurs: two-part comedy; written with Marcel Dubé in 1975; first published by Leméac, 1976.

Emile et une nuit: one-act; written in 1978; first published by Leméac, 1979; first produced by Théâtre du Rideau Vert, Montreal, 1979, under the direction of Jean-Joseph Tremblay.

Carol Bolt

Born Carol Johnson on August 25, 1941, in Winnipeg. Her father is a miner and a logger. The family lives in various places while she is growing up including McReary in Manitoba, Sudbury in Ontario, and Hudson Hope in British Columbia. In the late 50's she attends the University of British Columbia where she studies, among other things, playwriting. After graduating with a B.A. in 1961, she works briefly in Vancouver then moves to Britain for a year. On her return to Canada, she settles in Montreal. There, in 1963, she and a few friends start a small theatre where she works as stage manager and director until the theatre is closed because it doesn't meet fire regulations. She moves to Toronto where she meets David Bolt, an actor whom she eventually marries. She completes her first play, *Daganawida*, in 1970 and it is produced at Toronto Workshop Productions that year. Her second play, *Buffalo Jump*, premieres at Regina's Globe Theatre and is subsequently produced by Toronto's Theatre Passe Muraille. Her next seven scripts — several of them children's plays — receive productions at small theatres across the country. Her first major success is *Red Emma — Queen of the Anarchists*, a play about the early life of the revolutionary Emma Goldman, which is premiered by Toronto Free Theatre. The play is subsequently produced by the Manitoba Theatre Centre but its reception in Winnipeg is poor because many critics object to the play's subject matter. The play is, nonetheless, adapted for television and produced on CBC. Her next major play, *Shelter*, is premiered by Toronto's Firehall Theatre in 1974 and subsequently produced at the St. Lawrence Centre as well as at several regional theatres across the country. After lukewarm receptions for her next plays — *Bethune* and *Desperados* — a thriller, *One Night Stand*, proves to be extremely popular. Following its premiere at Toronto's Tarragon Theatre, it is produced by Theatre New Brunswick, Vancouver's Arts Club Theatre and Festival Lennoxville among others. As a television

film (produced by Allan King and the CBC), it receives three Canadian Film Awards in 1978. That same year, she is appointed writer-in-residence at the University of Toronto. A founding member of the Playwrights Co-op, she currently lives in Toronto with her husband and son.

Stage Writing

Daganawida: full-length play written in 1970; unpublished; first produced by Toronto Workshop Productions, 1970, under the direction of George Luscombe.

Buffalo Jump: two acts; written in 1970; first published by Playwrights Co-op, Toronto, in 1972; subsequently published by Playwrights Co-op, along with *Gabe* and *Red Emma* in *Playwrights in Profile* series, 1976; first produced by Globe Theatre, Regina, under the title *Next Year Country*, 1971, under the direction of Ken Kramer; subsequently produced by Theatre Passe Muraille, Toronto, 1972, under the direction of Paul Thompson.

Cyclone Jack: one-act children's play; written in 1971; first published by Playwrights Co-op, 1972; subsequently published by Simon and Pierre, Toronto, in *A Collection of Canadian Plays, Volume IV*, in 1975; first produced by Young People's Theatre, Toronto, 1972, under the direction of Timothy Bond with music by Paul Vigna; subsequently taken on a tour of Ontario; produced by Alberta Theatre Projects, 1973, under the direction of Douglas Riske; re-mounted by Young People's Theatre, 1976, for a tour of Ontario under the direction of Greg F. Rogers; adapted for television and broadcast by CBC, 1977.

Gabe: two acts; written in 1972; first published by Playwrights Co-op in *Playwrights in Profile* series, 1976; first produced by Algoma Youth Theatre, 1972; subsequently produced by Toronto Free Theatre, 1973, under the direction of Robert Handforth; produced by Manitoba Theatre Workshop, 1976, under the direction of Clarke Rogers.

My Best Friend is Twelve Feet High: one-act children's play; written in 1971; first published by Playwrights Co-op in 1972 in the same volume as *Tangleflags*; first produced by Young People's Theatre, 1972, under the direction of Ray Whelan with music by Jane Vasey; subsequently taken on a tour of Ontario; produced by Open Circle Theatre, Toronto, 1973, under the direction of Ray Whelan; produced by Huron Country Playhouse, Grand Bend, Ontario, 1976, under the direction of James Murphy.

Bluebird (based on Marie d'Aulnoy's story): narration for a Black Box production; written in 1972; unpublished; first produced by Black Box Theatre of Toronto and performed at St. Lawrence Centre, 1973; at the Nova Scotia Festival, 1974; at the National Arts Centre, Ottawa, 1975.

Pauline (based on the poems of Pauline Johnson): written in 1972; unpublished; first produced by Theatre Passe Muraille, 1973, under the direction of Paul Thompson.

Tangleflags: one-act children's play; written in 1972; first published by Playwrights Co-op in 1972 in the same volume as *My Best Friend is Twelve Feet High*; subsequently

published in separate volume by Playwrights Co-op in 1974; first produced by Young People's Theatre, 1974, under the direction of Ray Whelan; subsequently taken on a tour of Ontario; produced by St. Louis Community College, Missouri, 1977.

Maurice: one-act children's play; written in 1973; first published by *Performing Arts Magazine*, Winter, 1974; subsequently published by Playwrights Co-op, 1975; published by Gage, Toronto, in *Cues and Entrances, Canadian One-Act Plays*, 1977; first produced by Young People's Theatre and Prologue to the Performing Arts, 1974, under the direction of Timothy Bond; subsequently taken on a tour of Ontario.

Red Emma—Queen of the Anarchists: two acts; written in 1974; first published by Playwrights Co-op in 1974; subsequently published by Playwrights Co-op in *Playwrights in Profile* series, 1976; first produced by Toronto Free Theatre, 1974, under the direction of Martin Kinch; subsequently produced by Manitoba Theatre Centre, 1975, under the direction of Edward Gilbert; subsequently adapted for television and broadcast by CBC for *Performance*, 1976.

Shelter: three acts; written in 1974; first published by Playwrights Co-op, 1975; first produced jointly by University Alumnae Dramatic Club and Young People's Theatre; subsequently produced by Theatre London, 1975, under the direction of Eric Steiner; produced by Toronto Arts Productions at the St. Lawrence Centre, Toronto, 1975, under the direction of Eric Steiner; produced by Globe Theatre, Regina, 1975, under the direction of James Brewer.

Finding Bumble: a children's play; written in 1975; unpublished; first produced by Young People's Theatre, 1975, under the direction of Timothy Bond; subsequently taken on a tour of Ontario.

Bethune (Norman Bethune: On Board the S.S. Empress of Asia): written in 1975; unpublished; first produced by Muskoka Summer Theatre, Gravenhurst, Ontario, 1976, under the direction of Michael Ayoub.

Okey Doke: written in 1975; unpublished; commissioned and first produced by Queen's University Drama Department, Kingston, Ontario, 1976, under the direction of Bernard Burkom.

Desperados: full-length play; written in 1976; unpublished; first produced by Toronto Free Theatre, 1977, under the direction of Martin Kinch.

One Night Stand: full-length thriller; written in 1976; published by Playwrights Co-op, 1977; first produced by Tarragon Theatre, Toronto, 1977, under the direction of Eric Steiner; subsequently produced by Theatre New Brunswick, 1977, under the direction of Timothy Bond; produced by Arts Club Theatre, Vancouver, 1977, under the direction of Kathryn Shaw; produced by Festival Lennoxville, Quebec, 1978; under the direction of Richard Ouzounian; subsequently adapted as a television film and produced by Allan King and the CBC, 1977; recipient of three Canadian Film Awards, 1978.

TV Lounge: written in 1976; unpublished; first produced by Redlight Theatre, Toronto, 1977, under the direction of Steven Whistance-Smith.

Radio Writing

Guy and Jack: written in 1969; first produced by CBC, Regina, for *Saskatchewan Writers*, 1970, for regional broadcast.

Fast Forward: written in 1975; first produced by CBC for *Stage* series, 1976, for national broadcast.

Miscellaneous

Valerie: a television script; written in 1970; produced by CBC for *To See Ourselves*, 1971.

A Nice Girl Like You: television episode; written in 1974; produced by CBC for *Collaborators*, 1974.

Distance: a television script; written in 1973; produced by Educational Television in Ontario for *True North*, 1974.

Fidelity: a film script; written in 1975; produced by Allan King Associates.

B.A. Cameron (Cam Hubert)

Born Barbara Ann Cameron in 1938 in Nanaimo, British Columbia. Immediate relatives on both sides of her family are coal miners. As a child she develops a great love for story-telling and completes her first novel when she is 12. She leaves high school after Grade 12 — her last formal education — and marries Jacques Hubert. She takes her husband's surname, but decides to keep a shortened version of her maiden name, Cam, as her first name. She and her husband have three children of their own and care for over two dozen other foster children over a period of years. Her writing career comes to a standstill while she raises her various families. She resumes her writing in the 60's and completes a book of Indian poems entitled *Windigo*. Her interest in Indians is not merely literary: she founds Tillicum Theatre for native youth and her first play, *The Twin Sinks of Allan Sammy*, the story of an Indian's struggle to make it in the city, is premiered by the theatre in 1973. Her next two plays, *We're All Here Except Mike Casey's Horse* and *Echoes of Other Things*, are workshopped by the New Play Centre in Vancouver. An ardent feminist, she begins to deal with the lives and issues of women in her work. *Rites of Passage*, which examines the relationship of three generations of women, wins the New Play Centre Women's Playwriting Competition and is subsequently produced in Vancouver and in Toronto. Her next play, *The Trouble With the Women's Movement Is It Has No Sense of Humour At All*, takes a satiric look at feminist organizations while her first television script, *A Matter of Choice*, explores the issue of rape. The latter script is produced by CBC in 1977, the same year that her film script, *Dreamspeaker*, is aired. Both productions receive much acclaim, and *Dreamspeaker* wins six Etrog Film Awards including one for the script. Impressed by her explorations of social and familial themes, CBC broadcasts two more of her scripts, *They're Drying Up the Streets* (about drugs) and *The Home-coming*, in 1978. *Dreamspeaker* is released

as a novel that same year, along with another prose work, *Tem Eyos Ki and the Land Claims Question*. After divorcing her husband, she reverts back to her maiden name, B.A. Cameron, despite the fact that all her previous writing is under her married name. Still a resident of Nanaimo, she continues to write about social issues in both her prose and drama. Her major frustration — "there are no windmills in Canada to tilt."

Stage Writing

The Twin Sinks of Allan Sammy: one act; written in 1973; first published by Playwrights Co-op, Toronto 1973; subsequently published by Playwrights Co-op in *Five Canadian Plays*, 1978; first produced by Tillicum Theatre, British Columbia, 1973, under the direction of Jack Messinger.

We're All Here Except Mike Casey's Horse: two acts; written in 1973; first published by Playwrights Co-op, 1974; first workshopped by New Play Centre, Vancouver, 1975, under the direction of Pamela Hawthorn.

Echoes of Other Things: three acts; written in 1974; unpublished; first workshopped by New Play Centre, 1975, under the direction of Doris Chillcott.

Rites of Passage: full-length play; written in 1975; unpublished; first produced by New Play Centre, 1975, under the direction of Pamela Hawthorn; subsequently produced by The Great Canadian Theatre Company, Ottawa, 1978, under the direction of Svetlana Zylin; winner of New Play Centre's Playwriting Competition, 1975.

The Trouble With the Women's Movement Is It Has No Sense of Humour At All: one act; written in 1976; unpublished; first produced in West Vancouver, 1976.

Miscellaneous

Windigo: book of Indian poems; written in 1967; unpublished; winner of British Columbia Centennial Writing Competition; produced as a "dramatic event" by John Juliani at York University, 1974.

Dreamspeaker: film script; written in 1977; first produced by CBC-TV, 1977, under the direction of Claude Jutra; winner of six Etrog Awards including one for script; re-written as a novel; first published by Clarke Irwin in *Dreamspeaker and Tem Eyos Ki and the Land Claims Question*, 1978.

A Matter of Choice: television script; written in 1977; first produced by CBC-TV, 1977.

The Homecoming: television script; written in 1979; first produced by CBC-TV, 1979, under the direction of Gilles Carle.

They're Drying Up the Streets: television script; written in 1979; first produced by CBC-TV, 1979, under the direction of Robin Spry; winner of an ACTRA award in 1979.

Tem Eyos Ki and the Land Claims Question: novella; written in 1977; first published by Clarke Irwin in *Dreamspeaker and Tem Eyos Ki and the Land Claims Question*, 1978.

Paddy Campbell

Born on August 7, 1944, in Lancashire, England. Her father is a salesman. After moving to Canada with her family, she works at a number of jobs: as a secretary ("fired because I couldn't type"), a bank clerk ("fired because I couldn't balance"), and a puppeteer ("terminated by mutual agreement"). She becomes interested in the theatre and in the 60's works as an actress in radio plays and commercials in Vancouver, Edmonton and Regina. She also does a bit of choreography and tries her hand at design with Calgary's Arts Centre Company, a new group run by Douglas Riske. In 1967, she begins to write children's plays for the company and five of them are produced by the group that season. By 1970, when she leaves Calgary to spend a year in England, the company has done 10 of her works. On her return, she continues to write plays for children as well as for adults. Most of her work is done for and by Calgary's Alberta Theatre Projects, again under the direction of Douglas Riske. Between 1972 and 1974, she also teaches acting and educational drama at the University of Calgary. In 1974, she writes her most successful play to date, a musical called *Hoarse Muse* with William Skolnik. The show is first done in a school version and is then rewritten for Alberta Theatre Projects where it breaks all box office records. A founding member and national vice-chairman of the Guild of Canadian Playwrights as well as a regional representative for Playwrights Co-op, she and her husband currently live in Calgary. She also writes poetry which is "as yet unseen by other human eyes."

Vic LaVica

Stage Writing

The Enchanted Box: 45-minute children's play; written in 1967; unpublished; first produced by Arts Centre Company, Calgary, 1967, under the direction of Douglas Riske.

Maggie's Surprise: 45-minute "participation play designed for very young children aged 5-7 years"; unpublished; first produced by the Arts Centre Company, 1967, under the direction of Douglas Riske; subsequently produced by Holiday Theatre, Vancouver, 1968.

Spirit of the Mountain: 45-minute "participation play for children, based on Indian legend of the Thunderbird"; written in 1967; unpublished; first produced by the Arts Centre Company, 1967, under the direction of Douglas Riske.

Surprise II: 45-minute children's play "dependent on known space technology of the time"; written in 1967; unpublished; first produced by Arts Centre Company, 1967, directed by Douglas Riske; subsequently produced by Holiday Theatre, Vancouver, 1969, and Unicorn Theatre, London, England.

Buckskin and Chapperos: "science-fiction western" for children; written in 1968; unpublished; first produced by Arts Centre Company, 1968, under the direction of Douglas Riske; subsequently produced by the Edmonton Theatre for Children, 1970;

adapted as 30-minute television script, 1975; broadcast nationally by CBC, 1976.

Chinook: 45-minute "fantasy for children based on Canadian Indian legends"; written in 1968; first published by Playwrights Co-op, Toronto, in 1973; subsequently published by Playwrights Co-op in 1977 in the same volume as *Too Many Kings*; first produced by Arts Centre Company, 1968, directed by Douglas Riske; subsequently produced by Holiday Theatre, Vancouver, 1970; Citadel-on-Wheels (Edmonton), 1977; the Globe Theatre, Regina, 1979.

Ships and Sealing Wax: 60-minute play for children; written in 1968; unpublished; first produced by Arts Centre Company, 1967, under the direction of Douglas Riske; subsequently produced by Edmonton Theatre for Children, 1969.

Ariel's Promise: 45-minute play for children "written with three separate endings to be used depending on the participation of the audience"; written in 1969; first produced by Arts Centre Company, 1969, under the direction of Douglas Riske.

The Siege: 45-minute "anti-war" play for children; written in 1969; unpublished; first produced by Arts Centre Company, 1969, under the direction of Douglas Riske.

Too Many Kings: 45-minute participation play for children 5-7 years; written in 1969; first published by Playwrights Co-op in 1977 in the same volume as *Chinook*; first produced by Arts Centre Company, 1969, under the direction of Joyce Doolittle; subsequently produced by Theatre London, 1972.

The Bob Edwards Revue (later became the full-length musical **Hoarse Muse**): one act; written in 1973; unpublished; first produced by Alberta Theatre Projects, Calgary, in 1973, under the direction of Douglas Riske.

The History Show (Missionaries, Muskeg and Mounties): two acts; written in 1973; unpublished; first produced by Alberta Theatre Projects, 1973, under the direction of Douglas Riske; subsequently produced by Sunshine Company, 1975.

Madwitch: one-hour children's play; written in 1973; unpublished; first produced by Alberta Theatre Projects, 1973, under the direction of Douglas Riske.

Pioneer: two-act play "written for a company on a regional theme"; written in 1973; unpublished; first produced by Alberta Theatre Projects, 1973, directed by Douglas Riske.

Hoarse Muse: two-act musical; music composed by William Skolnik; written from 1973 to 1975(see *The Bob Edwards Revue* above); first published by Simon and Pierre, 1974; subsequently published in a collection, *Popular Performance Plays, Volume 1*, by Simon and Pierre, 1976; first produced by Alberta Theatre Projects, 1974, under the direction of Douglas Riske; subsequently revised and remounted by Alberta Theatre Projects in 1975.

Under the Arch: one-act "musical entertainment" originally written for children, later revised to a full-length adult version; music composed by William Skolnik; written in 1975; first published by *Canadian Theatre Review* (*CTR* 10), spring, 1976; first produced by Alberta Theatre Projects, 1975, under the direction of Douglas Riske; subsequently produced in 1976 by Alberta Theatre Projects, under the direction of Brian Rintoul.

Passengers: two-act play with music composed by William Skolnik; written in 1977; unpublished; first produced by Alberta Theatre Projects, 1977, under the direction of Douglas Riske.

The Yukon Show: 60 minutes; written in 1979 on commission from the Yukon Territorial Government; unpublished; first produced in the Yukon in 1979 under the direction of James Boyles.

Miscellaneous

The Eye Opener Man: 30-minute revue for television; written in 1976; broadcast regionally by CFAC, Calgary, in 1976 and 1977.

Roch Carrier

Born May 13, 1937, in Sainte-Justine de Dorchester, Quebec. Father a shopkeeper. From an early age his poetry and short stories are published in various journals and literary magazines. Moving to Montreal in the late 1950s he works at various jobs including wrapping food at Steinberg's. In 1957, he begins an undergraduate degree in literature at the Université de Montréal. However, not finding the atmosphere conducive to the kind of writing he wants to do, he leaves after only a year. From 1958 to 1961 he earns a living as a journalist and as a high school teacher while devoting his free time to writing novels, short stories and poetry.

In 1961 he leaves Canada for Europe. During the next four years he travels extensively and completes his undergraduate degree at the Sorbonne. He returns to Canada in 1964. That year also sees the publication of *Jolis Deuils: petites tragédies*, a collection of his short stories. He supplements his income by teaching high school and by public speaking engagements. *La Guerre, Yes Sir*, the best-known of his novels, is published in 1968. The first part of a trilogy, it is followed by *Floralie, ou-es tu?* in 1969 and *Il est par là, le soleil*, a year later. Translations of his short stories begin to appear in English.

Encouraged by director Jean-Louis Roux of Montreal's Théâtre du Nouveau Monde, he begins to adapt first *La Guerre* and then *Floralie* for the stage. The stage version of *La Guerre, Yes Sir* is produced by TNM in 1970. His ties with TNM are further strengthened when he becomes the theatre's general secretary, a post he holds until 1973. A year later *Floralie, ou-es tu?* is produced by the Theatre. During this period he continues to write novels and short stories as well as working on film versions of both *La Guerre* and *Floralie* which, despite interest, remain unproduced. In 1977, theatre director Jean Duceppe commissions him to prepare a stage adaptation of Carrier's most recent novel, *Il n'y a pas de pays sans grand-père*. The play is produced by Duceppe's company the following year.

Kéro

Although deeply concerned with the present-day problems and future development of Quebec, his works are seldom overtly political ("I create a character, give her life and let the audience analyze it from there, if they want ") and usually deal with earlier periods in Quebec history. Resisting attempts to tie him to any particular group or party he tells the Montreal Star in 1978, "Am I a Péquiste? I don't have a card...It's the role of the writer to be in the opposition and we need a real one here...Let me balance that by saying that the best and most positive thing to happen to Canada has been the victory of the Parti Quebecois." His feelings for Quebec are tempered with an internationalism which has led him to raise his children to be fluent in both English and German as well as their native French. He currently makes his home with his wife, Diane Gosselin, and their daughters, Capucine and Frédérique, in Longueuil, near Montreal, where he continues to write novels, short stories and film scripts.

Stage Writing

La Guerre, Yes Sir: originally written as a novel in 1967; first published by Editions du Jour, Montreal, in 1968; published in English by House of Anansi Press, Toronto, 1970, in a translation by Sheila Fischman; adapted for the stage in 1970; first published by Editions du Jour in 1972; first produced by Théâtre du Nouveau Monde, Montreal in 1970; produced in English at Stratford Festival in 1972 under the direction of Albert Millaire; adapted for the screen; unproduced.

Floralie, ou-es tu?: originally written as a novel in 1968; first published by Editions du Jour in 1969; published in English under the title *Floralie, Where Are You?* by House of Anansi Press, 1971, in a translation by Sheila Fischman; adapted for the stage in 1973; first published by Editions du Jour in 1974; first produced by Théâtre du Nouveau Monde in 1974 under the direction of Olivier Reichenbach.

Ce soir seulement, à l'Auberge de la Fortune, Marivaux! (adaptation of *L'Epreuve* by Marivaux): written in 1975; unpublished; first produced by Théâtre Populaire du Québec, 1975, at CEGEP Maisonneuve and then taken on tour of Quebec, directed by Jean Perraud.

Il n'y'a pas de pays sans grand-père: originally written as a novel in 1976; first published by Editions Alain Stanké, Montreal, in 1977; adapted for the stage in 1977; unpublished; produced by Compagnie Jean Duceppe, Montreal, in 1978 under the direction of Albert Millaire.

Novels

La Guerre, Yes Sir!: (see *Stage Writing*)

Floralie, ou-es tu?: (see *Stage Writing*)

Il est par la, le soleil: written in 1969; first published by Editions du Jour in 1970; published in English under the title *Is It The Sun, Philibert?* by House of Anansi Press, 1972, in a translation by Sheila Fischman.

Le deux-millième étage: written in 1972; first published by Editions du Jour in 1973; published in English under the title *They Won't Demolish Me!* by House of Anansi Press, 1973, in a translation by Sheila Fischman.

Le Jardin des delices: written in 1974; first published by La Presse, Montreal in 1975; published in English under the title *The Garden of Delights* by House of Anansi Press, 1978, in a translation by Sheila Fischman.

Il n'y'a pas de pays sans grand-père: (see *Stage Writing*)

Miscellaneous

Jolis Deuils: petites tragédies: short stories; first published by Editions du Jour in 1964; winner of the 1964 Prix littéraire du province du Québec.

Contes pour mille oreilles: short stories; written in 1968; first published in *Ecrits du Canada-francais*, 1969.

Le Martien de Noel: film script for children; written in 1970; unproduced.

Les Enfants du bonhomme dans la lune: short stories; written in 1978; first published by Editions Alain Stanké, Montreal, 1979; published in English under the title *The Hockey Sweater and Other Stories* by House of Anansi Press, 1979, in a translation by Sheila Fischman.

Tom Cone

Born March 25, 1947, in Miami, Florida.
Encouraged by his father and by his mother
("...who thought theatre would give me a
sense of maturity...little did she know..."),
he makes his acting debut at the age of six.
He also develops an early interest in poetry.
He begins his post-secondary education as
an English major at the University of
Miami and has his poetry published in local
literary journals. He then switches to
Ogelthorpe College and becomes the editor
of the school's literary magazine. Switching
schools once again, he enrols in Florida
State University and begins doing poetry
readings around the state. He also meets
Martin Esslin, who is teaching at Florida
State, and Esslin encourages him to try his
hand at playwriting.

He spends 1969 doing graduate work in
Italy, majoring in art history. Returning to
the States in 1970, he meets a group of
American poets, including Basil Bunting
(whom he describes as "A dark horse of the
30's generation who is not only interested in
writing but also in translating Persian
poetry"). He moves to Vancouver that
same year and supports himself through a
variety of jobs including work in a lumber
mill. In 1971, while working on the *Georgia
Straight Supplement*, he meets Stan Persky,
a Vancouver editor and poet, who helps
him to gain landed immigrant status in
Canada. The next year he enrols in the
Graduate Communications Program at
Simon Fraser University, only to drop out
before his final examinations. He then
begins writing short documentaries on
scientific and political themes for CBC
Radio and, after a year, he begins work
with CBC radio drama producer Don
Mowatt. Mowatt encourages him to try his
hand at dramatic scripts for radio and
produces all his radio work from that point
on.

At this same time, he also begins to write
for the stage and, when money is scarce,
models in art schools. In 1973, his first two
stage plays, *The Organizer* and *There*, are
produced at Simon Fraser University. In
the same year, he begins an important
association with director Pamela

Hawthorn at the Vancouver New Play
Centre. In 1974, he helps to found the
Westcoast Actors' Society which, with the
New Play Centre, co-produces his play
Whisper to Mendelsohn. The following year
he marries author Joyce Lannon; his play
Cubistique premieres at the New Play
Centre and is subsequently produced in
Toronto and New York; he writes a one-
man show, *Herringbone*, his most successful
work to date. Following its premiere at the
New Play Centre, *Herringbone* (starring
Eric Peterson) tours the country and is the
British Columbia submission to the 1976
Cultural Olympics in Montreal. Over the
next three years, the play is performed on
CBC-TV, at the Bathouse Theatre in
Seattle, and is optioned for Broadway.

In 1976 he becomes playwright-in-
residence for the Westcoast Actors'
company. His association with the New
Play Centre continues as director
Hawthorn stages his next three plays:
Beautiful Tigers, *Shotglass*, and *Stargazing*.
First produced at the Stratford Festival's
Third Stage, *Stargazing* is subsequently
mounted at New York's Circle Repertory
Theater and Washington's Arena Stage.

A founding member of the Guild of Canadian Playwrights, he has lectured at the University of Alberta, Dalhousie University, the University of Saskatchewan as well as in high schools and universities throughout British Columbia. Cone is an avid art collector who currently lives, with his wife, in Vancouver.

Stage Writing

The Organizer: one act; written in 1973; unpublished; first produced by Simon Fraser University in 1973 at the Vancouver East Cultural Centre under the direction of Michael Fletcher; subsequently produced by New Play Centre, Vancouver, in 1974, under the direction of Jace van der Veen; subsequently adapted for radio as a 45-minute script; produced by CBC, Vancouver, for national broadcast.

There: one act; written in 1973; first published by Playwrights Co-op in 1973; first produced by Simon Fraser University at Vancouver East Cultural Centre (1972), under the direction of Michael Fletcher; subsequently produced by Miami Dramatic Arts Center, 1974, under the direction of Carla Van Tosh; adapted for radio as a 17-minute script; broadcast nationally by CBC, Vancouver.

Cubistique: one act; written in 1974; first published in 1975 in *Westcoast Plays*; subsequently published by Pulp Press, Vancouver in *Three Plays by Tom Cone* (1976); first produced by the New Play Centre as part of the DuMaurier Festival (1974), under the direction of Jace van der Veen; subsequently produced by Toronto's Factory Theatre Lab, 1975, under the direction of Patricia Carroll Brown; produced at the VanDam Theatre, New York, 1976; subsequently adapted for radio as a 45-minute script; broadcast nationally by CBC, Vancouver, in 1975.

The Imaginary Invalid: translation and adaptation of the play by Molière with lyrics by John Gray; written in 1974; unpublished; first produced by Westcoast Actors' Society, Vancouver, in 1975 under the direction of John Gray.

Whisper to Mendelsohn: three acts; written in 1974 and 1975; first published by Playwrights Co-op; first produced by New Play Centre and Westcoast Actors' Society at Vancouver's Arts Club Theatre (1975) under the direction of Jace van der Veen.

Herringbone: first written in 1975 as a one-act play; first published by Pulp Press in *Three Plays by Tom Cone* (1976); first produced by New Play Centre as part of the DuMaurier Festival (1975), under the direction of John Gray; subsequently taken on a cross-country tour by City Stage, Vancouver, playing in Edmonton, Victoria, Calgary and, during 1976, in Montreal, where it represented British Columbia at the Cultural Olympics, directed by Ray Michal; adapted for television as a 30-minute script and broadcast by CBC; re-written as a full-length play in 1978; first produced by Festival Lennoxville in 1978.

Beautiful Tigers: one act; written in 1975 on commission from CBC Radio; first published in 1976 by Pulp Press in *Three Plays by Tom Cone*; first produced by New Play Centre as part of the DuMaurier Festival (1976), under the direction of Pam Hawthorn; subsequently taped from a live stage performance for national radio broadcast by NBC and CBC in 1977.

Shotglass: one act; written in 1976; unpublished; first produced by New Play Centre as part of the DuMaurier Festival (1977), under the direction of Pam Hawthorn.

1792: full-length play for children; written in 1977 with Joe Wiesenfeld and Brenda White; unpublished; first produced by Green Thumb Players, Vancouver, in 1978 under the direction of Pamela Hawthorn.

Stargazing: one act; written in 1977; first published by Playwrights Co-op in 1978; first produced by Stratford Festival at the Third Stage, 1978, under the direction of Pam Hawthorn; subsequently produced at Circle Repertory Theater, New York, 1978, and at Arena Stage, Washington, D.C., 1979; adapted for radio as a 45-minute script; broadcast regionally by CBC, Vancouver, in 1979.

The Writer's Show: collective creation; written in 1978; unpublished; produced by Tamahnous Theatre Workshop, Vancouver, in 1978.

Miscellaneous

Historical scripts: 20 radio scripts written for CBC, Vancouver.

Water Gong (with Alex Pauk): a short opera for seven characters on stilts; unpublished;

first produced by Tamahnous Theatre, Vancouver, in an evening of short pieces by 10 writers.

In Progress

Canada Dry: a full-length play; to be produced by New Play Centre and Westcoast Actors, Society.

Servant of Two Masters (a new version of the Goldoni play); commissioned by the Stratford Festival for production in 1980.

Michael Cook

Born February 14, 1933 in London, England of Catholic Anglo-Irish parents. The youngest of three children. Father a government civil servant with a keen interest in watercolour painting. After the death of his mother, he is sent to a series of boarding schools in and around London. At the Rudolf Steiner School, he appears in his first play. During the war, his father is in the service and there is virtually no family contact. Strong early memories of hiding in school shelters during the bombing of London. At the age of 15, he is expelled from school and he spends the following years working on a farm, in a restaurant as a waiter and as a houseboy. In 1949, he decides to join the Army himself and does so, though under age, by altering his birth certificate. He remains in the Army for 12 years visiting such places as Korea, Japan, Germany, Malaya and Singapore (in Singapore he is made part of an intelligence unit). He picks up typing skills while working as a chief clerk but spends a great deal of time involved in troop entertainments. His first script is a children's play done for the children of some of the servicemen. He acts in many shows and directs and writes a number of others. During this time he also writes an

autobiographical novel which "was rejected by every reputable publisher in the world." The novel is structured as a series of tape recorded monologues that have been found by the book's narrator. He tries his hand, as well, at writing radio plays and is particularly fascinated by the writings of Dylan Thomas, Giles Cooper and, later, Samuel Beckett and John Arden. In Singapore, he directs a production of Arden's *Sergeant Musgrave's Dance.* Almost all of his Army writing is in the comic field — short plays, sketches and revues ("what else can you write when you have to have a haircut twice a week?"). On numerous occasions he challenges official Army positions in published letters to the editor. Though as high as Staff Sergeant at one point in his Army career, he completes his service after 12 years with the rank of Sergeant.

After leaving the Army in 1961, he finds work in a ball-bearing factory and on a farm in the English Midlands. In 1962, he enrols in a teacher training course at Nottingham University's College of Education where his specialty is drama. He subsequently finds work teaching theatre and drama in a comprehensive school but decides after only three months to leave both the job and the country. He applies for and receives permission to emigrate to Newfoundland where he has an old Army friend. During Christmas 1965, he arrives in St. John's leaving behind as well his wife of 14 years, who has already formed another attachment, their eight children, his books, his furniture and his house in Nottinghamshire ("My Army days had gotten me used to simply picking up and moving my whole life. This was no different.") His first job in Canada is as a director for a production of Anouilh's *Antigone* being done by the Memorial University Dramatic Society. He later wins a Best Actor Award for his performance as the Common Man in Bolt's *A Man For All Seasons* which is done by the St. John's Players in a regional DDF final. Eventually, he is hired as a Drama Specialist by the Memorial University Extension Service where he directs, among others, *Mother Courage,* Gelinas' *Bousille and the Just* and his own comedy revue called *The J. Arthur Prufrock Hour.* The annual St. John's Summer Festival is evolved from these experiences and is eventually moved into the St. John's Arts and Culture Centre with him as artistic director. In 1966, he marries again, this time a girl from St. John's by whom he has two children. During this same period, he begins doing a weekly television and theatre column for the St.

John's *Evening Telegram* and in 1969, he begins teaching English literature at Memorial University. Already a produced radio playwright, in 1970 he begins writing seriously for the stage. In 1972, he divorces his second wife and the following year marries Madonna Decker, a Newfoundland girl from Fogo Island. They have three children. In 1975, he decides to take an extended leave of absence from his university teaching responsibilities to devote himself full-time to writing and moves to Random Island, about 140 miles from St. John's. Later that same year, he spends six months in Summerland, B.C. In the spring of 1977 he is awarded a Canada Council Short Term Grant to enable him to visit various European theatres that have expressed interest in his plays. That summer he is named senior playwright-in-residence at the Banff Festival. In 1978, he helps to organize a working visit by a contingent of Canadian theatre professionals to the Eugene O'Neill Theater Conference in Waterford, Connecticut where his play, *The Gayden Chronicles*, is workshopped with Kenneth Welsh and Denise Fergusson playing the leading roles. In 1979 he is a member of a group of Canadian playwrights who tour the United Kingdom. The trip is arranged by the Secretary of State. Active in several arts organizations across the country, he serves on the editorial advisory board of the *Canadian Theatre Review*, is vice-chairman of the Guild of Canadian Playwrights and a member of the Arts Council of Newfoundland and Labrador. In 1979, he is awarded a senior arts grant from the Canada Council and requests an extended leave of absence from Memorial University, again in order to devote himself to writing full-time. In the spring of 1980, his play, *The Gayden Chronicles*, is produced in Hollywood.

Stage Writing

Split: two-act drama; written in 1966; unpublished; only copy sent to Theatre Toronto "where it disappeared without trace"; unproduced.

Colour the Flesh the Colour of Dust: two-act historical drama; written between 1970 and 1971; first published by Simon and Pierre (Toronto) in 1972; subsequently republished in *A Collection of Canadian Plays, Vol. 1*, Rolf Kalman, editor, by Simon and Pierre in 1972; first produced by The Open Group (St. John's) in 1972 under the direction of the author, and subsequently by the Neptune Theatre, 1972, under the direction of Robert Sherrin and by Toronto Arts Productions at the St. Lawrence Centre, 1974, under the direction of Keith Turnbull.

The Head, Guts and Soundbone Dance: two-act contemporary drama; written in 1972; first published by *Canadian Theatre Review* in 1974 (*CTR* 1) and subsequently by Breakwater Books (St. John's) in 1975 and as part of *Three Plays by Michael Cook* in 1977; first produced by The Open Group at the Arts and Culture Centre, St. John's, 1973, directed by Tony Chadwick and subsequently by the Saidye Bronfman Centre in Montreal, 1974, under the direction of Roy Higgins; by Theatre Three in Edmonton, 1975, under the direction of Richard Roberts; by Theatre New Brunswick in Fredericton, 1974, under the direction of Walter Learning; and by the Globe Theatre, Regina, 1977, under the direction of the author; filmed by CBC-TV for its *Opening Night* series, 1974, where it was directed by Ray McConnell.

Jacob's Wake: two-act drama of the near future; written in 1974; first published by Talonbooks in 1975; first produced by The Open Group, 1974, under the direction of Tony Chadwick, and subsequently by Festival Lennoxville, 1975, under the direction of William Davis; scheduled for production by the Performance Circle, Fox Island, Washington, 1980.

Not As A Dream: one-act drama; written in 1975 on commission from Dalhousie University for their acting classes; published by Doubleday, Toronto, 1980, along with *Fisherman's Revenge* as part of an anthology of Newfoundland plays; produced at Dalhousie University in

Halifax, 1976, under the direction of Lionel Lawrence.

Quiller: one-act drama; written in 1975; first published by the Playwrights Co-op in the same volume as *Tiln* in 1975, and subsequently by Talonbooks as part of *Tiln and Other Plays*, 1976; anthologized by Breakwater Books as part of *The Blasty Bough*, 1975, and by Gage (Toronto) as part of *Cues and Entrances*, 1977; first produced by the Breakwater Theatre Company, 1975, directed by Al Pittman and subsequently by the Centaur Theatre in Montreal, 1977, under the direction of John Juliani; also produced in British Columbia and Mexico.

On the Rim of the Curve: one-act drama about the last of the Beothuks; written between 1974 and 1975; first published by Breakwater as part of *Three Plays by Michael Cook* in 1977; first produced by the Avion Players (Gander) in 1977 under the direction of Carmel Doyle.

Therese's Creed: one-act monologue; written in 1976; first published by Talonbooks as part of *Tiln and Other Plays*, 1976 and subsequently by Breakwater as part of *Three Plays by Michael Cook,* 1977; first produced by the Centaur Theatre in Montreal, 1977, under the direction of John Juliani; subsequently produced by Open Circle Theatre, Winnipeg, 1979; and by Rising Tide Theatre, Newfoundland, under the direction of the author; other productions in Victoria, British Columbia and Ontario.

Special Providence: two-act comedy; written in 1976; unpublished; re-written, 1979; unproduced.

The Gayden Chronicles: three-act historical drama; written on commission from Festival Lennoxville between 1975 and 1976; first published by *Canadian Theatre Review* in 1977 (*CTR* 13); subsequently published by Playwrights Canada, Toronto, 1979; workshopped by Festival Lennoxville, 1976, under the direction of William Davis; workshopped, 1978, by the Eugene O'Neill National Playwrights

Conference; first produced by The Cast Theatre, Hollywood, California, 1980.

Fisherman's Revenge: one-act farce for children; written in 1976 on commission from the Newfoundland Travelling Theatre Company; published by the Playwrights Co-op; subsequently published by Doubleday, 1980, along with *Not as a Dream*, as part of an anthology of Newfoundland plays; produced by the Newfoundland Travelling Theatre Company, 1976, under the direction of Dudley Cox.

All the Funny People Are Dead: full length; unpublished; first workshopped at the Banff School of Fine Arts in 1977; completed in 1979; unproduced.

Radio Writing

How to Catch a Pirate: 60 minutes; written in 1966; produced by CBC, St. John's, in 1966 for national broadcast.

A Walk in the Rain: 60 minutes; written in 1967; produced by CBC, St. John's, in 1967 for national broadcast.

No Man Can Serve Two Masters: 60 minutes; written in 1967; produced by CBC, St. John's, in 1967 for national broadcast.

The Concubine: 60 minutes; written in 1968; produced by CBC, Toronto, in 1968 by Esse Ljungh for national broadcast.

Or the Wheel Broken: 60 minutes; written in 1968; produced by CBC, St. John's, in 1968 for national broadcast.

The Truck: 60 minutes; written in 1969; produced by CBC, St. John's in 1969 for national broadcast.

A Time For Doors: 60 minutes; written in 1969; produced by CBC, St. John's, for national broadcast.

To Inhabit the Earth Is Not Enough: 60 minutes; written in 1970, produced by CBC, St. John's, in 1970 for national broadcast.

Journey into the Unknown: 60 minutes; written in 1970; produced by CBC, St. John's, in 1970 for national broadcast.

Ballad of Patrick Docker: 30 minutes; written in 1971; produced by CBC, St. John's, in 1971 for national broadcast.

Waiting: 30 minutes; written in 1971; unproduced.

Tiln: 30 minutes; written in 1971; first published as a part of an anthology entitled *Encounter, Canadian Drama in Four Media* by Methuen in 1973; subsequently published in the same volume as *Quiller* by Playwrights Co-op in 1975; published by Talonbooks as part of *Tiln and Other Plays* in 1976 and by Commcept Publications, Vancouver, in *Transitions I—Short Plays*, 1978; first produced by CBC in 1971.

Apostles for the Burning: 90 minutes; written in 1972; first produced by CBC, St. John's, 1972 for national broadcast and subsequently in German by Radio Berlin in 1977; also produced by Radio Switzerland, 1978.

There's a Seal at the Bottom of the Garden: 60 minutes; written in 1973; produced by CBC, St. John's, in 1973 for national broadcast.

Colour the Flesh the Colour of Dust: a 90-minute adaptation of the stage play; written in 1973; produced by CBC, St. John's, in 1973 for national broadcast.

The Head, Guts and Soundbone Dance: a 60-minute adaptation of the stage play; written in 1974; produced by CBC, St. John's, in 1974 for national broadcast.

Love Is a Walnut: 30 minutes; written in 1975; first produced by CBC, St. John's, for national broadcast and subsequently by Earplay, University of Wisconsin in 1975.

Travels with Aunt Jane: a 30-minute episode commissioned for the CBC series; written in 1975; produced by CBC, Toronto, in 1975 for national broadcast.

The Producer, the Director: 30 minutes; written in 1976; produced by CBC, Calgary, in 1976 for national broadcast.

Knight of Shadow: 40 minutes; written in 1976; produced by CBC, Calgary, in 1976 for national broadcast.

Ireland's Eye: 60 minutes; written in 1976; commissioned by CBC Toronto, as part of the *Kunst Kopf* series; produced by CBC, St. John's, in 1977 for national broadcast.

On the Rim of the Curve: a 90-minute adaptation of the stage play; written in 1975; produced by CBC, St. John's, in 1977 as the final program for the CBC Tuesday Night series, for national broadcast.

Quiller: 60 minutes; written in 1975; unproduced.

The Gentleman Amateur: two 30-minute scripts; written in 1977; scheduled for production by CBC, St. John's, for regional broadcast in 1977.

C.F.A.: a 30-minute television episode commissioned for the CBC comedy series, *Up at Ours.*

At Ours: written in 1978; produced by CBC, St. John's, for regional broadcast.

Christn.as Special: 60-minute television script commissioned by CBC, St. John's, for regional broadcast in 1978.

Daniel My Brother: 30-minute television script; written in 1979; commissioned by CBC, St. John's and produced as part of series *Up at Ours.*

Miscellaneous

Our Man Friday: a series of 30-minute satirical television scripts; written and hosted by the author for CBC, St. John's (regional broadcast) between 1969 and 1970.

Newfoundland Dramatized School Broadcasts: a series of 15-minute programs (more than 50) written between 1967 and 1970; produced by CBC Radio, St. John's, for regional broadcast (1967-1970); includes a serialized adaptation of Ibsen's *Enemy of the People.*

Autobiographical Novel: untitled; written between 1964 and 1965; unpublished.

The Fogo Island Caper: a children's novel; written between 1969 and 1970; unpublished.

The Collaborators: a 60-minute episode for the television series; written in 1975 on commission by CBC-TV; unproduced.

The M.T.B.: a 30-minute thriller; written in 1978; commissioned by CBC, Toronto.

Numerous articles published in national journals and magazines including *Canadian Theatre Review, Maclean's, Performing Arts in Canada, Ten Cent Review,* and *Vie des Arts.*

In Progress

The Apocalypse Sonata: a stage play commissioned by Globe Theatre, Regina, for production in 1980.

The Island of Fire: a satirical novel.

Secondary Sources

A short essay by Cook in *Transitions I: Short Plays*, Commcept, 1978, pp. 245-247. Long essay in *Stage Voices* (Geraldine Anthony, ed.), Doubleday 1978, pp. 208-232.

John Coulter

Born in 1888, in Belfast, Northern Ireland, of Protestant parents. At the age of four he begins his education at the Belfast Model School. After a year at school he is determined to become an artist. On graduating from the Model School, this inclination leads him to enter the Belfast School of Art and Technology. It is here that he first becomes interested in theatre. After receiving several prizes in the "National Art Competition of South Kensington" in London, he wins a research scholarship to the School of Technology and Art at the University of Manchester. During this period, he concentrates on creating tapestries.

In 1912, he returns to the Belfast School of Art and Technology as a lecturer on textile design. A year later he becomes a resident master and teacher of art and English literature at Coleraine Academical Institute. Pursuing his interest in theatre, he moves to Dublin in 1914 where he takes a teaching position at Wesley College. In Dublin he makes innumerable visits to the Abbey Theatre and is deeply influenced by the plays of Yeats, Synge and other leaders of the Irish literary renaissance. *Conochar*, his first stage play, is published in 1917.

On his return to Ulster two years later, he tries to organize a theatre group to dramatize the history, culture and problems of the area. Due to unstable conditions resulting from increased Irish nationalist activity during this period, however, he is forced to abandon his plans. Disappointed, he moves to London where he works as a freelance writer for the BBC and various newspapers as well as preparing a series on modern drama for the *Irish Times* of Dublin. *Sally's Chance*, the first of his plays to receive a professional production, is directed by Sir Tyrone Guthrie for the BBC in 1925. The play is later re-titled *The House in the Quiet Glen.*

While in London he meets John Middleton Murray, editor of the magazine *The Adelphi*. With Murray's sponsorship, he becomes managing editor of *The New Adelphi* magazine in 1927. At the offices of the magazine, he meets Canadian Olive

Clare Primrose, author of poetry and short stories. They are married soon after emigrating to Canada in 1936. In 1937, his play *The House in the Quiet Glen* wins several awards at the Dominion Drama Festival. Becoming a Canadian citizen, he divides his time almost equally for the rest of his life between Ireland and Canada. In 1938 he gives a lecture entitled *The Art of Playwriting* at the University of Toronto's Hart House Theatre. Later that year, he moves to New York to write for the CBS radio program, *The Living History Series.*

After his return to Canada in 1940, his play *Holy Manhattan* is produced by Toronto's Arts and Letters Club. In 1944, committed to the development of Canadian drama, he presents the "Artists Brief" to the Turgeon Committee of the House of Commons. This document provides impetus for the formation of the Massey Commission which, in its turn, led to the eventual birth of the Canada Council. That same year, he helps to found the Canadian Arts Council, a forerunner of the Canadian Conference of the Arts.

Throughout the 40's, 50's and 60's, his works are produced on radio, stage and television throughout Canada, the United States and Great Britain. In 1975, he writes

In My Day, a book of memoirs. His collected works form the Coulter Archives at Hamilton's McMaster University.

Stage Writing

Conochar: two acts; written in 1916; first published by W. and G. Baird, Belfast, in 1917; first broadcast in a revised version titled *Conachar's Queen* by BBC Radio, Belfast, in 1934.

The House in the Quiet Glen: one act; written in 1925; first published in same volume as *The Family Portrait* by Macmillan Company of Canada, Toronto, in 1937; subsequently published by CTR Publications, 1980, in *Canada's Lost Plays: The Developing Mosaic* with an introduction by the author; first broadcast by BBC Radio, Belfast, as *Sally's Chance*, in 1925, under the direction of Tyrone Guthrie; first produced by Toronto Masquers at the Margaret Eaton Hall, Toronto, in 1937; produced on the stage in the Dominion Drama Festival, at Hart House Theatre, Toronto, 1937, where it wins all but one award; subsequently broadcast by CBC Radio, Toronto, in 1940.

The Family Portrait: three acts; originally titled *The Folks in Brickfield Street*; written in 1926; first published in same volume as *The House in the Quiet Glen* by Macmillan Company of Canada, 1937; first broadcast by BBC Radio, Belfast, in 1935; first produced by Ulster Group Theatre under the title *The Folks in Brickfield Street*; produced on stage by Lennox Robinson as an Abbey Theatre School Production at the Abbey Theatre, Dublin, in 1937; subsequently produced at Hart House Theatre, Toronto, in 1938; the Group Theatre, Belfast, in 1948; broadcast by CBC Radio, Toronto, in 1938, under the title *The Stars in Brickfield Street*, and by CBC-TV's *GM Theatre* in 1956, under the title *The Sponger*.

Holy Manhattan: three acts; written in 1940; unpublished; first produced by the Arts and Letters Club, Toronto, in 1940 under the direction of E.G. Sterndale Bennett; subsequently produced by CBC Radio, Toronto, in 1941, under the title *This is My Country*; produced by CBC-TV Toronto, in 1955, under the title *Come Back To Erin*.

Pigs: one act; written in 1940; unpublished; first produced by the Arts and Letters Club at Hart House Theatre in 1940 as part of a revue entitled *Fair Well of all Things*; subsequently produced by CBC Radio in 1940; later produced by BBC Radio and Radio Telefis Eireann, under the title *Cloghabenn Fair.*

Christmas Comes But Once a Year: one act; written in 1942 for Christmas stage production by the Arts and Letters Club; unpublished.

The Churchill of England: living newspaper play; written in 1942; rewritten as biography, *Churchill*; published serially by *Maclean's* and in book form by Ryerson Press, Toronto, in 1944; first produced by Arts and Letters Club in 1942.

Transit Through Fire: a libretto for an opera in six scenes; commissioned by CBC Radio for music by Healey Willan; written 1942; first published by the Macmillan Company of Canada in 1942; subsequently republished in an abridged form by Hurtig Publishers in *Colombo's Book of Canada* in 1978; produced in concert form by University of Toronto at Convocation Hall in 1942; also broadcast by CBC Radio in 1942.

Dierdre: originally titled *Dierdre of the Sorrows*; a libretto for an opera commissioned by CBC Radio for music by Healey Willan; three acts; written in 1943; first published under original title by Macmillan Company of Canada in 1944; subsequently published as *Dierdre* by Macmillan Company of Canada in 1965; and again, in a souvenir edition in 1966; first broadcast by BBC Northern Ireland; broadcast by CBC Radio, Toronto, in 1946; first produced on stage by Royal Conservatory of Music at the Macmillan Theatre, Toronto, in 1965; subsequently produced by the Canadian Opera Company at the O'Keefe, Toronto, 1966.

Mr. Oblomoff: adapted from the novel by Ivan Goutcharov; three-act comedy;

written in 1947; unpublished; first produced by Arts and Letters Club in 1946 and later in 1958; subsequently produced by the Group Theatre, Belfast, 1959, and by the University of Western Ontario at the Talbot Theatre, London, 1967; broadcast by BBC Radio and in translation in many countries; broadcast by CBC Radio in 1961 and by CBC-TV in 1962.

The Drums are Out: three acts; written in 1947; first published by DePaul University Press, Chicago, in 1971, with lengthy introduction by the author; first produced by the Abbey Theatre, in 1948; subsequently produced at the Dominion Drama Festival where it was named Best Play; first broadcast by CBC Radio, Toronto, in 1951, rebroadcast by CBC Radio, Toronto, as part of the series *Radio Showcase*, in both 1967 and 1969; produced by CBC-TV, Toronto, as part of the series *FM Theatre*, in 1969.

Riel: drama in two parts; written in 1949; first published by Ryerson Press, Toronto, in 1962; subsequently published by Cromlech Press, Hamilton, in 1972; first produced by New Play Society, Toronto, in 1950, starring Mavor Moore; first broadcast by CBC Radio, Toronto, in 1951, as part of the series *Wednesday Night*; revised version produced by the National Arts Centre, Ottawa, in 1975, under the direction of Jean Gascon; produced by CBC-TV in 1961, starring Bruno Gerussi; later broadcast by several British, European and American television stations.

Sleep My Pretty One: modern dramatic verse; written in 1950; unpublished; option to produce bought by Sir Laurence Olivier in 1951; rehearsed reading given at St. James' Theatre, London, in 1951, arranged by Laurence Olivier; rehearsed reading given at the Royal Court Theatre, London, with Irene Worth, in 1954; subsequently produced by Centre Stage, Toronto, in 1961.

The Crime of Louis Riel: written in 1960; first published by Playwrights Co-op, Toronto, in 1976; first produced at the Dominion Drama Festival, London, Ontario, in 1966, where it wins the Festival's regional prize for Best Canadian Play.

The Trial of Louis Riel: documentary drama based on transcripts of the actual trial; written in 1960 on commission from the Regina Chamber of Commerce to mark the Canadian Centennial in 1967; first published by Oberon Press, Ottawa, in 1968; produced annually as a summer tourist attraction by the Regina Chamber of Commerce, its 14th consecutive year of production being 1980.

A Capful of Pennies: three acts; written in 1967; unpublished; first produced at Central Library Theatre, Toronto, 1967 by Aries Productions.

While I Live: two parts; written in 1971; unpublished; unproduced.

Francois Bigot: A Rediscovery in Dramatic Form of the Fall of Quebec: two parts; written in 1978; first published by Hounslow Press, Toronto, 1978; bought by CBC Radio; stage production in preparation.

Living Together: sequence of two plays **(Edie, Helen, Hal** and **Willie, Sinton, Jill)** "variations on a theme"; written in 1979; unpublished; to be produced by Theatre Passe Muraille, Toronto, in 1980.

Mr. Kean of Drury Lane: "a play based on the off-stage life of the celebrated Edmund Kean"; completed in March 1980.

Radio Writing

A Tale of Old Quebec: written in 1935 on commission by BBC Radio; broadcast to Canada in 1935.

Tales of the Towns: series written in 1935-1936 on commission by BBC Radio; broadcast by BBC Radio from 1935-1936.

The Home Counties: series written in 1936-1937 on commission by BBC Radio; broadcast by BBC Radio from 1936-1937.

Quebec in 1670: written in 1940; broadcast by CBS Radio, New York, in 1940.

The Trial of Joseph Howe: written in 1942; broadcast by CBC Radio in 1942.

Miscellaneous

Radio Drama Is Not Theatre: published by the Macmillan Company of Canada in 1937.

Prelude to a Marriage: autobiography; published by Oberon Press, 1979.

In My Day: memoirs; published by Hounslow Press, 1980.

Reviews, articles and short stories for *The New Adelphi* (London), BBC Radio, CBC Radio, *Theatre Arts Monthly*, *Saturday Night*, *Curtain Call*, *Canadian Review of Music and Art*, and *Opera Canada*.

Secondary Sources

Book-length study, *John Coulter*, by Geraldine Anthony; Twayne, Boston, 1976

A section on Coulter included in *Stage Voices*, (Anthony, ed.), Doubleday, 1978, pp. 2-26.

"Portrait of Can-lit's Anonymous Parent," *Maclean's*, July 1979.

Robertson Davies

Born August 28, 1913, in Thamesville, a small community in southwestern Ontario. His father, William Rupert Davies, a Liberal senator, is owner of the *Thamesville Herald* and later the *Peterborough Examiner*.

Both his parents participate in amateur shows at the small Ferguson Opera House in Renfrew, where he sees his first theatrical performances. They also take him to Toronto and Detroit to see touring productions. He later attends Upper Canada College in Toronto and subsequently Queen's University in Kingston. He receives his B.Litt. in English from Oxford's Balliol College in 1938. His thesis, *Shakespeare's Boy Actors*, is published the following year. He remains in England working as both an actor and "a literary handyman" to Tyrone Guthrie at the Old Vic. He also lectures on dramatic literature at the Old Vic School.

Returning to Canada in 1940 after extensive travel in Europe and Australia, he becomes literary editor of *Saturday Night* magazine, a post which he holds for two years. During this period he writes *Shakespeare for Young Players*, his second

Peter Paterson

book on theatre, which is published in 1942, and marries Brenda Mathews, a director whom he had met at the Old Vic. Although from 1942 to 1962 his career does not directly involve him in theatre — he is first editor and then publisher of the *Peterborough Examiner* — his interest in playwriting continues. He also finds time to write fiction, including the book, *The Diary of Samuel Marchbanks*, which is published in 1947. His first volume of stage plays, entitled *Eros at Breakfast and Other Plays*, is published in 1949. An active member of the Peterborough Little Theatre, in 1949 he wins the Dominion Drama Festival's Louis Jouvet Prize for directing the Little Theatre's production of *The Taming of the Shrew*. During the 1950's, he and Toronto drama critic Herbert Whittaker work out a plan to make the Dominion Drama Festival less competitive.

In 1950, he is asked by the Massey Commission to do a special study on the state of Canadian theatre. In this report, he acknowledges the role of amateur dramatics but stresses the need for a strong professional theatre. The Massey Commission's final report, which calls for the establishment of a council for the arts, letters, humanities and social sciences, reflects many of his ideas.

Appointed a governor of the Stratford Festival on its establishment in 1953 (a position he retains until 1971), he and Tyrone Guthrie write books describing what has been accomplished after each of the first three seasons—*Renown at Stratford*, 1953; *Twice Have the Trumpets Sounded*, 1954; and *Thrice the Brinded Cat Hath Mew'd*, 1955.

That same year, *Leaven of Malice*, a novel, wins him the Stephen Leacock Medal For Humour. As well, his play, *Hunting Stuart*, is performed at the Crest Theatre in Toronto. *Love and Libel*, a stage version of *Leaven of Malice*, is produced on Broadway in 1960. With the failure of this play, he decides to spend more time on non-dramatic writing. The next year, he wins the Royal Society of Canada's Lorne Pierce Medal for his contribution to Canadian literature. In 1963, he is appointed Master of the University of Toronto's Massey College, where he helps establish the Graduate Centre for the Study of Drama. He is made a fellow of the Royal Society of Canada in 1967. In the same year, his *The Centennial Play* is performed in Lindsay, Ontario. In 1970, his novel, *Fifth Business*, reflecting his theatrical background, is published as the first part of a trilogy. The second part, *The Manticore*, published in 1972, wins the Governor General's Award

for fiction.

In 1973, Director Leon Major asks him to write a play for Toronto Arts Productions. The result is *Question Time*, which the theatre produces in 1975. *Pontiac and the Green Man*, his contribution to the University of Toronto's sesquicentennial celebrations, is produced at the University's MacMillan Theatre in 1977.

He has been awarded 13 honorary degrees from universities in Canada. Married, he currently make his home in Toronto.

Stage Writing

A Play of Our Lord's Nativity: an adaptation from the Medieval Pageant of Shearmen and Tailors; written in 1946; unpublished; first produced by the Coventry Players, Peterborough, in 1946; subsequently produced by Upper Canada College Preparatory School at Grace Church on the Hill, Toronto, in 1974.

Overlaid: one act; written in 1947; first published by Samuel French in 1948; subsequently reprinted by Samuel French in 1949 in *Eros at Breakfast and Other Plays*; by Longmans, Toronto, 1958, in *Curtain Rising*; by Clarke Irwin, 1960, in *Canada On Stage;* by Clarke Irwin, 1966, in *At My Heart's Core and Overlaid*; by Methuen, Toronto, 1973, in *Encounter, Canadian Drama in Four Media*, Eugene Benson ed.; by Commcept, Vancouver, 1978, in *Transitions I: Short Plays*, first produced by the Ottawa Drama League, Ottawa, in 1947, under the direction of Michael Meiklejohn; has received several productions across the country, both amateur and professional; subsequently adapted for CBC Radio, for the series *Stage* in 1964, and for CBC-TV, for the series *First Person* in 1960; winner of the Ottawa Drama League Workshop Competition in 1947.

Eros at Breakfast: one act; written in 1948; first published by Clarke Irwin, Toronto, in 1949 in *Eros at Breakfast and Other Plays*; subsequently released in the paperback volume, *Four Favourite Plays*, by Clarke Irwin in 1968; first produced by the Ottawa Drama League in 1948; has received several productions across the country, both amateur and professional; the 1948 production is winner of the Gratien Gélinas Award for Best Canadian Play in the Dominion Drama Festival.

Hope Deferred: one act; written in 1948; first published by Clarke Irwin, Toronto, in 1949, in *Eros at Breakfast and Other Plays*; subsequently published by CTR Publications, 1980, in *Canada's Lost Plays: The Developing Mosaic* with an introduction by the author; first produced by the Montreal Repertory Theatre Studio in 1948.

The Voice of the People: one act; written in 1948; first published by Clarke Irwin, Toronto, in 1949, in *Eros at Breakfast and Other Plays*; subsequently released in paperback by Clarke Irwin in 1968 in the paperback volume *Four Favourite Plays*; by The Book Society, Agincourt, Ontario, 1968, in *Voice of the People*; by Macmillan, Toronto, 1968, in *Upstage and Down*; by Gage, 1977, in *Cues and Entrances—Ten Canadian One-Act Plays.*

At the Gates of the Righteous: one act; written in 1948; first published by Clarke Irwin, Toronto, in 1949, in *Eros at Breakfast and Other Plays*; subsequently released in the paperback volume, *Four Favourite Plays*, by Clarke Irwin in 1968.

Fortune, My Foe: three acts; written in 1948; first published by Clarke Irwin, Toronto, in 1949; subsequently released in the paperback volume, *Four Favourite Plays*, by Clarke Irwin in 1968; first produced by the International Players, Kingston, in 1949, under the direction of Arthur Sutherland; subsequently adapted for CBC Radio and CBC-TV for the series *CBC Theatre* in 1953; winner of the Gratien Gélinas Award for Best Canadian Play in the Dominion Drama Festival in 1949.

At My Heart's Core: three acts; written in 1950; first published by Clarke Irwin, Toronto, in 1950 in the same volume as *Overlaid*; subsequently released in paperback by Clarke Irwin, in 1966; first produced by the Peterborough Summer Theatre, Peterborough, in 1950 under the direction of Michael Sadlier; subsequently

adapted for CBC Radio and CBC-TV for the series *CBC Theatre* in 1953.

King Phoenix: three acts; written in 1950; first published by New Press, Toronto, 1972, in *Hunting Stuart and Other Plays*; first produced by the North Toronto Theatre Guild in 1950, under the direction of Herbert Whittaker.

A Masque of Aesop: one act; written in 1952; first published by Clarke Irwin, Toronto, in 1952; first produced at Upper Canada College, Toronto, in 1952 under the direction of G. Galt.

A Jig for the Gypsy: three acts; written in 1954; first published by Clarke Irwin, Toronto, in 1954; first produced at the Crest Theatre, Toronto, in 1954, under the direction of Herbert Whittaker; subsequently produced at the Questors Theatre, London, England, in 1954; and at Festival Lennoxville, Lennoxville, Quebec, in 1973.

Hunting Stuart: three acts; written in 1955; first published by New Press, 1972, in *Hunting Stuart and Other Plays*; first produced at the Crest Theatre, Toronto, in 1955, under the direction of Robert Gill; subsequently produced at Festival Lennoxville, Lennoxville, Quebec, in 1975, under the direction of Malcolm Black.

Bartholomew Fair: adapted from the play by Ben Jonson; three acts; written in 1956; unpublished; unproduced.

General Confession: three acts; written in 1958; first published by New Press, 1972, in *Hunting Stuart and Other Plays*; unproduced.

Love and Libel: adapted from the author's own novel, *Leaven of Malice*; three acts; written in 1960; unpublished; first produced by the Theater Guild of New York, toured Toronto, Boston, Detroit and New York City in 1960, under the direction of Tyrone Guthrie.

A Masque of Mr. Punch: one act; written in 1962; first published by the Oxford University Press, Toronto, in 1963; first produced at Upper Canada College,

Toronto, in 1962, under the direction of Michael Carver.

The Centennial Play: full-length; written in 1966 by Davies, W.O. Mitchell, Arthur L. Murphy, Eric Nicol and Yves Thériault with music by Keith Bissell; unpublished; first produced by Ottawa Little Theatre, 1967, in association with Canadian Festival of the Arts, under the direction of Peter Boretski.

Leaven of Malice: adapted from the playwright's novel of the same name; three acts; written in 1972; unpublished; first produced at Hart House Theatre, University of Toronto, in 1973, under the direction of Martin Hunter; subsequently produced at the Shaw Festival, Niagara-on-the-Lake, Ontario, in 1975, under the direction of Tony Van Bridge.

Question Time: two-act fantasy; written in 1975; first published by Macmillan of Canada, Toronto, in 1975; first produced by Toronto Arts Productions at the St. Lawrence Centre in 1975, under the direction of Leon Major.

Pontiac and the Green Man: two acts; written in 1977; unpublished; first produced by the University of Toronto at the MacMillan Theatre, Toronto, in 1977, under the direction of Martin Hunter; this play includes excerpts from the play *Ponteach or The Savages of America*, by Major Robert Rogers, and was written as part of the University's Sesquicentennial celebrations.

Miscellaneous

Shakespeare's Boy Actors: first published by J.M. Dent, London, in 1939; subsequently published by Russell and Russell, New York, in 1964.

Shakespeare for Young Players: first published by Clarke Irwin, Toronto, in 1942.

The Diary of Samuel Marchbanks: fiction; first published by Clarke Irwin, Toronto, in 1947; revised edition, with added "Preface"

published in paperback by Clarke Irwin, Toronto, in 1966.

The Table Talk of Samuel Marchbanks: fiction; first published by Clarke Irwin, Toronto, in 1949; subsequently published by Chatto and Windus, London, 1951; released in paperback by Clarke Irwin, Toronto, in 1967.

Tempest Tost: first published by Clarke Irwin, Toronto, in 1951; subsequently republished by Rinehart, New York, in 1952; Chatto and Windus, London, in 1952; and released in paperback by Clarke Irwin, in 1965.

Renown at Stratford: overview of Stratford's first season written in collaboration with Tyrone Guthrie and Grant MacDonald; first published by Clarke Irwin, Toronto, in 1953.

Twice Have the Trumpets Sounded: overview of Stratford's second season written in collaboration with Tyrone Guthrie and Grant MacDonald; first published by Clarke Irwin, in 1954.

Leaven of Malice: novel, first published by Clarke Irwin, Toronto, in 1954; subsequently republished by Clarke Irwin in 1964.

Thrice the Brinded Cat Hath Mew'd: overview of Stratford's third season written in collaboration with Tyrone Guthrie, Boyd Neel and Tanya Moisevitch; first published by Clarke Irwin, in 1955.

A Mixture of Frailties: novel; first published by Macmillan, Toronto, in 1958; subsequently published by Weidenfeld and Nicolson, London, in 1958, and by Scribner's, New York, in 1958; translated into German and published as *Glanz und Schwäche*, by Paul Neff Verlag, in 1960; translated into Dutch and published as *Eon Lied voor Monica*, by W.C. Stok, in 1962.

A Voice from the Attic: first published by McClelland and Stewart, Toronto, in 1960; simultaneously published by Alfred Knopf, New York; published as *The Personal Art: Reading for Good Purpose* by Secker and Warburg, London, in 1961; reprinted under the original title by McClelland and Stewart, in 1972, and by Viking Press Compass Books, New York, 1972.

Samuel Marchbanks' Almanack; fiction; first published by McClelland and Stewart, Toronto, in 1967; released in paperback by McClelland and Stewart in 1968.

Ste,•.en Leacock: a critique; first published in the Canadian Writers Series by McClelland and Stewart in 1970; reprinted and slightly revised as "Introduction" in *Feast of Stephen*, an anthology of some of the less familiar writings of Stephen Leacock, by McClelland and Stewart, 1970.

Fifth Business: a novel; first published by Macmillan of Canada, in 1970; subsequently published by Viking Press, New York, in 1970; Macmillan, London, in 1971; Signet Books (New American Library), New York, in 1971; and by Penguin Books, New York, in 1977; published in a Polish translation entitled *Piata Osoba Dramatu* by Instytut Wydawniczy, Warsaw, in 1973; and in a French translation entitled *Cinquième Emploi*, by Le Cercle du Livre de France, Montreal, in 1975.

The Manticore: a novel; first published by Macmillan of Canada, Toronto, in 1972; subsequently published by Viking Press, New York, in 1972; Macmillan, London, in 1973; Curtis Books, New York, in 1974; Penguin Books, New York, in 1976; published in French under the title *Le lion avait un visage d'homme*, by Le Cercle du Livre de France, Montreal; winner of the 1972 Governor General's Award for fiction.

Brothers in the Black Art: 60-minute television play; written in 1974; first produced by CBC-TV, Toronto, in 1974, for national broadcast.

World of Wonders: a novel; first published by Macmillan of Canada, Toronto, in 1975; subsequently published by Viking Press, New York, in 1976; W.H. Allen, London, in 1977; and Penguin Books, New York, in 1977.

One Half of Robertson Davies: essays; first published by Macmillan, Toronto, in 1977; subsequently published by Viking Press, New York, in 1978; and by Penguin Books, New York, in 1978.

Critical reviews and essays in *Peterborough Examiner*, *Saturday Night*, and on BBC.

Secondary Sources

Buitenhuis, Elspeth MacGregor, *Robertson Davies*, (Toronto: Forum House, 1972).

Grant, Judith Skelton, *Robertson Davies*, (Toronto: McClelland and Stewart, 1978).

Morley, Patricia, *Robertson Davies*, (Toronto: Gage Educational Publishing, 1977).

Journal of Canadian Studies, Vol. XII, No. 1, February 1977—a special issue devoted to Davies.

Section on Davies included in *Stage Voices*, Geraldine C. Anthony (ed.), (Toronto: Doubleday, 1978) pp. 56-84.

James DeFelice

Born January 6, 1940, in Lynn, Massachusetts. His father is "one of the early leaders in the Labour Movement." He works his way through Northeastern University by working as a sports writer for the Boston *Globe*. After graduation, he decides on a career as a professional actor and director.

Appearing on stage in theatres throughout Canada and the northern United States, he also tries his hand at playwriting. His first work, *The Elixir*, is written in 1961. In 1964, he writes *When the Wind Blew Cold at Rosie's Place*. Over the years his acting credits include plays at Edmonton's Theatre 3, Northern Light and Torches Theatre, as well as frequent roles in radio and television. As a director he works in Boston, Bloomington and New Brunswick, as well as in various theatres in Edmonton.

After a break of nine years, he returns to playwriting with *Fools and Masters* in 1973 and, from that point on, begins writing regularly for the stage. In 1978, he receives an Etrog Award for his screen adaptation of *Why Shoot The Teacher*. A year later, he receives an Alberta Achievement Award for "Excellence in Theatre Arts" and an Outstanding Alumni Award from Northeastern University. Currently teaching in the Department of Drama at the University of Alberta, he is married, the father of two children, and continues to make his home in Edmonton.

Stage Writing

The Elixir: one act; written in 1961; first published in *First Stage*, Lafayette, Indiana, 1963; revised; subsequently published by Playwrights Co-op, Toronto, 1973; first produced by University of Alberta, Edmonton, 1973, under the direction of Ken Agrell-Smith.

When the Wind Blew Cool at Rosie's Place: three acts; written in 1964; unpublished; first produced at Arena Theatre, Medford, Massachusetts, 1965, under the direction of Marston Balch.

Fools and Masters (originally titled **The Jumper**): one act; written in 1973; first published by Playwrights Co-op, 1975; first produced by University of Alberta, in 1973, under the direction of Patrick Dunn; subsequently produced by Factory Theatre Lab, Toronto, 1975, under the direction of Alex Dmitriev; adapted for radio in 1976 by CBC, Calgary, for national broadcast.

Alice Through the Looking Glass: two-act "musical adaptation with L. Reese"; unpublished; first produced by Theatre 3, Edmonton, 1974, under the direction of the author.

Winnie the Pooh: one-act musical adaptation with L. Reese; written in 1976; unpublished; first produced by Northern Light Theatre, Edmonton, 1976, under the direction of Scott Swan.

Take Me Where the Water's Warm: three acts; written between 1977 and 1978; first published by Playwrights Co-op, 1978; first produced by Northern Light Theatre, 1979, under the direction of Scott Swan.

A Yard of Pucks: two acts; written between 1977 and 1978; unpublished; scheduled for production by Workshop West, Edmonton, 1980, under the direction of Gerry Potter; adapted for radio; produced by CBC Calgary, 1979, for the program *CBC Stage*.

Miscellaneous

Filmguide to Odd Man Out: "a detailed analysis of the classic Carol Reed film"; published by Indiana University Press, 1975.

Why Shoot the Teacher: feature film based on the novel by Max Braithwaite; written in 1974; produced by Fil Fraser, Hanna, Alberta, 1976; winner of an Etrog Award in 1978.

Wings of Time: 30 minutes; written in 1975; produced by National Film Board of Canada, 1975, under the direction of Tom Radford.

In Residence: one hour; written in 1979; broadcast by CBC Radio in 1980 as part of the series *Soundstage.*

Prisoners in the Snow: television script; written in 1979; scheduled for national broadcast by CBC, Edmonton, 1980.

In Progress

The Secret World of Og: a screenplay.

Kepler: a stage play.

The Dandelion War: a radio play.

Rex Deverell

Born July 17, 1941, in Toronto. His father is a carpenter; his mother a nurse. He grows up in Orillia and becomes interested in acting and directing while still in high school there. He later goes on to McMaster University where he gets his B.A. (General Arts) in 1963 and, with a growing interest in the church, his Bachelor of Divinity Degree in 1966. For his Divinity School thesis, he submits his first play, *The Invitation*. The play is subsequently published by both the Religion and Theatre Council and by a literary magazine at the University of Western Ontario. Western also awards the play first prize in a university playwriting competition.

After graduation, he spends a year in New York at the Union Theological Seminary and, upon his return home, he accepts a position as pastor of a small Baptist congregation in southwestern Ontario. Retaining his church position for the next three years, he continues to write plays, many of which are produced for local and regional church conferences. In 1970,

he helps script an adaptation of *The Brothers* for Toronto's Studio Lab Theatre, where his wife, Rita, is working as an actress.

His work with Studio Lab turns his attention more and more to writing. In 1971, Studio Lab produces one of his children's plays, *Sam and the Tigers*. In 1972, the Globe Theatre in Regina produces another of his children's plays, *Shortshrift*. In 1975, turning his energies almost completely to theatre, he is asked to become the Globe's writer-in-residence, a position he holds for several years. The father of one child, he presently makes his home in Toronto, though retaining strong ties to Regina.

Stage Writing

The Invitation: one-act play "in the style of Ionesco as translated by a preacher"; written in 1966; first published by the Religion and Theatre Council, Toronto, in 1966; subsequently published by the University of Western Ontario literary magazine, 1968; first produced by McMaster Divinity College, McMaster University, Hamilton, 1966, under the direction of the author; awarded first prize in University of Western Ontario Playwriting Competition (1966).

The Lemonade Was Too Sweet (or **Betwixt Blackouts**): one-act play dealing with the "theme of real time and its interrelationship with theatrical time"; written in 1968; unpublished; first produced by Black River Playhouse, Chester, New Jersey, 1969, under the direction of Clint Betz.

Bits Pieces and Visions: one-act revue; written in 1968; unpublished; directed by the author at a church conference in 1968.

The Village of New Wine: one act; written in 1969; unpublished, unproduced.

The Brothers (with Ernest Schwarz and Studio Lab Company): full-length comedy; written in 1970; unpublished; first produced by Studio Lab Theatre, Toronto, in 1970, under the direction of Ernest Schwarz.

Bus Station: one-act revue; written in 1970; unpublished; directed by the author at a church conference in 1970.

Sam and the Tigers (with Ernest Schwarz): one-act play for children; written in 1971; unpublished; first produced by Studio Lab Theatre, 1971, directed by Ernest Schwarz.

A Truly Great Offer: one act; written in 1972 with Rita Deverell; first published by United Church of Canada, Toronto, 1973, in *The Fold-Out, Hang-Up, Push-Out Global Think and Do Thing*, Series 2, No. 4; unproduced.

The Jack and Jill Play: one act; written in 1972; unpublished; first produced by Walmer Road Baptist Church, Toronto, in 1972, directed by the author.

Shortshrift: one-act children's play in which "a small prairie town loses its place on the map"; written in 1972; first published by Playwrights Co-op, Toronto, in 1973; first produced by Globe Theatre, Regina, 1972, under the direction of James Brewer; subsequently produced by Theatre Calgary, Citadel Theatre, Edmonton, and the Charlottetown Festival; produced by Globe Theatre in 1978 under the direction of James Brewer.

Soup: one-act play for children; written in 1972; unpublished, unproduced.

The Copetown City Kite Crisis: one-act play for children; written in 1973; first published in 1974 by Playwrights Co-op; first produced by the Globe Theatre, Regina, in 1973, directed by Ken Kramer.

Power Trip: two-act anthology of the playwright's own work, "and scenes from classic plays, philosophers, and biographies on the theme of power" for high school students; written in 1973; unpublished; first produced by Globe Theatre in 1975 under the direction of Ken Kramer.

Sarah's Play: one-act play for children; written in 1974; first published in 1975 by Playwrights Co-op; subsequently published by Nelson in *Rowboats and Rollerskates*, 1977; first produced by Globe Theatre in 1973, under the direction of Robert Syme; subsequently produced by Theatre Calgary.

Harry Oddstack and the Case of the Missing King: two-act Christmas entertainment;

written in 1975; unpublished; first produced by Globe Theatre, 1975, directed by Ken Kramer.

The Shinbone General Store Caper: one-act play for children; written in 1975; first published along with *Underground Lake* and *Uphill Revival* by Playwrights Co-op, 1977; first produced by Globe Theatre in 1975, under the direction of Ken Kramer; subsequently produced by Citadel on Wheels/Wings.

Underground Lake: one act; written in 1975; first published along with *Shinbone General Store Caper* and *Uphill Revival* by Playwrights Co-op, 1977; first produced by Globe Theatre in 1974, directed by Ken Kramer.

For Lands Sake: one-act revue; written in 1976; unpublished; first produced by Globe Theatre for a conference on Land Use, Department of Environment; later rewritten as a musical revue, with music and lyrics by Geoffrey Ursell; produced by Globe Theatre in 1978 under the direction of Kim McCaw; taken on a school tour.

Next Town: Nine Miles: three-act "entertainment for families, consisting of three of the small prairie town plays, *Shortshrift, Copetown City Kite Crisis,* and *Shinbone General Store Caper*, and using one character to link the three communities together"; written in 1976; unpublished; first produced by Globe Theatre in 1976 for the Montreal Olympics cultural program.

The Uphill Revival: two-act play for high school audiences; written in 1976; first published along with *Underground Lake* and *Shinbone General Store Caper* by Playwrights Co-op, 1977; first produced by Globe Theatre in 1977, directed by James Brewer.

Boiler Room Suite: two acts; written in 1977; first published by Playwrights Co-op in 1978; subsequently published by Talonbooks, Vancouver, 1978; first produced by Globe Theatre, 1977, under the direction of Ken Kramer; also produced in 1977 by Citadel Theatre, Edmonton under the direction of Lawrence Seligman; subsequently produced by Theatre Calgary

and by Arts Club/Carousel, Vancouver in 1978 under the direction of Rick McNair; recipient of the Canadian Authors Association Literary Award in 1978.

In Short Supply: one act; written in 1978; unpublished; first produced by Globe Theatre, 1978, directed by Ken Kramer.

Superwheel: two-act musical revue; music and lyrics by Geoffrey Ursell; written in 1977; first published by Coteau Books, 1979; first produced by Globe Theatre, 1977, directed by Ken Kramer; subsequently remounted by the same theatre in 1978 under the direction of Ken Kramer.

The Mark on the Corner of Scarth and 11th: full-length; first produced by Globe Theatre, 1979.

You Want Me To Be Grown Up Don't I?: 50 minutes; Globe Theatre, school tour, 1979.

Radio Writing

Night Bird: 30 minutes; written in 1979; unpublished; unproduced.

Bus Trip: 30 minutes; written in 1971; unpublished; unproduced.

Dreams and Things: three 30-minute episodes; adaptations of fantasy and science fiction novels; written in 1972 and 1973; unpublished; first produced by CBC, Regina, for regional broadcast in 1972 and 1973.

Travels with Aunt Jane: 30-minute episode in series; written in 1974; unpublished; first produced by CBC, Vancouver, in 1974, for national broadcast.

Worthington: 30 minutes; written in 1974; unpublished; commissioned by CBC; unproduced.

Maple Creek: Mounties, Indians and Railroads: 30 minutes; written in 1977; unpublished; produced by CBC, Regina, for regional broadcast in 1977.

Blizzard: 30 minutes; written in 1978; unpublished; first produced by CBC, Regina, for regional broadcast in 1978.

From War to Wilderness: 30 minutes; written in 1978; unpublished; first produced by CBC, Regina, for regional broadcast in 1978.

Love Scenes: 60 minutes; written in 1978; first produced by CBC, Regina, for national broadcast in 1978.

Miscellaneous

Verse and Worse: 30-minute television episode for series; written in 1974; first produced by CBC, Ottawa, for *Hi Diddle Day* series, and broadcast nationally.

What's a Moosejaw?: 30-minute television script; written in 1978; first produced by CBC, Regina, for regional broadcast in 1978.

In Progress

A full-length play about love and hostility.

Guy Dufresne

Born April 17, 1915 in Montreal, one of four sons. Father a family doctor. Receives his primary and secondary schooling at L'Académie Bonsecours and L'Académie Querbes. Completes his education at the Collège Sainte-Marie and also at the Collège Jean-de-Brébeuf, from which he receives a liberal arts degree. Due to ill health and his dislike of large cities, he abandons Montreal to become an apple grower in Frelighsburg, in the eastern townships of Quebec. In 1939, he marries Anne-Marie Lucien. They have two daughters; Andrée, born in 1942, and Madeleine, born in 1945. When in 1945 a sudden frost destroys the apple crop, the family is left with no income for the next 18 months. At this time CBC Montreal (Radio-Canada) has just launched its first writing competition and in the hope of recouping some of his losses, he submits *Le Contrabandier*, a short story which wins first prize. This leads to a second career as a writer for radio and later television. The main subjects of his work are Quebec history and present-day life in rural Quebec. He writes, "Je me méfie de l'abstrait au théâtre. J'aime le concret. Je préfère donc

les situations et les personnages, aux thèmes." *Le Jeu sur la presqu'ile*, his first stage play, is produced in 1950. Recent works include *Décembre*, a 90-minute television drama produced by Radio-Canada in 1978 and *Je cherche ton visage,* a television play produced in 1979. He and his wife still make their home in Frelighsburg.

Stage Writing

Le Jeu sur la presqu'ile: written in 1950; unpublished; first produced at Parc Lafontaine in 1950; adapted for radio and produced by CBC in 1950.

Le Cri de l'engoulevent: two acts; written in 1959; rewritten in 1969; first published by Editions Leméac in the Théâtre Canadien series, 1969; first produced by the Comédie Canadienne in 1960; subsequently produced by la Nouvelle Compagnie Théâtrale in 1961 under the direction of Gilles Pelletier and by Théâtre Populaire du Québec in 1970; first produced for television under the title *Chemin privé* in 1961; translated as *The Call of the Whippoorwill* by Philip London and Laurance Bérard and published by New Press, Toronto, 1972.

Les Traitants: written in 1960; first produced by CBC-TV in 1960 for French broadcast; revised stage version written in 1968; first published by Editions Leméac in the Théâtre Canadien series, 1969; first produced by Théâtre du Nouveau Monde in 1969 under the direction of Albert Millaire.

Docile: two-act comedy; written between 1967 and 1968; first published by Editions Leméac in the Répertoire Québécois series, 1972; first produced by the Comédie-Canadienne in 1968 under the direction of Gratien Gélinas.

Radio Writing

Le Ciel par-dessus les toits: written in 1947; unpublished; first produced by CBC Radio in 1948; two extracts produced on CBC-TV in 1954.

Tessa Maloney: written in 1949; an adaptation of a novel by Marie LeFranc; unpublished; first produced on CBC Radio in 1949.

Perrette et le trio des petits: written in 1951; unpublished; first produced on CBC Radio in 1951.

Deux-zero-sonnez-quatre: written in 1951; unpublished; first produced by CBC Radio in 1951.

Felix Poutre: written in 1952; an adaptation of a play by Louis Frechette; unpublished; first produced by CBC Radio in 1952.

Selkirk: written in 1952; unpublished; first produced by CBC Radio in 1952.

Le Choc des idées: written in 1953; unpublished; first produced by CBC Radio in 1952.

Burins d'histoire: written in 1953; unpublished; first produced on CBC shortwave in 1954.

Les Feux de la Saint-Jean: written in 1954; unpublished; first produced by CBC Radio in 1954.

Le 13 Avril: 30 minutes; written in 1954; unpublished; first produced by CBC Radio in 1954.

Le Jeu de la voyagere: adaptation of a poem by Rina Lanire; written in 1954; unpublished; first produced by CBC Radio in 1954.

L'Hotel-Dieu: 30 minutes; written in 1954; unpublished; first produced by CBC Radio in 1954.

L'Acadie: written in 1954; unpublished; first produced by CBC Radio in 1954.

Chronique de Frélibourg: four episodes; written in 1955; unpublished; first produced by CBC Radio in 1955.

Wahata: 30-minute historical drama; written in 1962; unpublished; first produced by Radio Canada in 1962.

Un Train passe: series of five 30-minute episodes; written in 1969; unpublished; first produced by CKAO Radio in 1969.

Affrontement: 120-minute drama about generation and class conflict; written in 1974; unpublished; first produced by CBC-TV in 1974 for regional broadcast.

La Veille de...: historical series; ten 60-minute episodes; written between 1974 and 1977; unpublished; first produced by CBC-TV between 1974 and 1977 for regional broadcast.

Décembre: 120-minute drama about rock musicians in Montreal; written in 1977; unpublished; first produced by CBC in 1978.

Le Chemin des patriots: six 60-minute episodes on the life of Wilfred Nielson (1805-1838); unpublished; to be given first production by CBC.

Television Writing

Eux nivres: written in 1953; unpublished; first produced by CBC-TV in 1953.

Cap-aux-Sorciers: a series; written between 1955 and 1958; selected episodes published by Editions Leméac in 1969 in the Beaux Textes series under the title *Cap-aux-Sorciers*; first produced by CBC-TV between 1955 and 1958.

L'Ile-aux-pommes: written in 1954; unpublished; first produced by CBC-TV in 1954.

La Neilleuse: written in 1954; unpublished; first produced by CBC-TV in 1954.

Kebec: written in 1958; unpublished; first produced by CBC-TV in 1958.

A la romance: written in 1959; unpublished; first produced by CBC-TV in 1959 for national broadcast.

Mesure de guerre: written in 1960; unpublished; first produced by CBC-TV in 1960.

Kanawio: a series; written between 1960 and 1961; unpublished; first produced by CBC-TV between 1960 and 1961.

Chemin privé: adaptation of *Le Cri de l'engoulevant*; produced by CBC-TV in 1961.

Septième-nord: a series; written between 1963 and 1967; unpublished; first produced by CBC-TV between 1963 and 1967.

Les Trois Soeurs: adaptation of Chekhov's *The Three Sisters*; written in 1965; unpublished; first produced by CBC-TV in 1965.

Des souris des hommes: adaptation of Steinbeck's *Of Mice and Men*; written in 1966; unpublished; first produced by CBC-TV in 1966.

Les Forges de Saint-Maurice: a serial; written between 1969 and 1970; unpublished; first produced by CBC-TV in 1972; one episode, *Ce maudit lardier*, published by Leméac in 1975.

Johanne et ses vieux: 30 minutes; written in 1976; unpublished; first produced by CBC-TV in 1976 for regional broadcast.

Ces dames de l'estuare: translation and adaptation of *Ladies in Retirement*; written in 1977; unpublished; first produced by CBC-TV in 1977 for regional broadcast; directed by Paul Beouin.

Je cherche ton visage: drama about loss of faith; written in 1978; unpublished; to be given first production by CBC-TV in 1979.

Miscellaneous

Les Ordres: film script; written in 1971; produced under the direction of Michel Brault.

Couleurs des jours mêlés: poetry collection; written in 1950.

Ondes courtes: poetry collection; written in 1950.

Jeremie: scenario for ballet; written in 1972; first published by Leméac, 1973; first produced by Ballets Jazz, Montreal, 1973.

La Tragédie est un acte de foi: critical writings on theatre; written in 1972; first published by Leméac, 1973; winner of Prix David, 1973.

Textes et documents: poetry and prose collection; written in 1972; first published by Leméac, 1973.

Secondary Sources

Only the most significant are listed.
In English:

Hamblet, Edwin C., *Marcel Dubé and French-Canadian Drama*, Exposition Press, New York, 1970.

In French:
Amyot, Michel, *Le Drame de l'impuissance dans le théâtre de Marcel Dubé*, MA thesis Université de Montréal, 1963.
Godin, Jean-Cleo and Mailhot, Laurent, *Le Théâtre québécois*, 1970, pp. 81-108.
Laroche, Maximilien, *Marcel Dubé*, Editions Fides, 1970.

Marcel Dubé

Born January 3, 1930, in Montreal, one of eight children. Father an accountant. Receives his primary education in three French Catholic schools near his home in a crowded neighbourhood in the city's east end. His first exposure to theatre comes when he is taken to see an amateur production mounted in a nearby parish hall. He and his friends recreate this and other performances in their backyards, with the price of admission set at one clothespin. He completes both secondary and undergraduate studies at the Jesuit Collège Sainte-Marie where he majors in the classics. His family's means are modest and he is the first of the Dubés to have a post-secondary education. He is, however, an indifferent student, more interested in ice hockey than books.

Kéro

1948 marks the opening, in Montreal, of Gratien Gélinas' historic play *Tit-Coq*. Dubé is so impressed by the production that he sees it five times, realizing that *Tit-Coq* is indicative of the future direction of theatre in Quebec. Later that year, he becomes founder and also director of La Jeune Scène, a cultural-theatrical group which sponsors lectures on theatre and produces plays on an amateur basis. In the same year, *Couleurs des jours mêlés,* his first collection of poetry, wins recognition from l'Association Catholiques des Jeunes Canadiens. He sees his first professional production in 1949 when Anouilh's *Antigone* is mounted by Les Compagnons de Saint-Laurent at Montreal's Théâtre du Gésu. Having read Quebec poets Emile Nelligan and Hector Saint-Denys-Garneau as well as the complete works of playwrights Jean Anouilh, Jean Giraudoux and Anton Chekhov, he decides on a career as a writer. In 1950, he completes *Ondes courtes*, his second collection of poetry.

Until this time, his interests are mainly literary. Through reading newspapers, he gradually becomes aware of the atmosphere of change and unrest sweeping Quebec during the 1950's. This growing political awareness is reflected in his writing. His first play, *Le Bal triste*, is produced by La Jeune Scène in 1950. Although the play is a failure, he receives encouragement from Louis-Georges Carrier, one of Quebec's foremost theatre directors. After graduating from Collège Sainte-Marie in 1951, he enrols as a graduate student in the Faculté des Lettres at l'Université de Montréal. While at university, he supports himself by writing radio and television scripts for Radio-Canada. In 1952, his play *De l'autre côté du mur* wins first prize at the Western Quebec Drama Festival in Saint John, New Brunswick. At this point he is forced to choose between the theatre and his academic studies since his final examinations coincide with the Saint John competition and the university refuses to allow him to take the exams later. After considerable soul-searching, he chooses to pursue his theatrical ambitions. In 1953, his play *Zone*, also produced by La Jeune Scène, wins the Grand Prize for the best new Canadian play of the year at the DDF finals in Victoria. The play then enjoys a three-week run at Montreal's Théâtre des Compagnons.

By this time Dubé is becoming well-known, both as a spokesman for and one of the main architects of Quebec's blossoming cultural scene. A fervent cultural nationalist, in 1953 he makes the following statement about the purpose and contribution of Quebec writers: "Writing must affirm, in spite of all obstacles, the legitimacy and autonomy of the French-Canadian people; we must cut our cultural ties with France and assume the task of living our own lifestyle . . ." Although welcoming recognition from France, Dubé writes for and about Quebec. He feels that to be truly honest a playwright must root himself in his own culture. He must recognize his true identity and the identities of those with whom he lives. By 1956, La Jeune Scène is in financial difficulty. Dubé is forced to

disband the troupe and assume its $10,000 debt himself.

In order to support himself and pay off the debt, he devotes most of his time during the mid-1950's and early 60's to writing for radio and television. These scripts are produced by Radio-Canada. His only stage plays during this period are *Chambres à louer*, 1954, winner of the Grand Prize at the DDF finals in Regina, Saskatchewan; *Le Naufragé* and *Le Barrage*, both of which are staged in Montreal in 1955; and *Le Temps des lilas* produced by Théâtre du Nouveau Monde in 1958.

In 1958 he becomes a member of the editorial board of *Ecrits du Canada Français*. Though he feels it important that an artist retain his political independence, for a time he serves as speech writer for Quebec Liberal Premier, Jean Lesage. As well, he works for a time in 1962 and '63 as an editorial writer for the magazine *Perspectives*.

Still deeply committed to the creation of a national drama for Quebec, he returns to the stage in 1965 with *Les Beaux Dimanches*. In 1966, he is awarded the Société Saint-Jean Baptiste's Victor Morin Prize for his contribution to Quebec theatre. During the next 10 years he writes 13 plays including *L'Eté s'appelle July, L'Impromptu de Québec, Pauvre amour, Un Matin comme les autres, Virginie, Hold Up, De l'autre côté du mur, Port au Persil, La Vie quotidienne d'Antoine X, Paradis perdu, Avant de t'en aller*, and *Portés disparus*, and in 1967 he receives a grant from the Ministre des Affaires Culturelles to prepare a complete edition of his plays. As well as dramatic works, he is also the author of novels, essays and poetry. Dubé is married and makes his home today in Montreal.

Stage Writing

Le Bal triste: one-act; written in 1949; unpublished; first produced by La Jeune Scène, 1950, under the direction of the author; subsequently produced by Collège de Montréal, Montreal, 1950.

De l'autre côté du mur: one-act; written in 1951; first published by Leméac,

Montreal, 1973, in a volume including *Rendez-vous du lendemain, Le Visiteur, L'Aiguillage, Le Père idéal* and *Les Frères ennemis*; first produced by La Jeune Scène, 1952 under the direction of the author; winner of first prize at the Western Quebec Drama Festival, 1952; subsequently performed at the Dominion Drama Festival finals, Saint John, New Brunswick, 1952.

Zone: three-acts; written in 1952; first published in *Ecrits du Canada Français*, Vol. II, 1955; subsequently published by Editions de la Cascade, Montreal, 1956 and Leméac, 1968; first produced by La Jeune Scène, 1953, under the direction of the author; subsequently produced at Théâtre des Compagnons, Montreal, 1953, also under the direction of the author; winner of both first prize at the Western Quebec Drama Festival and the Grand Prize at the DDF finals in Victoria in 1953; adapted for radio and television; produced by CBC television, Montreal, 1953, for regional broadcast; subsequently produced by Ford Radio Theatre; produced by Théâtre de Marjolaine, Eastman, Quebec, in 1960 under the direction of Georges Campeau.

Chambres à louer: full-length; written in 1953; unpublished; first produced by La Jeune Scène, 1954, under the direction of the author; winner of both first prize at the Western Quebec Drama Festival and the Grand Prize at the DDF finals in Regina, Saskatchewan, 1954; adapted for radio and television; produced by CBC-TV, Montreal, 1954, for regional broadcast; produced as a series by CKAC Radio, 1955-56.

Le Barrage: full-length; written in 1954; unpublished; first produced by Théâtre Club, Montreal, 1955.

Le Naufragé: full-length; written in 1954; revised version published by Leméac, 1971; first produced by Théâtre-Club, 1955.

Le Temps des lilas: two-act; written in 1957; first published by Institut Littéraire du Québec, 1958 in the same volume as the television play *Un Simple Soldat*; subsequently published by Leméac, 1969, and re-issued in 1973; first produced by

Théâtre du Nouveau Monde, Montreal, 1958 under the direction of Jean Gascon; adapted for television; produced by CBC-TV, Montreal, 1962, for regional broadcast.

L'Aiguillage: one act; written in 1959; first published by Leméac in 1973 in the same volume as *Rendez-vous du lendemain, De l'autre côté du mur, Le Visiteur, Le Père ideal* and *Les Frères ennemis*; unproduced.

Le Visiteur: one act; written in 1959; first published by Leméac in 1973 in the same volume as *L'Aiguillage, Rendez-vous du lendemain, De l'autre côté du mur, Le Père ideal* and *Les Frères ennemis*; unproduced.

Les Frères ennemis: one act; written in 1960; first published by Leméac in 1973 in the same volume as *L'Aiguillage, De l'autre Côté du mur, Rendez-vous du lendemain, Le Visiteur* and *Le Père ideal*; unproduced.

Les Beaux Dimanches: three-act; written in 1964; first published by Leméac, 1968; first produced by Comédie-Canadienne, Montreal, 1965, under the direction of Louis-Georges Carrier.

L'Est un saison: full-length; written in 1964 with Louis-Georges Carrier and Claude Léveillée; unpublished; first produced by Comédie-Canadienne, 1965, under the direction of Louis-Georges Carrier.

Au retour des oies blanches: full-length; written in 1965, first published by Leméac, 1969; subsequently published in English under the title *The White Geese* by New Press, Toronto, 1972 with translation by Jean Remple; first produced by Comédie-Canadienne, 1966 under the direction of Georges Groulx.

Port au Persil: full-length; written in 1967; unpublished; unproduced.

Un Matin comme les autres: full-length; written in 1967; first published by Leméac, 1971; first produced by Comédie-Canadienne, 1968, under the direction of Louis-Georges Carrier.

La Vie quotidienne d'Antoine X: full-length; written in 1967; unpublished; produced on stage, 1968.

Pauvre amour: full-length; written in 1967; first published by Leméac, 1969; first produced by Comédie-Canadienne, 1968, under the direction of Louis-Georges Carrier.

Hold-Up: full-length; written in 1968 with Louise-Georges Carrier; first published by Leméac, 1969; first produced by Théâtre de Marjolaine, Eastman, Quebec, 1969 under the direction of Louis-Georges Carrier.

Le Coup de l'étrier: one-act; written in 1968; first published by Leméac, 1970, in same volume as *Avant de t'en aller*; first produced by Théâtre du Rideau Vert, Montreal, 1969, on a double bill with *Avant de t'en aller*, under the direction of Georges Groulx and Yvette Brind'Amour.

Avant de t'en aller: one-act; written in 1968; first published by Leméac, 1970, in same volume as *Le Coup de l'etrier;* first produced by Théâtre du Rideau Vert, 1969, on a double bill with *Le Coup de l'étrier*, under the direction of Yvette Brind'Amour.

Virginie: four parts; written in 1968; first published by Leméac in 1974; first produced by Compagnie Jean Duceppe, Montreal, in 1974.

Paradis perdu: 23 short scenes; written in 1970; first published by Leméac, 1972, in same volume as revised version of TV script *L'Echéance du vendredi;* unproduced.

Portés disparus: full-length; written in 1971; unpublished; first produced on stage, 1972.

Le Père ideal: one act; written in 1972; first published by Leméac in 1973 in the same volume as *L'Aiguillage, Rendez-vous du lendemain, De l'autre Côté du mur, Le Visiteur* and *Les Frères ennemis*; unproduced.

Rendez-vous du lendemain: one act; written in 1972; first published by Leméac in 1973 in the same volume as *L'Aiguillage, De l'autre côté du mur, Le Visiteur, Le Père ideal* and *Les Frères ennemis*; unproduced.

L'Impromptu de Québec ou Le Testament: full-length; written in 1973; first published by Leméac, 1974; first produced by Théâtre de Marjolaine, 1974, under the direction of Albert Millaire.

L'Eté s'appelle Julie: full-length comedy; written in 1974; first published by Leméac, 1975.

Dites le avec des fleurs: comedy; written in 1975 with Jean Barbeau; first published by Leméac in 1976.

Le Réformiste ou L'Honneur des hommes: full-length; written in 1976; first published by Leméac, 1977; first produced by Théâtre du Nouveau Monde in 1977 under the direction of Fernand Déry.

Television Writing

L'Etranger: written in 1952; produced by CBC-TV, Montreal, 1953, for regional broadcast.

La Lettre: written in 1953; produced by CBC-TV, Montreal, 1954, for regional broadcast.

La Bicyclette: written in 1953; produced by CBC-TV, Montreal, 1954, for regional broadcast.

Pour cinq sous d'amour: written in 1954; produced by CBC-TV, Montreal, 1955, for national broadcast.

Florence: written in 1955; original version unproduced; revised version published by Leméac, 1970; revised version produced by CBC-TV, Montreal, 1957; adapted for the stage; produced by Comédie-Canadienne, 1960, under the direction of Louis-Georges Carrier.

Un Simple Soldat: written in 1955; first published by Institute Littéraire du Québéc in 1958; subsequently published by Editions de l'Homme, Montreal, 1967; produced by CBC-TV, Montreal, 1957, for regional broadcast; revised for the stage; produced by Comédie-Canadienne, 1958, under the direction of Jean-Paul Fugère; revised; new version produced by Comédie-Canadienne,

1967, under the direction of Jacques Létourneau.

La Fin du rêve: written in 1957; produced by CBC-TV, Montreal, 1958, for regional broadcast; rewritten in 1969 and broadcast by CBC-TV Montreal as part of the series *Le Monde de Marcel Dubé*.

Médée: written in 1958; first published by Lémeac in 1973; produced by CBC-TV, Montreal, 1958, for regional broadcast.

La Cellule: written in 1959; first published by Leméac in 1973; produced by CBC-TV Montreal in 1959 for regional broadcast; rewritten in 1969 and broadcast by CBC-TV Montreal as part of the series *Le Monde de Marcel Dubé*.

Equation à deux inconnus: written in 1958; produced by CBC-TV, Montreal, 1959, for regional broadcast; adapted for the stage; produced in 1967.

L'Echéance du vendredi: written in 1959; revised version published by Leméac, 1972, in the same volume as the stage play *Paradis perdu*; produced by CBC-TV, Montreal, 1962, for regional broadcast.

Bilan: written in 1959; revised stage version published by Leméac, 1968; first produced by CBC-TV, Montreal, 1960, for regional broadcast; revised for the stage; produced by Comédie-Canadienne, 1965; subsequently produced by Théâtre du Nouveau Monde, 1968, under the direction of Albert Millaire.

La Côté de Sable: television series, written between 1960 and 1962; produced by CBC-TV, Montreal, 1960-62, for regional broadcast.

Aux Voyageurs: written in 1960 with Georges Dor; produced by CBC-TV, Montreal, 1962, for regional broadcast.

Les Frères Ennemis: written in 1961; first published by Leméac, 1973, one of five short pieces (originally radio and television scripts) including *Rendez-Vous de Lendemain, Le Visiteur, L'Auguillage* and *Le Pere ideal* in same volume as the stage play *D'l'autre cote du Mur.*

De 9 à 5: television series; written between 1963 and 1965; produced by CBC-TV, Montreal, 1963-65, for regional broadcast.

Le Monde de Marcel Dubé: television series; written between 1968 and 1972; extracts published by Leméac, 1971, under the title *Entre Midi et Soir*; produced by CBC-TV, Montreal, 1968-72, for regional broadcast.

Octobre: television play; first published by Leméac in 1977.

Radio Writing

Pleure, pauvre Guillaume: written in 1950; produced by Radio-Canada, 1951.

Cartes postales: written in 1950; produced by Radio-Canada, 1951.

Pivart, le malin: written in 1950; produced by Radio-Canada, 1951.

L'Anneau: written in 1951; produced by Radio-Canada, 1952.

La Radonée fantastique: written in 1952; produced by Radio-Canada, 1953.

Un bord de la rivière: written in 1953; produced by Radio-Canada, 1954.

Un Bouquet d'immortelles: written in 1955; produced by Radio-Canada, 1956.

Le Cage: translation of *Crack-Up* by Mac Shoub; written in 1959; produced by Radio-Canada, 1959.

Manuel: dramatic text in four parts; written in 1967; first published by Leméac, 1973; produced by CBFT Radio, 1968.

David Fennario

Born in 1947 as David Wiper in Point St.
Charles, an English working-class district in
Montreal. The second of six children.
Father a housepainter. Although a good
student he leaves school at the age of 16,
seeing no future for himself either as an
intellectual or as a "bourgeois" worker.
Filled with romantic dreams, he drifts into
the 60's street scene and supports himself by
doing odd jobs, spending his spare time
among poets, artists and hippies in the
coffee houses of Montreal and Toronto.

During this same period, a girlfriend
gives him the nickname Fennario, taken
from his favourite line in the Bob Dylan
song *Pretty Peggy-O*. In 1966, he spends 30
days in jail on a vagrancy charge. His
companion and future wife, Elizabeth,
works as a waitress while he himself takes a
series of odd jobs. Laid off from a job in the
shipping department of the Montreal
Simpsons in 1969 and feeling that years of
drifting have brought him to a dead-end, he
decides to return to school. In 1972, while
still a student at Dawson College, he
submits as a creative writing assignment a
journal that he has been working on for
several years. His teacher is so impressed by
the writing that she helps get it published by
the college under the title, *Without A
Parachute*. Shortly thereafter, he leaves
school again. He distributes the book
himself to bookstores in and around
Montreal. One of the 1,000 copies of the
book is bought by Maurice Podbrey,
artistic director of Montreal's English-
language Centaur Theatre. Podbrey,
impressed by the book, asks Fennario to
write a play for Centaur. Hesitant, having
seen only one play in his life, he spends two
years on a Canada Council grant as the
Centaur's writer-in-residence, watching
plays go through the rehearsal process to
finished production.

His first play, *On the Job*, is premiered by
the Centaur in 1975. Based on his own
experiences, it is set in the shipping room of
a large garment manufacturing company.
Remounted by the Centaur in 1976, it is
later produced by CBC-TV. The play is also
a finalist in the Chalmers Outstanding

Canadian Play Awards. That same year, he
and Elizabeth are married.

The Centaur premieres his next three
plays, *Nothing to Lose, Toronto,* and
Balconville, which wins the Chalmers Award
for the outstanding Canadian play of 1979.
As with *On the Job*, these plays too draw on
Fennario's own experiences and are set in
milieux with which he is familiar.
Considered immediately as a "political"
writer, he points out that "the politics have
to come out of the characters or else it
doesn't work." He tells the *Toronto Star* in
1978, "because of my background, just the
fact that I'm writing plays is a political
thing." An active member of the Socialist
Labour Party, he and his wife, now an art
student, currently make their home in the
same working-class neighbourhood in
which Fennario grew up. He continues as
well in his post as playwright-in-residence
at the Centaur.

Stage Writing

On the Job: full-length drama; written in
1974; first published by Talonbooks,
Vancouver, in 1976; first produced by
Centaur Theatre, Montreal in 1975 under

the direction of David Calderisi, re-mounted by Centaur in 1976; subsequently produced by the Arts Club Theatre, Vancouver, in 1976 under the direction of Bill Millerd; adapted for television and broadcast by CBC in 1976.

Nothing to Lose: full-length drama; written in 1975; first published by Talonbooks in 1977; first produced by Centaur Theatre in 1976 under the direction of Guy Sprung; re-mounted by Centaur in 1978, a production later taken on tour in Quebec and Ontario.

Toronto: full-length play about theatre life; written in 1977, unpublished; first produced by Centaur in 1978 under the direction of Eric Steiner.

Balconville: full-length bilingual drama; written in 1978; scheduled for publication by Talonbooks in 1980; first produced by Centaur Theatre in 1979 under the direction of Guy Sprung; winner of the 1979 Chalmers Award for the outstanding Canadian play of the year.

Miscellaneous

Without a Parachute: originally written in 1972 as a journal novel; privately published through Dawson College, Montreal; subsequently published by McClelland and Stewart; adapted for the stage and first produced by Theatre Passe Muraille, Toronto, in 1979.

Jacques Ferron

Born January 20, 1921, in Louiseville, Quebec, one of five children of a notary. Mother dies of tuberculosis when he is 11 years old. Receives his secondary education at Collège Brébeuf in Montreal after which he takes a degree in medicine at Laval College. While still a student, he marries Madeleine Thérien. After graduation in 1945, he enlists in the Canadian Army as a captain. He completes his first novel, written in the style of Anatole France, *La Gorge de Minerve*, that same year, but the book is not published.

After the war, he and his wife move to Rivière-Madeleine, a tiny village in the Gaspé where he decides to set up as a general practitioner, a field of practice which he feels will allow him enough freedom to pursue his writing at the same time. In 1947, his wife gives birth to their first child, a daughter. Shortly thereafter, he develops tuberculosis. His writing continues, though, and he completes two novels: *Martine* and *La Barbe de François Hertel*. A satirist, his attacks are often focused on those he knows best — doctors, a profession he calls "...la mafia des diplomes". In 1948, he is forced, because of

Kéro

ill health and a reduction in his government grant, to move his practice to Ville-Jacques Cartier, a working class suburb of Montreal. In the same year, he becomes a Communist. While his practice is still small, he writes *L'Ogre*, his first stage play. Dissatisfied with the state of Canadian medicine, he volunteers for service during the Korean War in the hope that on the battlefield his medical skills will be put to better use. He is, however, refused because of the tuberculosis.

This same period also sees the end of his marriage to Madeleine Thérien and his subsequent remarraige to Madeleine Lavalée with whom he has three children. Soon after the marriage, he enters the hospital to be treated for his continuing illness. Finally cured, he returns to Ville-Jacques Cartier to resume his practice. As well as writing and medicine, he becomes active politically, running as a candidate for office in 1955. In 1962 he is awarded the Governor General's Prize for *Contes du pays incertain*, a collection of short stories dealing with the problems of maintaining Quebec's cultural identity, a driving force behind his work.

In 1963 he founds a new political party using a rhinoceros as its symbol. From 1965 onwards, the Rhinoceros Party fields candidates in all federal elections as a satirical protest as much as anything else. In 1966, he becomes resident doctor at Saint-Jean-de-Dieux Hospital, a post which he holds through the present. In 1973 he is awarded the Prix-France Canada by l'Association des Ecrivains de la Langue française for this novel, *Les Roses sauvages*.

Remaining active as a physician, a playwright, and a political satirist, he runs in the 1979 election on a platform which promises to make the War Measures Act permanent so as to give the Army something to do, issue Rolls Royces to all Army officers, repatriate the Queen, lower the voting age to 14 and give unemployment insurance recipients more money than they'd get if they'd been working. Previous promises from the Rhinoceros leader included covering the town of Mount Royal with Plexiglass to ward off separatism and bad weather, and legalizing bribes.

Stage Writing

L'Ogre: full-length; written in 1948; first published by Cahiers de la File Indienne, Montreal, in 1949; first produced by Théâtre-Club, Montreal. 1958.

Le Licou: one-act comedy; written in 1950; first published by Editions d' Orphée, 1951; in same volume as the novel, *La barbe de François Hertel*; subsequently reprinted separately by Editions d'Orphée, 1959; unproduced.

Le Dodu: full-length comedy; written in 1952; first published by Editions d' Orphée, Montreal, in 1953; first published by Théâtre-Club, 1958.

Lella Mariem: full-length; written in 1953; extracts published in *l' Amerique Francais,* (Vol. 12, No. 3), 1954; first act published in *Le Devoir*, March 31, 1966; unproduced.

Les Rats: full-length; written in 1953; extracts published in *L'Amérique français,* (Vol. 12, No. 5), 1954; unproduced.

Tante Elise ou la prix de l'amour: one-act comedy; written in 1956; first published by Editions Orphée, 1957; unproduced.

Le Cheval de Don Juan: full-length; written in 1958, first produced by Editions d'Orphée, 1959; first produced by College Séraphique, Verdun, Montreal in 1959.

Les Grands Soleils: full-length; written in 1958; first published by Editions d'Orphée in 1959; first produced by Théâtre-Club in 1958; revised version produced by Théâtre du Nouveau Monde, Montreal in 1968.

L'Américaine ou le triomphe de l'amitié: one-act; written in 1958; first published in *Situations* (Vol. 1, No. 7), 1959; first produced by Théâtre des Auteurs, Montreal in 1961.

Cazou ou le prix de la virginité: one act; written in 1962; first published by Editions d'Orphée, 1963; unproduced.

La Tête du roi: full-length; written in 1962; first published by AGEUM, Montreal, 1963; unproduced.

La Sortie: one act; written in 1964; first published by *Ecrits de Canada français*,

(Vol. 19), 1965; unproduced.

Théâtre 1: collection of plays containing *Les Grands Soleils, Tante Elise* and *Don Juan crétin*; published by Librairie Déom, Montréal in 1968.

Théâtre 2: collection of plays containing *Le Dodu, La Tête du roi, L' Impromptu des deux chiens* as well as the short story *La Mort de Monsier Borduas* and an essay entitled *Le Permis du dramaturge*: published by Librairie Déom in 1975.

Novels

Martine: written in 1947; unpublished.

La Gorge de Minerve: written in 1945; unpublished.

La Barbe de François Hertel: written in 1950; first published by Editions d'Orphée, 1951, in same volume as the play *Le licou*; subsequently published by Editions du Jour, Montreal, in 1970, in same volume as the novel *Cotnoir*.

Cotnoir: written in 1969; first published by Editions d'Orphée in 1962; subsequently published by Editions du Jour, 1970, in same volume as *La Barbe de François Hertel*; *Cotnoir* subsequently published in English under the title *Dr. Cotnoir* by Harvest House, Montreal, in 1973, translated by Pierre Cloutier.

La Charette: written in 1967; first published by Editions du Jour, Montreal, 1968.

Le Ciel de Québec: written in 1968; first published by Editions HMH, 1969.

L'Amélanchier: written in 1969; first published by Editions du Jour, 1970.

Le Salut de l'Irland: written in 1969; first published by Editions du Jour, 1970.

Les Roses sauvages suivi d'une lettre d'amour soigneusement présentée: written in 1970; first published by Editions du Jour, 1971; subsequently published in English by McClelland and Stewart, Toronto, in 1976, translated by Betty Bednarski; winner of the 1973 Prix France-Canada.

La Chaise du maréchal ferrant: written in 1971; first published by Editions du Jour, 1972.

Le Saint-Elias: written in 1971; first published by Editions du Jour, 1972; subsequently published in English under the title *The Saint Elias* by Harvest House, in 1973, translated by Pierre Cloutier.

Short Stories

Le Mariage d'Hercule: short story; written in 1941; first published in *l'Amérique français*, (No. 6), 1942.

Contes du pays incertain: short stories; written in 1961; first published by Editions d'Orphée in 1962.

Contes anglais et autres: short stories; written in 1963; first published by Editions d'Orphée, 1964; subsequently published by Editions HMH, Montreal, 1964.

La Nuit: story; written in 1964; first published by Editions Parti Pris, Montreal, 1965; revised version entitled *Les Confitures de coings* published in a collection of short stories under the same title including *Papa Boss* and *La Créance* by Editions Parti Pris, 1972.

Papa Boss: short story; written in 1965; first published by Editions Parti Pris, 1966; reprinted in *Les Confitures de coings*, a collection of short stories also including *Les Confitures de coings* (revised version of *La Nuit*) and *La Créance*, by Editions Parti Pris, 1972; published in English by Coach House Press, Toronto in 1977 in the collection entitled *Quince Jam* including *Quince Jam* and *Credit Due*, in translation by Ray Ellenwood.

Contes inédits: short stories; written in 1967; first published by Editions HMH, 1968.

La Mort de Monsieur Borduas: short story; written in 1967; first published in *Les Herbes rouges*, (No. 1), 1968.

Contes: reprint of *Contes du pays incertain* and *Contes anglais et autres* as well as four new stories; first published by Editions HMH, 1968.

Histoirettes: short stories; written in 1968; first published by Editions du Jour, 1969.

Le Coeur d'une mère: short story; written in 1968; first published in *Ecrits du Canada français*, (Vol. 25), 1969.

Les Confitures de coings: a selection of short stories including *Papa Boss, Les Confitures de coings* (a new version of *La Nuit*) and *La Créance*; first published by Editions Parti Pris, 1972; subsequently published under the title *Quince Jam*, a collection including *Papa Boss* and *Credit Due*, by Coach House Press, Toronto, translated by Ray Ellenwood.

Tales from the Uncertain Country: selection of short stories from *Contes du pays incertain, Contes anglais et autres* and *Contes inédits*; first published by House of Anansi Press, Toronto, 1972, translated by Betty Bednarski.

Du Fond de mon arrière-cuisine: short stories; written in 1972; first published bv Editions du Jour, 1973.

Miscellaneous

Le Permis du dramaturge: essay; first published in *La Barre du Jour*, (Vol. 1, Nos. 3,4,5), 1965; subsequently reprinted in *Theatre 1*, a collection of plays including *Les Grands Soleils, Tante Elise* and *Don Juan cretin*, by Librarie Déom in 1968.

Escarmouches I: short essays; written in 1974; first published by Leméac, Montreal, 1975.

Escarmouches II: short essays; written in 1974; first published by Leméac, Montreal, 1975.

Secondary Sources

Godin, Jean-Cleo and Mailhot, Laurent, *Le Theatre quebecois*, Editions HMH, 1970, pp. 151-172.

Varasse, Andre, "*Le Théâtre de Jacques Ferron: à la rechereche d'une identite*" in *LAQ*, 1969, pp. 219-230.

Boucher, Jean-Pierre, *Jacques Ferron au pays des amélanchiers*, Les Presses de l'Université de Montréal, 1973.

Marcel, Jean, *Jacques Ferron malgré lui*, Editions du Jour, 1970.

de Roussan, Jacques, *Jacques Ferron*, Les Presses de l'Université du Québec, 1971.

Taschereau, Yves, *La Médecine dans l'oeuvre de Jacques Ferron*, Editions de l'Aurore, 1975.

Charlotte Fielden

Born in Toronto in 1934. Her first
involvement in theatre is as a student at the
University of Toronto where she is directed
by Robert Christie and fellow student Leon
Major in productions at the University
College Playhouse and Hart House
Theatre. A poet as well as an actress, she
receives an Epstein Award for Creative
Writing. In 1951, she earns a degree in
speech and drama from the Royal
Conservatory of Music in Toronto. At the
University of Toronto, she receives several
awards for her theatre work. She graduates
in 1955 with a B.A. in English, and is soon
hired by the Stratford Festival. She appears
there in several productions, including
Tyrone Guthrie's *The Merchant of Venice* in
which she plays Jessica.

That fall, she moves to France where she
works as a translator for the U.S. Army and
studies at the Marcel Marceau School of
Mime. Returning to Canada in 1958, she
settles in Montreal and works as an actress
and a mime, both on stage and in television.
In the 60's, she begins to write full-time,
mostly for television. Between 1966 and
1968, she writes a novel, *Crying As She Ran*,
which is published by Macmillan in 1970. In
1973, she writes *The Nowhere Girl*, her first
stage play, which leads to the creation of
her own theatre, the Melanie, which she
founds with Ais Snyder in Montreal. The
first "feminist" theatre in Montreal, the
company also works in community centres,
schools and prisons. In 1976, *One Crowded
Hour* wins a National Playwriting for
Women Award sponsored by Playwrights
Co-op. This is followed by an Ontario Arts
Council playwriting grant in 1977. The
same year, she ends her association with
Melanie. A teacher as well as an actress and
writer, she has taught at l'Université de
Sherbrooke, Dalhousie University, Queen's
University, Concordia University and
l'Université de Québec. Recipient of three
Canada Council writing grants, she now
lives in Toronto.

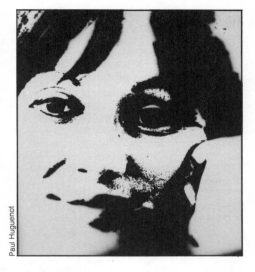

Paul Huguenot

Stage Writing

The Nowhere Girl: written in 1973;
unpublished; unproduced.

One Crowded Hour: three-act monologue;
written in 1975; first published by the
Playwrights Co-op, 1977 in *Women Write
for the Theatre, Volume Two*; first produced
by the Melanie Theatre, Montreal, 1975,
under the direction of Ais Snyder;
subsequently produced by the Théâtre de
Quat'Sous, Montreal, in a translation by
Rene Dionne; film adaptation is completed
in 1977; winner of a Women Write for the
Theatre Award.

The Honeymoon: three acts; unpublished;
first produced by the Melanie Theatre,
Montreal, in 1976, under the direction of
Ais Snyder.

Summer Holidays (translation/adaptation
of the play by Serge Sirois): unpublished;
first produced by the Melanie Theatre,
Montreal, 1976, under the direction of
Monique Lepage.

Will the Real Punch and Judy Please Stand Up: written between 1978 and 1979; unpublished; unproduced.

Miscellaneous

Chez Hélène: several 15-minute television shows for children; written during the 1960's; produced by CBC for national broadcast.

Crying as She Ran: novel; written between 1966 and 1968; first published by Macmillan of Canada, 1970.

Family Court: several 30-minute television dramas; written during the 1970's; produced by CBC for national broadcast.

A Message from Sarah: novel; sequel to *Crying as She Ran*; unpublished;

Matthew, Mark, Luke and John: screen play; unproduced.

Several short stories and articles published in *Tamarack Review*, *Impulse*, and *Canadian Theatre Review*.

In Progress

Stage Plays: **The Morning Needs Me, The Hacks, The Dodo, Me and New Orleans** (a musical-comedy in collaboration with Robert Swerdlow).

Timothy Findley

Born October 30, 1930, in Toronto. Father a businessman. In the early 50's, he attends the Central School of Speech and Drama in London. After graduation, he appears in numerous shows on the West End, ranging from *The Matchmaker* to *Hamlet*. Back in Canada, he appears in Stratford's inaugural season in 1953 and subsequently at Toronto's Civic Theatre and later at the Crest.

In the mid 60's, he leaves acting and begins to write novels. *The Last of the Crazy People* is published in 1967, followed two years later by *The Butterfly Plague*. At the same time, he begins to write for television and radio as well as doing documentary profiles on people in the arts for CBC. In 1971-1972 he writes seven episodes for the CBC-TV series, *Jalna*. The next year he writes the eight episodes for CBC's *The National Dream* for which he receives an ACTRA award. Between 1976 and 1978 he writes for *The Newcomers*, a series dealing with Canada's immigrants. One of these scripts, *The Newcomers: 1832*, wins an award from the Canadian Film and

Rolf Kalman

Television Association. His third novel, *The Wars*, receives both the Governor General's Award for Fiction and the City of Toronto Book Award. Divorced, he currently makes his home in Cannington, Ontario.

Stage Writing

Can You See Me Yet?: two-act drama about the efforts of a mental patient to examine the cause of her insanity; written in 1974-1975; first published by Talonbooks, Vancouver, 1977; first produced by the National Arts Centre, Ottawa, 1976, under the direction of Marigold Charlesworth.

John A. — Himself: two-act historical play with music by Berthold Carriere about "the last days of John A. MacDonald in the style of Victorian theatre, with the traditional change of sexes as in classical pantomime"; written in 1978; unpublished; first produced by Theatre London, 1979, under the direction of Peter Moss.

Radio Plays

Missionaries: 90 minutes; written in 1971; unpublished; first produced by CBC, Toronto, for national broadcast.

Adrift: 30 minutes; written in 1972; unpublished; first produced by CBC, Toronto, for national broadcast.

The Journey: 90 minutes: written in 1973; first produced by CBC, Toronto, for national broadcast; winner of the Armstrong Award for Radio Drama.

River through Time: 90-minute play in blank verse; unpublished; first produced by CBC, Toronto, for national broadcast.

Television Writing

The Paper People: 90-minute film for television; written in 1967; produced by CBC, Toronto, 1968, for national broadcast.

Jalna: seven 60-minute episodes for the television series based on the novels by Mazo de la Roche; written in 1971-72; produced by CBC, Toronto, for national broadcast in 1972 and 1973.

The National Dream with William Whitehead: eight 60-minute episodes for the television series; written in 1973; produced by CBC, Toronto, 1974, for national broadcast; winner of an ACTRA award.

The Newcomers: two 60-minute episodes for the television series; written from 1976-1978; produced by CBC, Toronto, 1978-1979, for national broadcast; *Newcomers: 1832* won a Canadian Film and Television Association Award.

Other People's Children: 90 minutes; written in 1978; produced by CBC, Toronto.

Novels

The Last of the Crazy People: written in 1964; first published in 1967 by Meredith Press, New York; subsequently published by Bantam Books, U.S. and Canada; Macdonald, Great Britain; Corgi (paperback), Great Britain; Laurentian Library, Macmillan.

The Butterfly Plague: written in 1967-1968; first published by Viking Press, New York, 1969; subsequently published by Bantam Books, U.S. and Canada; Andre Deutsch, Great Britain; Corgi (paperback) Great Britain.

The Wars: written in 1977; first published by Clarke Irwin, Canada, 1977; subsequently published by Delacourt, U.S.; Penguin (paperback), Canada, Great Britain and Commonwealth; Dell (paperback) U.S.; Macmillan, Great Britain; Piper, West Germany; Fayard, France; Ritzzoli, Italy; publication pending in Holland, Denmark, Sweden, Finland, Norway, Spain, Portugal, Israel, South America; winner of the Governor General's Award for fiction, and the City of Toronto Book Award.

In Progress

The Tin Wreath: tentative title for a novel.

Song: a television mini-series; three 90-minutes episodes.

Larry Fineberg

Born in 1945 in Montreal, the only child of an orthodox Jewish family. Father the owner-operator of a meat-packing plant. His first theatrical experience is a children's performance of *Little Black Sambo* ("...I became utterly fascinated and captivated by the fact that magic and illusion that was more interesting than real life, could be put on the stage..."). After attending West Hill High School, he enrols at McGill University, but fails to complete his first year.

Transferring to Emerson College, Boston, he majors in English literature, minoring in philosophy. He also does a number of courses in theatre. For a year, he holds a part-time job as an usher at the Colonial Theater, one of Boston's well-known pre-Broadway tryout theatres. During this same period, he and several friends form an investment group which puts small sums of money into backing Broadway productions. From this, he learns much about the business side of theatre.

His participation in the investment group leads to a meeting with Broadway composer-producer Frank Loesser, who offers him a job as his personal assistant after Fineberg's graduation in 1967. A few months later, he begins a three-and-a-half year stint as assistant director for various Broadway plays ("I did everything from helping actors to doing the director's laundry"). As a break from Broadway, he spends the summer of 1968 in England as assistant director to Robert Kidd for the West End production of *Summer*. While in England, he also meets playwright Edward Bond ("someone whose work I admire very much"). Moving to New York late in 1968, he becomes assistant director to Martin Charnin (composer of the musical *Annie*) and works on an unproduced play by Gore Vidal entitled *A Drawing Room Comedy* before producing Bond's *Early Morning* at Cafe Le Mama in 1970.

He returns to Toronto in 1972 when his first play, *Stonehenge*, is produced at Factory Theatre Lab. His next play, *Hope*, commissioned by Toronto Free Theatre, is produced there later that year. He remains close to both Factory and Toronto Free over the next years but works as well with Theatre Passe Muraille and the Tarragon. Young People's Theatre produces his children's musical *Waterfall* in 1974. That same year, he writes a new libretto for the opera *Carmen* for the San Francisco Opera Company and is the recipient of a Canada Council Junior Arts Grant. The 1975 New Theatre production of his play, *Human Remains*, is a runner-up in the Chalmers Canadian play competition that year. At the same time, the Stratford Festival commissions him to adapt Constance Beresford-Howe's novel, *Eve*, into a stage play. After the production opens, he travels to the Banff School of Fine Arts to teach a course in playwriting. In 1977, he helps to found the Guild of Canadian Playwrights and becomes Chairman of the Playwrights Co-op. As playwright-in-residence at the Stratford Festival in 1978, he prepares a new version of *Medea*, which is produced at the Third Stage, as well as a workshop production of his comedy, *Devotion*.

In 1979, he tells *CTR*, "Canadian plays still desperately need to do three things: stop being afraid of invention and imagination, stop relying on historical events for plays, stop writing any play that doesn't make an audience re-assess its life." He currently makes his home in Toronto.

Stage Writing

Hope: two-act comedy; written in 1972; first published by Playwrights Co-op, Toronto, 1972; republished by Playwrights Co-op in an anthology in 1978, along with *Death, Human Remains* and *Stonehenge*; first produced by Toronto Free Theatre, Toronto, 1972, under the direction of John Palmer.

Stonehenge: three-act comedy; written in 1972; first published by Playwrights Co-op in 1972; revised version published by Playwrights Co-op in 1975; republished by Playwrights Co-op in 1978 in an anthology along with *Hope, Human Remains* and *Death*; first produced by the Factory Theatre Lab, Toronto, 1972, under the direction of Eric Steiner; subsequently produced by Vancouver East Cultural Centre, 1974, under the direction of Jackie Crossland.

Death: one-act drama; written in 1972; first published by Playwrights Co-op in 1972; subsequently published by Fineglow Press, Toronto, 1973, in *Now in Paperback, Six Canadian Plays of the 1970's*; also published in *Performing Arts in Canada*, Vol. 10, No. 2, (Summer 1973); republished by Playwrights Co-op in 1978 in an anthology along with *Human Remains, Hope* and *Stonehenge*; first produced by the Factory Theatre Lab, Toronto, 1972, under the direction of Timothy Bond; subsequently produced by the WPA Theater, New York, 1974; and the Colonade Theater, New York, 1979, under the direction of Michael Lessac; adapted for television and nationally broadcast by CBC, Toronto, 1976, starring Donald Pleasance.

A Crazy Play: one act; written in 1974; unpublished; unproduced.

All the Ghosts: two acts; written in 1974; unpublished; first produced by Theatre Passe Muraille, Toronto, 1974, under the direction of Louis del Grande, starring Jane Mallet.

Lady Celeste's Tea: one act; written in 1974; first published in a limited edition by Playwrights Co-op, 1974; first produced by Theatre Passe Muraille for the Gnatcan Festival, Toronto, 1974, under the direction of Paul Bettis.

Waterfall: with music by William Skolnik; one act; written in 1974 on commission from Young People's Theatre, Toronto; first published by Playwrights Co-op, 1974; first produced by Young People's Theatre, Toronto, 1974, under the direction of Timothy Bond; subsequently produced by the Playhouse Theatre Centre, Vancouver, 1974, under the direction of David Latham.

Medea: one act; written in 1975; first published by Theatre Books, Toronto, 1978; first workshopped by Stratford Festival in 1975 under the direction of Don Shipley; first produced by the Stratford Festival, 1978, under the direction of John Palmer; produced by Theatre 2000, Ottawa, 1979; winner of first prize at 1979 St. Lawrence Centre Drama Festival.

Eve (stage adaptation of Constance Beresford-Howe's novel): full-length; written in 1975-76; first published by Theatre Books, Toronto, 1977; first produced by the Stratford Festival, 1976, under the direction of Vivian Matelon, starring Jessica Tandy; subsequently produced by the Centaur Theatre, Montreal, 1977, under the direction of Maurice Podbrey; by the Hartford Stage Company, Connecticut, 1977, under the direction of Irene Lewis; winner of the 1976 Chalmers Award for an Outstanding Canadian Play.

Fresh Disasters: with music by Glen Morley; two acts; written in 1975-76; unpublished; first produced by the Young People's Theatre at Tarragon Theatre, Toronto, 1976, under the direction of Stephen Katz.

Human Remains: one-act drama; first published by Playwrights Co-op in 1976; republished by Playwrights Co-op in 1978 in an anthology along with *Hope, Stonehenge* and *Death*; first produced by New Theatre, 1975, under the direction of Stephen Katz.

Devotion: two-act comedy; unpublished; workshopped by Stratford Festival, 1978.

Life on Mars: two-act comedy about "sex, marriage and show business"; written in 1978-79; unpublished; first produced by the Toronto Free Theatre, 1979, under the direction of Eric Steiner.

Miscellaneous

Carmen: new version of the opera libretto; written for the San Francisco Opera Company in 1974; unpublished; first produced by the San Franciso Opera Company in 1974.

Sanity: 30-minute television drama; written in 1976; commissioned by BBC, London; unpublished; unproduced.

Dixie Diamond Detectives: mini-series for radio; written in 1979; produced by CBC, Winnipeg, 1979.

In Progress

An Illustrated History of the World: full-length comic stage play to be written for the Juilliard School.

Cutler: a film script; "a contemporary mystery in the Raymond Chandler tradition set in Toronto."

Men Obsessed: a comic play; "it offers a humorous look at five contemporary males from 35-40 years of age."

Star Quality: a two-hour radio play "about a husband and wife acting team"; to be produced by CBC, Winnipeg, 1980, for the series *Festival Theatre*.

The Last Chronicles of Ballyfungus: a musical comedy based on the novel by Mary Manning; to be written in collaboration with American lyricist Dennis Green and composer Scott Oakley.

David E. Freeman

Born January 7, 1945, in Toronto, one of three children. Father a security guard at IBM; mother a housewife. A victim of cerebral palsy resulting from brain damage at birth, he attends Toronto's Sunnyview School for handicapped children, where, encouraged by one of his teachers, he begins to write poetry and short stories. He also writes his first play there, an adaptation of Dickens' *Christmas Carol*. After graduating from Sunnyview at age 17 he immediately begins working at the Interfraternity Adult Cerebral Palsy Workshop where he spends his time sanding blocks and separating nuts and bolts. Years of frustration and boredom spent performing such menial tasks provide the impetus behind his first play, *Creeps*, which is set in the washroom of a sheltered workshop for cerebral palsy

Rosemary O'Shaugnessy

victims. It explores life in the workshop where the aim "is not to provide a living wage but rather to occupy idle hours."

In 1966, a year after writing the play, he leaves the workshop to enroll as a student of political science at McMaster University in Hamilton. *Creeps* remains unproduced for several years and while a student he does not write any more plays. It is only after graduating with a B.A. in 1971 that he begins, once again, to write for the stage. In 1972 *Creeps* is finally produced, amid unanimous praise, by Toronto's Factory Theatre Lab. It is subsequently produced at the new Tarragon Theatre and helps the company get through its first crucial season. It also turns Freeman into what he himself terms "a spastic Shakespeare". The play wins three awards: one from the Canadian Rehabilitation Council for the Disabled (1972), the Chalmers Award as Best Canadian Play of the year (1972) and, after its New York premiere, the New York Drama Desk Award for Outstanding New Playwrights (1973). He uses the money from the Chalmers Award to travel extensively in England in an effort to learn more about theatre.

The following years see his plays produced across the country, plays which gradually move away from the "handicapped" as subject matter into more universal areas. In 1975, he moves to Montreal where he currently makes his home. He lives with Francine, also a C.P. victim. As he told an interviewer (*The Canadian*, February 18, 1978), "if you want to talk to me today, talk to me as a playwright, not about my disabilities."

Stage Writing

Creeps: full length drama "set in the washroom of a sheltered workshop for cerebral palsy victims where disabled people go and work at their own pace without pressure from the competitive outside world"; written in 1965; first published, 1972, by the University of Toronto Press; first produced by Factory Theatre Lab, Toronto, 1971, directed by Bill Glassco; subsequently produced at the Tarragon Theatre, 1972, directed by Bill Glassco; at the Folger Theatre, Washington, D.C. and Playhouse 2, New York; winner of the 1972 Chalmers Award for Best Canadian play of the year; winner of the 1973 New York Drama Desk Award for Outstanding New Playwright; winner of one of six prizes given at the 1979 Edinburgh "fringe" Festival.

Battering Ram: two-act drama "...about a volunteer worker who brings home a cripple. This play concerned people who are handicapped by their inability to look at themselves honestly"; written in 1972; first published by Playwrights Co-op in 1972; subsequently published by Talonbooks, Vancouver, in 1974; first produced by Factory Theatre Lab, Toronto, in workshop in 1972 under the direction of Victor Sutton; subsequently produced by Tarragon Theatre, Toronto, in 1973 under the direction of Bill Glassco and taken on a national tour; produced in workshop by the Manhattan Theatre Club, New York, in 1976.

You're Gonna Be Alright, Jamie-Boy: two-act drama about "the death of television and its subsequent effects on a working-class family"; written in 1973-74; first published by Talonbooks, 1974; first produced by Tarragon Theatre in 1974, under the direction of Bill Glassco and played later that year at Centaur Theatre, Montreal; produced on television for the CBC "Opening Night" series; subsequently produced by the American National Theatre Academy in 1977.

Flytrap: two-act comedy-drama about "the loneliness and alienation of a middle-aged couple"; written between 1973 and 1976; unpublished; first produced by the Saidye Bronfman Centre, Montreal, 1976, under the direction of Robert Robinson.

Miscellaneous

The Poker Player: screenplay about handicapped teenaged campers and the solutions their volunteer counsellors concoct for their problems; developed for the Canadian Film Development Corporation; unproduced.

The World of Can't: article in *Maclean's*, 4 July 1964.

This Is What It's Like To Be a CP: article in *MacLean's*, 19 September 1965.

On and From Schools: article in *Toronto Educational Quarterly*.

How I Conquered Canada: article in *Star Weekly*, 13 November 1965.

The Good, the Bad, and the Ugly: article in *The Silhouette*, 25 January 1968.

Adam and Eve: article in *The Silhouette*, 1969.

Hello, Darkness: two-hour radio play, written in 1978 on commission from CBC; unproduced.

In Progress

The Bee-Hive: play

Jungle of Lilacs: a play

The Mask Factory: a novel about the changes students go through while in university in the 60's.

The Thank you Child: a novel dealing with "the pain of finding out what normality is and isn't."

Secondary Sources

Section on Freeman included in *Stage Voices* (Geraldine Anthony ed.), Doubleday, 1978. pp. 251-274.

David French

Born January 18, 1939, in Coley's Point, Newfoundland, one of five children. Father a carpenter. In 1945, the family emigrates to Toronto. Growing up in a household whose reading material consists entirely of the Bible and a copy of the Prayer Book, he is almost totally unexposed to culture of any sort. A gang member, he is keenly interested in sports and hates school. His attitude changes, however, when, as a rowdy schoolboy of 15, an exasperated teacher gives him a copy of Mark Twain's *Tom Sawyer* in the hope of keeping him quiet during class. By the time he finishes the book, he decides to become a writer and soon begins producing poetry and short stories. His first published poem appears in *The Canadian Boy*, a magazine put out by the United Church.

After graduating from high school in 1958, he begins a series of odd jobs including picking fruit, working as a sailor in Vancouver and working as a janitor in Toronto's Rochdale College ("we were always finding dope under the radiators..."). Deciding at this point to become an actor, he studies at several

Nir Bareket

Toronto theatre schools including a workshop run by Al Saxe of New York's Group Theatre. During this period he continues to write poetry and short stories. In 1959, he travels extensively throughout the United States and spends some time as an acting student at California's Pasadena Playhouse. He is offered a scholarship for further study but refuses, knowing already that he would rather write than act. ("I hate the term self-expression, but that's what it boils down to. I only write about the things that are hurting me inside.") Back in Toronto in 1960, he continues his training at the Lawlor School of Acting. He supports himself by working as a professional actor, mainly in CBC-TV dramas.

In 1962, fearful of making the transition from actor to writer, he joins the CBC as a mailboy. In the same year, his first script, *Beckons the Dark River*, is bought by the network for the television series, *Shoestring Theatre*. By 1965, he is able to give up acting, concentrating instead on his writing. In the next few years he completes over a dozen plays for radio and television. For several years, he also writes for the CBC children's television series, *Razzle Dazzle*.

After nine years, he leaves his $300-a-week position with the CBC for a $40-a-week job at the Post Office and the necessary free time to write a novel. In 1972, he visits Prince Edward Island. Here he begins to think about his family's experience of moving from Newfoundland to Toronto and to turn his memories into a play. That play, *Leaving Home*, is produced to rave reviews at Toronto's Tarragon Theatre. The play is also a finalist for the Chalmers Award for an Outstanding Canadian Play of 1972. It receives 35 subsequent productions across Canada. This is the beginning of an important collaboration between French and Tarragon Theatre director Bill Glassco, who is to stage the initial productions of all French's subsequent plays. The next year, 1973, he completes *Of the Fields, Lately*, a sequel to *Leaving Home*, which wins the Chalmers Award. After three abortive attempts to conclude his "trilogy about the Mercer family," he turns to other plays including *One Crack Out*, written in 1975; an adaptation of Anton Chekhov's *The Seagull*; and, in 1979, his first comedy *Jitters*.

Married, he divides his time between Toronto and a summer home in Prince Edward Island.

Stage Writing

Leaving Home: full-length drama; written in 1972; first published by New Press and General Publishing, Toronto, in 1972; first produced by the Tarragon Theatre, Toronto, 1972, under the direction of Bill Glassco; finalist for the 1977 Chalmers Play Award.

Of the Fields, Lately: full-length drama; written in 1973; first published by Playwrights Co-op, Toronto, in 1973; subsequently published by New Press, Toronto, 1975; first produced by the Tarragon Theatre, Toronto, 1973, under the direction of Bill Glassco; winner of the 1973 Chalmers Outstanding Canadian Play Award.

One Crack Out: three-act drama; written in 1975; first published by Playwrights Co-op, Toronto, in 1975; subsequently published by New Press in 1976; first produced by the Tarragon Theatre, 1975, under the direction of Bill Glassco.

The Seagull (a translation of the Chekhov play): written in 1976; first published by Playwrights Co-op in 1977; subsequently published by General Publishing, 1978; first performed by the Tarragon Theatre, Toronto, 1977, under the direction of Bill Glassco.

Jitters: three-act comedy about the theatre; written in 1978; first published by Playwrights Co-op in 1979; to be published by Talonbooks, 1980; first produced by the Tarragon Theatre, Toronto, 1979, under the direction of Bill Glassco; subsequently produced at the Long Wharf Theatre, New Haven under the direction of Bill Glassco; Broadway production scheduled for 1980; Chalmers Award finalist in 1979.

Radio Writing

Angeline: 30 minutes; written in 1966; first produced by CBC Radio, Toronto, in 1967, for national broadcast.

Invitation to a Zoo: 30 minutes; written in 1966; first produced by CBC Radio, Toronto, 1967, for national broadcast.

Winter of Timothy: 30 minutes; written in 1967; first produced by CBC Radio, Toronto, 1968, for national broadcast.

Television Writing

Beckons the Dark River: 30 minutes; written in 1962; first produced by CBC-TV, Montreal, 1963, for regional broadcast.

The Willow Harp: 30 minutes; written in 1962; first produced by CBC-TV, Montreal, in 1964, for regional broadcast.

After Hours: 30 minutes; written in 1964; first produced by CBC-TV, Montreal, in 1964, for regional broadcast.

A Ring for Florrie: 30 minutes; written in 1964; first produced by CBC-TV, Montreal, 1964, for regional broadcast.

Sparrow on a Monday Morning: 30 minutes; written in 1965; first produced by ETV Philadelphia in 1966; produced by CBC-TV Montreal, in 1967, for regional broadcast.

A Token Gesture: 30 minutes; written in 1969; first produced by CBC-TV, Toronto, in 1970, for national broadcast.

The Happiest Man in the World: an adaptation of a short story by Hugh Garner; 30 minutes; written in 1971; first produced by CBC-TV, Toronto, in 1972, for national broadcast.

A Tender Branch: 30 minutes; written in 1971; first produced by CBC-TV, Toronto, in 1972, for national broadcast.

Miscellaneous

A Company of Strangers: a novel, written in 1968; unpublished.

Several short stories and poems in *The Canadian Boy*, the *Montrealer*, and for CBC Radio.

A Day of Hockey: a short story; first published in *First Flowering*, an anthology edited by Anthony Frisch, Kingswood House, Toronto, 1956.

Secondary Sources

Section on French in *Stage Voices*, (Geraldine Anthony, ed.), Doubleday, 1978, pp. 234-250.

Ken Gass

Born September 10, 1945, in Abbotsford, British Columbia. He studies creative writing and theatre at the University of British Columbia, earning a B.A. in 1967 and an M.A. in 1968. After moving to Toronto, he teaches English at Parkdale Collegiate and works as a free-lance director at both Theatre Passe Muraille and John Herbert's Garret Theatre. Increasingly interested in new and experimental plays, he helps organize a *Festival of Underground Theatre* at the St. Lawrence Centre in 1970. The program includes four of his own experimental works, collectively entitled, *Light*.

Later that year, a $3,000 bank loan allows him to found Factory Theatre Lab in a disused candle factory above a garage on Dupont Street. The Factory is dedicated to the production of new Canadian plays, the first English-language theatre in the country to devote itself totally to indigenous work. Gass' own play *Red Revolutionary*, an adaptation of Charles Mair's *Tecumseh*, is produced at Factory in 1971. In 1973, he takes his company to England, offering up a Festival of Canadian plays. Over the next six years, he runs the factory almost single-handedly, teaches at York University and George Brown College, runs new play workshops, directs at the University of Toronto, Vancouver's Arts Club Theatre and at both the Playroom and Act Inn in London, England. *Hurray for Johnny Canuck* is produced by the Factory in 1975, under his own direction. This is followed a year later by a historical fantasy he writes, *The Boy Bishop*. Also premiered at the Factory under his direction, the play receives wide acclaim. He tells the *Toronto Star*, "It explores my own love-hate relationship with Canada. I've tried to plant a few flowers in what I consider to be our country's cultural desert. Like the Boy Bishop, I've attempted to create a new order in the wilderness and, like him, I've realized the futility of effecting an overnight change. Obsessed revolutionaries often get shot down." The play is a finalist in the Chalmers Competition for the Outstanding Canadian

Play of 1975. The following year, he directs *Revolutionary Project*, a collective creation, at Factory Theatre Lab. His next play, *Winter Offensive* (set in Germany during a party given by Mrs. Adolf Eichmann), opens a year later and provokes a major debate centred on obscenity and censorship in the arts. The play, he later writes, was simply about "a contemporary society in collapse." In 1977, he resigns his position as artistic director of Factory Theatre Lab, saying that he needs a rest. Married to actress Rosemary Donnelly and the father of one child, he currently makes his home in Toronto.

Stage Writing

Light: four short experimental plays; written in 1969; unpublished; first produced at the Festival of Underground Theatre at St. Lawrence Centre, Toronto, in 1970, under the direction of the author.

Red Revolutionary (adaptation of Charles Mair's *Tecumseh*): full-length; written in 1970; unpublished; first produced by Factory Theatre Lab, Toronto, in 1971, under the direction of the author;

subsequently produced by Arts Club, Vancouver, 1971, under the direction of the author.

Hurray for Johnny Canuck: two-act "cartoon" written in 1974; first published by Playwrights Co-op, Toronto, 1975; subsequently reprinted by Playwrights Co-op in 1978 in the anthology *Five Canadian Plays*; first produced by Factory Theatre Lab, 1974, under the direction of the author; subsequently produced by Young Peoples' Theatre, Toronto, for a provincial tour in 1975, under the direction of the author.

The Boy Bishop: two-act historical fantasy; written in 1976; first published by *Canadian Theatre Review*, Toronto, in 1976 (CTR 11); first produced by Factory Theatre Lab, 1976, under the direction of the author; finalist in the 1976 Chalmers competition for best new Canadian play.

Revolutionary Project (in collaboration with John Mills-Cockell and the cast): full-length; written in 1976; unpublished; first produced by Factory Theatre Lab in 1976 under the direction of the author; subsequently adapted for radio and broadcast by CBC in 1977.

Winter Offensive: full-length historical fantasy; written between 1976 and 1977; first published by Playwrights Co-op, 1978; first produced by Factory Theatre Lab in 1977 under the direction of the author.

Stage Directing

Two Programs of Short Plays: 1969; production at Theatre Passe Muraille, Toronto.

Horseshoe House (Ivan Burgess): 1970; production at Garrett Theatre, Toronto.

Act of Violence (Stan Ross): 1970; production at Factory Theatre Lab.

Snails (Michael Mirolla): 1971; production at Factory Theatre Lab.

Ambush at Tether's End (George F. Walker): 1971; production at Factory Theatre Lab.

Sacktown Rag (George F. Walker): 1972; production at Factory Theatre Lab.

Cowboy Island (Brian Shein): 1972; production at Factory Theatre Lab.

Penetration (Lawrence Russell): 1973; production at Playroom Theatre, London, England.

We Three, You and I (Bill Greenland): 1973; production at Factory Theatre Lab; 1973 production at Act Inn Theatre, London, England.

Demerit (George F. Walker): 1974; production at Factory Theatre Lab.

Prince of Naples (George F. Walker): 1974; production at Factory Theatre Lab.

Measures Taken (Bertolt Brecht): 1976; production at Factory Theatre Lab.

Miscellaneous Writing

Several critical articles for periodicals and newspapers including the *Canadian Theatre Review*.

Sceneworks: anthology of five plays previously published by Playwrights Co-op; edited by the author with extensive study and production notes; first published by Playwrights Co-op in 1977.

Michel Garneau

Born April 25, 1939, in Montreal, the son of a judge. After studying at several Jesuit schools (Collège Brébeuf, Collège Sainte-Marie and Collège Saint-Denis), he enrols in the acting program at a school run by Montreal's Théâtre du Nouveau Monde. He later studies at Montreal's Conservatory of Dramatic Art. In 1955, he begins a career as a radio announcer in Trois Rivières. In 1956, after working briefly at a Montreal radio station, he begins to write, starting with radio scripts but soon turning to poetry. In 1958, his first poetry collection, *Eau de Plui*, is published. In 1960, he is hired by CBC-TV to work as an announcer as well as a script-writer, and between 1961 and 1968 he writes over a hundred programs for regional and, in some cases, national broadcast, particularly for the show *Images en tête*. He also begins to sing professionally at this time, appearing on television with the musical group "Les Cailloux". In 1962, his second book of poetry is published and, shortly thereafter, he writes his first play, *Sur le Matelas*, which is premiered by Les Jeunes Comédiens du Nouveau Monde at a Montreal prison, and subsequently taken on a tour of Quebec. Over the next decade he publishes 10 more volumes of poetry and achieves a wide reputation as both a poet and playwright. In 1967, he writes his first English script, *Who's Afraid of James Wolfe*, which is produced by CBC-TV in Toronto. In 1967 and 1968, he moves to Paris working primarily for Radio-Canada (CBC-TV in Montreal) on a free-lance basis.

On his return to Montreal, he continues to write for the stage and his work is produced by Les Jeunes Comédiens du Nouveau Monde and Théâtre Populaire. At this time he also begins to produce his own plays. In collaboration with François Berd and Michelle Rossignol, he presents the program *Rencontre-Animation-Théâtre* on a tour of Quebec in 1969 and 1970. In 1973, he is hired as dramaturge for the National Theatre School's French Section and for the next five years, while holding this position, he writes several plays for the

school, including an adaptation of *The Tempest* and a poetic version of the epic *Gilgamesh*. In 1973 he also serves as dramaturge for Lionel-Groulx College in Ste. Thérèse, Quebec, and his play, *Quatre à Quatre*, is premiered there that year. One of his most successful plays, *Quatre à Quatre* subsequently receives other productions in Quebec and is later produced in Paris at Théâtre de la Commune Aubervilliers in both 1976 and in 1977. The play is also translated into English as *Four by Four* and produced by Toronto's Tarragon Theatre as well as by the Saidye Bronfman Centre in Montreal. Continuing to work as a singer, in 1975 he composes and performs the music for the recording *Allô Toulmônd*. The same year he adapts both *Macbeth* and Lorca's *The House of Bernarda Alba*. During this same period he writes *Les Voyagements* and *Rien que la mémoire* for the Quebec theatre group Voyagements, and *L'usage du coeur dans le domaine réel* for another company —La Rallonge.

He continues to make his home in Montreal.

Stage Writing

Sur le Matelas: two acts; written in 1962; first published by Editions de l'Aurore, Montreal, in 1974; first produced by Théâtre le Galendor in 1972, and by Théâtre de Quat'Sous, Montreal, in 1973, under the direction of Gilles Renaud.

Hostay de Croum (Saperlipocresse et Crisse Porlipopette): one act; written in 1968; unpublished; first produced by Théâtre Populaire du Quebec, at a Quebec prison in 1968; subsequently taken on a provincial tour; re-mounted by Théâtre Populaire in 1971.

Beu-meu: one act; written in 1968; unpublished; first produced by Théâtre Populaire at a Quebec prison in 1968; subsequently taken on a provincial tour; re-mounted by Théâtre Populaire in 1971.

Le Ravi: one act; written in 1968; first produced by Théâtre d'Aujourd-hui, Montreal, in 1968.

Des Chevaux, des rois, des dames, et des fous: a collective creation; unpublished; first produced by Les Jeunes Comediens du Nouveau Monde, in 1970.

Les Grands Moments: one act; written in 1970; first produced by Les Jeunes Comédiens du Nouveau Monde as part of a larger production entitled *Des Chevaux, des rois, des dames, et des fous* at a Montreal prison, 1970; revised 1972; subsequently produced by the French section of the National Theatre School, Montreal, 1973.

Dix-sept: one act; written in 1972; unpublished; first produced by the French Section, National Theatre School, Montreal in 1972.

Le Tempête (adaptation of Shakespeare's *The Tempest*): full-length; written in 1973; unpublished; first produced by the French Section of the National Theatre School in 1973.

Le Bonhomme sept heures: written in 1973 with music by André Angelini; unpublished; first produced by the French Section of the National Theatre School in 1974; subsequently produced by Théâtre de Quat'Sous in 1974, under the direction of André Brassard.

Quatre à Quatre: full-length; written in 1973; first published by Editions de l'Aurore in 1974; subsequently published by Editions VLB, Montreal, in 1979; first produced by Collège Lionel-Groulx in 1973 under the direction of Jean-Luc Bastien; subsequently produced by Théâtre Quat'Sous, Montreal, in 1974, under the direction of André Brassard; produced by Théâtre de la Commune Aubervilliers, Paris, in 1976 and 1977, under the direction of Gabriel Garran; translated into English by Keith Turnbull and Christian Bedard as *Four by Four*; produced by Tarragon Theatre, Toronto, in 1974, under the direction of Keith Turnbull; produced at the Saidye Bronfman Theatre, Montreal, in 1975, under the direction of Daniele J. Suissa.

Le Chanson d'amour de cul: monologue; written in 1974; unpublished; first produced by Patriote de Sainte-Agathe under the direction of Gilles Renaud; rewritten as a full-length play; first published by Editions de l'Aurore in 1974; first produced by Théâtre du Nouveau Monde in 1974, under the direction of the author.

Gilgamesh: poetic drama in 12 parts with music by André Angelini; originally written for radio in 1974; first produced by Radio-Canada in 1974; rewritten for stage in 1975; first published by Editions VLB, Montreal, in 1976; first produced by the French section of the National Theatre School in 1974, under the direction of Roger Blay.

Strauss et Pesant (et Rosa): one act; written in 1974; first published by Editions de l'Aurore in 1974; first produced by Théâtre d'Aujourd'hui, Montreal, in 1974, under the direction of André Pagé; subsequently produced by Théâtre de l'Atelier, Sherbrooke, Quebec, in 1975, under the direction of Pierre Gobeil, and by Théâtre de Nouvel-Ontario, Sudbury, in 1976, under the direction of Jacques Desnoyers.

Le Groupe: one act; written in 1975; unpublished.

Macbeth (an adaptation of Shakepeare's play): full-length; written in 1975; first published by Editions VLB in 1978; first produced by Théâtre de la Manufacture, Montreal, in 1978, under the direction of Roger Blay.

Abriés et Desabriées: written in 1975 with music by the author and André Angelini; first published by Editions VLB in 1979 in the same volume as *L'Usage du coeur dans le domaine réel*; first produced by the French section of the National Theatre School in 1975; subsequently produced by Théâtre de la Manufacture, Montreal, in 1977, under the direction of Daniel Simard.

La Maison de Bernard Alba (adaptation of Lorca's *House of Bernarda Alba*): full-length; written in 1975; unpublished; first produced by La Compagnie des Deux Chaises at Place des Arts, Montreal in 1975, under the direction of André Brassard.

Sers-toi d'tes antennes: children's play; written in 1975; unpublished; first produced by Organisation O, in 1977.

L'Usage du coeur dans le domaine réel: one act; written in 1975; unpublished; first produced by La Rallonge, Montreal, in 1975.

Les Voyagements: one-act comedy; written in 1975; first published by Editions VLB in 1977 in the same volume as *Rien que le mémoire*; first produced by Voyagements at Maison des Arts de la Sauvegarde, Montreal, in 1975, under the direction of Robert Duparc.

Les Célébrations: one-act comedy; written in 1976; first published by Editions VLB in 1977 in the same volume as *Adidou Adidouce*; first produced by Théâtre du Horla, St. Bruno, Quebec, in 1976, under the direction of Robert Duparc and Danielle Panneton; adapted for radio, first produced by Radio-Canada in 1977.

Il n'ya rien de plus nouveau que le soleil: one act; written in 1976; unpublished.

Joséphine la pas fine et Itoff le Toff: children's play; written in 1976; unpublished; first produced by Théâtre de la Marmaille a Théâtre du Gésu, Montreal, in 1976.

Pourquoi tu dis ça?: one act; unpublished; first produced by La Marmaille and Nouvelle Compagnie Théâtrale at Théâtre du Gésu, Montreal, in 1976, under the direction of Monique Rioux.

De la poussière d'étoiles dans les os: full-length; written in 1976; unpublished; first workshopped in Ste. Thérèse, Quebec, in 1976; subsequently produced by Lionel-Groulx College in 1976.

Rien que la mémoire: one-act comedy; written in 1976; first published by Editions VLB in 1977 in the same volume as *Les Voyagements*; first produced by Voyagements et Maison des Arts—la Sauvegarde in 1976, under the direction of Robert Duparc; adapted for radio and first produced by Radio-Canada in 1977.

Adidou, Adidouce: full-length; written in 1977; first published by Editions VLB in 1977 in the same volume as *Les Célébrations*; first produced by Voyagements et Maison des Arts de la Sauvegarde in 1977, under the direction of Michel Demers; subsequently produced by Théâtre de l'Atelier in 1977.

Miscellaneous

Eau de pluie: poetry; written in 1957; first published by Compte d'auteur, Montreal, in 1958.

Langage O: poetry; written in 1961; first published by Editions à la page, Montreal, in 1962.

Le Pays: poetry; written in 1962; first published by Editions Déom, Montreal, in 1963.

Who's Afraid of James Wolfe: television script; written in English in 1967; first produced by CBC-TV, Toronto, in 1967.

Langage 1, Vous pouvez m'acheter pour 69¢: poetry; written in 1971; first published by Compte d'auteur, 1972.

Langage 2, Blues des élections: poetry; written in 1971; first published by Compte d'auteur in 1972.

Langage 3, L'Animal humain: poetry; written in 1971; first published by Compte d'auteur in 1972.

Elégie au Génocide des Nasopodes: poetry; written in 1973; first published by Editions de l'Aurore in 1974.

Langage 4, J'aime la litterature, elle est utile: poetry; written in 1973; first published by Editions de l'Aurore in 1974.

Langage 5, Politique: poetry; written in 1973; first published by Editions de l'Aurore in 1974.

Moments: poetry; written in 1973; published be Editions Danielle Laliberté, Montreal, in 1974.

La Plus Belle Ile: poetry; written in 1974; first published by Editions Parti-Pris, Montreal, in 1975.

Allô Toulmônd: a recording; sung and composed music; produced by Capital-EMI, Montreal, in 1975.

Le Théâtre sur commande: theatre essay; written in 1975; first published by Editions Centre d'essai des auteurs dramatiques in "Entretien No. 1", 1975; subsequently published in part, in *Jeu*, No. 3, 1976.

Les Petits Chevals amoureux: poetry; written in 1976; first published by Editions VLB in 1977.

Pour travailler ensemble: essay; written in 1977; first published by Editions La Fondation du théâtre publique in 1978.

Secondary Sources

A long, first-person essay/poem by Garneau dealing with his approach to writing appeared in *Stage Voices*, ed. by Geraldine Anthony, Doubleday.

Gratien Gélinas

Born December 8, 1909, in the Village of
Saint-Tite, Quebec. Father a harness-maker
who moves his family to Montreal soon
after his son's birth to take a job as an
insurance agent. A natural performer, the
young Gélinas creates comic monologues
for presentation at family gatherings. At the
age of 12, he is sent to Terrebonne, a school
run by the congregation of the Blessed
Sacrament as a training ground for boys
preparing to enter the priesthood. After a
year, when it becomes apparent that his
interests lie elsewhere, he transfers to the
Collège de Montréal. As well as being an
excellent student, he develops a flair for
comedy and is active in the school's
dramatic society.

Shortly after leaving the Collège in 1929,
he founds the Troupe des Anciens au
Collège de Montréal, an amateur theatre
group composed of recent graduates of the
school. As the Depression develops,
though, he is forced to abandon his plans
for further study. After working briefly as a
yardgoods salesman in a Montreal
department store, he is hired by the
accounting department of an insurance
company. At the same time he takes on a
second job as a shoe salesman and attends
evening courses in business at the Ecole des
Hautes Etudes Commerciales. He marries
Simone Lalonde with whom he subsequently has six children. Acting continues
as a major hobby and he performs several
roles in both English and French at the
Montreal Repertory Theatre. Occasionally
he plays minor parts on radio programs.
His professional acting career is launched in
1932 when he lands the leading part in the
Radio-Canada serial, *Le Curé de village.* He
later creates a series of satirical sketches
entitled *Télévise-mois ça* which he then
performs at the cabaret, Ici Paris. His
growing reputation as a "one-man
entertainment machine" leads to invitations
to perform for various groups and social
clubs.

His big break comes in 1937 when,
having been offered his own weekly radio
show, he leaves his day job for a full-time
career as performer and writer. The series,

entitled *Fridolin*, attracts a large following
over the years as audiences identify with the
title character, a French-Canadian,
working-class "everyman" around whom
the shows revolve. In 1938, he adapts
Fridolin into a series of stage revues called
Fridolinons. Performed annually at the
Théâtre Monument National in Montreal
until 1946, the revues become increasingly
popular with workers as well as with
Quebec's intellectuals.

In 1948, *Tit-Coq*, his first full-length stage
play, is premiered at the Théâtre Monument
National. An English translation of
the play is later produced at the Théâtre du
Gésu in 1950. Three years later, a film of
Tit-Coq is made with its author in the
leading role. In 1949, he receives an
honorary doctorate from the Université de
Montréal and publicly states his belief that
Quebec theatre must ". . . bring together in
one and the same emotion, the great and
the humble, the rich and the poor, the
ignorant and the learned." His contribution
to the development of French-Canadian
consciousness is once again acknowledged
when, in 1949, he is awarded the Grand
Prize by the Society of Dramatic Authors.
In 1951, he receives a second honorary
doctorate, this time from the University of

71

Toronto. In 1954, he both writes and performs on the weekly Radio-Canada television series *Les Quat'Fers en l'air*. Two years later he presents his last Fridolinon revue.

That same year — 1956 — is spent at the Stratford Festival where he plays leading roles in *Henry V* and *The Merry Wives of Windsor*. He also becomes vice-president of the Greater Montreal Arts Council, a post which he holds until 1963. In 1958, he is elected president of the Canadian Theatre Centre, a branch of the International Theatre Institute. He also founds the Comédie-Canadienne, dedicated to the production of Canadian plays. In 1959, the theatre produces his second full-length play, *Bousille et les justes*. The English version (*Bousille and the Just*) is also produced by the Comédie-Canadienne. As with his earlier plays, Gélinas has a hand in directing both versions.

In 1960, he helps found the National Theatre School in Montreal. He returns to the satirical revue form in 1964 with *Le Diable à quatre*, premiered by the Comédie-Canadienne the following year. In 1966, his next play, *Hier, les enfants dansaient* is produced by the Comédie-Canadienne. The play is produced in English (*Yesterday, the Children Were Dancing*) at the Charlotte-town Festival in 1967 under the direction of both Gélinas and the play's translator, Mavor Moore. The same year, he is awarded the Victor Morin Prize by the Société Saint-Jean Baptiste and the Order of Canada for his contribution to theatre in Quebec and Canada. In 1969, he is named president of the Canadian Film Development Corporation, a position he holds through the 70's. In 1980, he is given the Toronto Drama Bench Award for Distinguished Contribution to the Canadian Theatre. He currently makes his home in Oka, Quebec.

Stage Writing

Télévise-moi ça: series of satirical monologues; written between 1932 and 1937; unpublished; first produced at the cabaret, Ici Paris, Montreal; subsequently performed at various charitable and amateur events.

Fridolinons: satirical revues; written between 1938 and 1946 and also in 1956; unpublished; produced annually at Théâtre Monument National.

Tit-Coq: three-act drama; written in 1948; first published by Beauchemin in 1950; subsequently published by Editions de l'Homme, 1968; first published in English by Clarke Irwin in 1967, in a translation by Kenneth Johnstone; first produced at the Théâtre Monument National in 1948 under the direction of the author and Fred Barry; first produced in English at the Théâtre du Gésu in 1950, also directed by the author and Fred Barry; adapted as a film script and produced in 1953 starring the author.

Bousille et les justes: four-act drama; written in 1959; first published by Editions de l'Homme in 1967; first published in English by Clarke Irwin in 1961, in a translation by Kenneth Johnstone; first produced by Comédie-Canadienne at Festivals de Montréal in 1959, under the direction of the author and Jan Donat; first produced in English by Comédie-Canadienne in 1961, directed by the author and Jan Donat.

Le Diable a quatre: satirical revue; written in 1964; unpublished; produced by Comédie-Canadienne in 1964.

Hier, les enfants dansaient: two-part drama; written in 1965; first published by Editions Leméac in the Théâtre Canadien series, 1968; first published in English by Clarke Irwin as *Yesterday, the Children Were Dancing* in 1967 in a translation by Mavor Moore; first produced in French by Comédie-Canadienne in 1966; first produced in English by the Charlottetown Festival in 1967 under the direction of the author and Mavor Moore.

Miscellaneous

Fridolin: weekly radio show; written between 1937 and 1941; unpublished; produced by radio CKAC, Montreal, between 1937 and 1941.

Les Quat'Fers en l'air: weekly television show; written in 1954; unpublished;

produced by Radio-Canada in 1954.

"Pour un theatre national et populaire":
speech given on the occasion of receiving an
honorary degree from the Université de
Montréal, January 31, 1949; published in
Action Universitaire, April 1949. English
version published in the appendix of Renate
Usmiani's book, *Gratien Gélinas* (Gage,
Toronto, 1976).

"Why Broadway Turned me Down":
Saturday Night, March 6, 1951.

"Discrimination and Canada's Future":
Labour Gazette, March 1955.

"Credo of the Comédie-Canadienne":
Queen's Quarterly LXVI, Spring 1959.

"Jeune auteur, mon camarade": *Revue
Dominicaine,* November 1960.

In Progress

An edition of collected *Fridolin* revues.

Secondary Sources

Usmiani, Renate, *Gratien Gélinas*, Gage,
Toronto, 1976.

Jean-Claude Germain

Born June 16, 1939 in Montreal. Father a
commercial traveller and grocer. Mother a
milliner. While still a student (history
major) at the Université de Montréal, he
founds his own company which he calls,
Théâtre Antonin Artaud. After graduation
in 1959, he supports himself primarily as a
journalist and theatre critic for such
publications as *Petit Journal* and
Dimensions magazine. An outspoken
cultural nationalist, he becomes executive
secretary of Quebec's newly-formed Centre
d'essai des auteurs dramatiques in 1968, a
post that he holds until 1971. In 1969, with
a group of friends he founds Théâtre du
Même Nom. During this period he directs
several of his own plays including *Diguidi,
Diguidi, Ha! Ha! Ha!, Les Enfants du
Chenier dans un autre grand spectacle adieu*
and *La Mise à la Morte de la Miss des Miss.*
At the same time he also works as author
and director with Enfants du Chenier
(1969-1971) and P'tits Enfants l'Aliberte
(1971-1975). In 1972, with Germain as
director, the two companies begin
operating under the collective name
Théâtre d'Aujourd'hui. The same year, he
becomes a member of the administrative
council of l'Association des Directeurs de

Theatre and begins teaching playwriting at
the National Theatre School. He continues
to do critical articles during this time, some
appearing in *Maclean's* and in 1976, he edits
a special issue on Quebec theatre for the
Canadian Theatre Review. He also writes an
eloquent defence of cultural separatism
entitled *Théâtre Québécois: A Protestant*

Theatre. For his contribution to Quebec theatre over many years, he is awarded Societé Saint-Jean Baptiste's Victor Morin Theatre Prize in 1977. He tells the *Montreal Star* in light of the Parti Quebecois victory the previous year, "...the underdog is dead. The perennial, sympathetic loser can no longer survive here...From now on the theatre we write must be of a conscious type, dealing with real facts. Drama will be a revelation of our strength, not our weakness. If we are crushed, the failure will result from having tried to measure up to reality by practical means..." Married to actress Nicole Leblanc, he still lives today in Montreal.

Stage Writing

Diguidi, Diguidi, Ha! Ha! Ha!: full-length; written in 1969; first published by Leméac, Montreal, in 1972 in same volume as *Si les sansoucis s'en soucient, ces sansoucis-ci s'en soucieront-ils?*; first produced by Théâtre du Même Nom in 1969; subsequently produced by Théâtre d'Aujourd'hui; directed by the author.

Les Enfants du Chenier dans un autre grand spectacle adieu: full length; written in 1969; unpublished; first produced in 1969 by Théâtre d'Aujourd'hui and Théâtre du Même Nom under the direction of the author.

La Mise à la mort de la Miss des Miss: full length; written in 1970 first produced by Théâtre d'Aujourd'hui and Théâtre du Même Nom in 1970, directed by the author.

Les Tourtereaux ou la vieillesse frappe à l'aube: full length; written in 1970; first published by Editions de l'aurore in 1974; first produced by Théâtre Cocktail in 1970, under the direction of the author.

Rodeo et Juliette: full-length; first version written in 1970; second version written in 1971; first version produced at Théâtre Place du Canada in 1970, directed by the author; second version produced by Théâtre d'Aujourd'hui and Théâtre du Même Nom in 1971, directed by the author.

Si Aurore m'etait contée: full-length; written in 1970; unpublished; first produced by Théâtre d'Aujourd'hui and Théâtre du Même Nom in 1970, directed by the author.

La Garde Monée, un episode dans la vie canadiénne de Don Quickshort: full-length; first version written in 1971, second version written in 1975 under the pseudonym Claude-Jean Magnier; third version written in 1978, retitled *Don Quickshort l'Homme a la Manque*; unpublished; first version produced by Comédie dex Deux Rives, Ottawa, 1971, directed by the author; second version produced by the Centre d'essai at the Université de Montreal, in 1975 under the direction of the author.

Le pays dan l'pays: full-length; written in 1971; unpublished; first produced by Théâtre du Même Nom in 1971, under the direction of the author; subsequently produced at Théâtre du Gésu in 1971 under the direction of the author.

Le Rois des Mises à bas prix: full-length; written in 1971; first published by Leméac, in 1978; first produced by Théâtre du Même Nom in 1971, directed by the author.

Les Jeunes s'toute des fous: full-length; written in 1971; unpublished; first produced by Théâtre d'Aujourd'hui and Théâtre du Même Nom in 1972, directed by the author.

Si les sansoucis s'en soucient, ces sansoucis-ci s'en soucieront'ils?: full-length; written in 1971; first published by Leméac in same volume as *Diguidi, Diguidi, Ha! Ha! Ha!*; first co-produced by Théâtre d'Aujourd'hui and Théâtre du Même Nom in 1971, directed by the author.

Dede Mesure: full-length; written in 1972; unpublished; first produced by Théâtre d'Aujourd'hui and Théâtre du Même Nom in 1972 under the direction of the author.

La Charlotte électrique: full-length; written in 1972; unpublished; first produced by Théâtre du Même Nom in 1972 under the direction of the author.

Nous Autes aussi ont fait ça pour rire: full-length; written in 1972; unpublished; first produced at Théâtre Patriote in 1972 under the direction of the author.

Les Méfaits de l'acide: full-length; written in 1973 under the pseudonym Claude-Jean Mangier; unpublished; first produced by Théâtre d'Aujourd'hui in 1973 under the direction of the author.

L'Affront Commun: full-length; written in 1973; unpublished; first produced by Théâtre d'Aujourd'hui in 1973 under the direction of the author.

Les Hauts et les bas de la vie d'une diva: Sarah Ménard par eux-mêmes: two-part play; written in 1974; first published by Editions VLB in 1975; first produced by Théâtre d'Aujourd'hui in 1975 under the direction of the author; subsequently toured throughout Quebec and played at the Kennedy Centre, Washington, D.C. as part of a Festival of Theatre in the Americas.

Beau bon pas cher ou la Transe du bon boule: full-length; written in 1975; unpublished; first produced by Théâtre d'Aujourd'hui in 1975 under the direction of the author.

Un pays dont la devise est: je m'oublie: full-length "grandgigne epic"; written in 1975; first published by Editions VLB in 1976; first produced by Théâtre d'Aujourd'hui in 1976 under the direction of the author.

Les Faux Brillants de Félix-Gabriel Marchand: three acts; written in 1971; first published by Editions VLB in 1977; first produced by Théâtre d'Aujourd'hui in 1977 under the direction of the author.

L'école des reves: full-length; written in 1978; unpublished; first produced by Théâtre d'Aujourd'hui in 1978 under the direction of the author.

Mamours et conjugat: full-length; written in 1978; unpublished; first produced by Théâtre d'Aujourd'hui in 1978 under the direction of the author.

Miscellaneous

Le Temps d'une prière: television script; written in 1972 in collaboration with Jacques W. Benoit; unproduced.

Canadiens, Canailles, Canayens: seven 30-minute episodes for television; written in 1973 and 1974; produced by Ontario Educations Authority for regional broadcast, directed by Harry Fishback.

Les Jeunes s'toute des fous!: six 30-minute television scripts; written in 1973; produced by Ontario Education Communications Authority for regional broadcast, directed by Harry Fishback.

The Bullfrog: 60-minute television drama; written in 1975; produced by CBC as part of "Performance" series in 1975 for national broadcast.

Le Temps d'une vente: film script; written in 1974; produced by the National Film Board under the direction of Jacques Gagne.

Théâtre Québécois: A Protestant Theatre: major essay; written in 1976; published in *Canadian Theatre Review*, No. 11, summer 1976.

Germain has also written songs and music for playwrights such as Michel Garneau, Jacques Ferron, Germain Gauthier, Michel Robidoux and Jacques Michel. Some of the songs have been recorded or presented in concerts by artists such as Pauline Julien, Louise Forestier, Jacques Michel and Nicole Leblanc.

In Progress

Le Buffet impromptu ou las nosse chez les proprietaire de bungalows: adaptation of a Brecht work; begun in 1976, unfinished.

Joanna Glass

Born Joanna McClelland, October 1936, in Saskatoon, the daughter of Kate and Morrill MacKenzie McClelland. A fifth-generation Canadian, she is the niece of Howard Stanley McClelland, Saskatchewan's first aviator. After graduating from high school, she spends a year as an advertising writer for CKOM Radio in Saskatoon. At age 19, she moves to Calgary to take a similar job at television station CHCT. Here she begins a second career as an actress starting with an acting workshop run by Betty Mitchell. Her portrayal of Anne Boleyn in Robert Bolt's *Anne of a Thousand Days*, Dr. Mitchell's entry in the 1957 Dominion Drama Festival, results in her being offered an Alberta Arts Council Scholarship to study at the Pasadena Playhouse in California. Her studies at the Playhouse are followed by a brief stint as a contract player at Warner Brothers.

Phyllis Crowley

In 1959, she marries a physicist, Dr. Alexander Glass, and from this point on she becomes a permanent resident of the United States. During the next few years, motherhood takes precedence over writing. A daughter is born in 1963 and in 1965 she gives birth to twins (a son and a daughter). She also travels in England, France and Italy during this period.

In the late 60's, she begins to write seriously. Looking back on this period in her life, she once said, "I lamented that I would never be a confessional writer like Sylvia Plath or an 'angry young writer' because by the time I got down to it (writing), my anger was more frustration than rage, and my confessions were boring, even to me. Be it blessing or curse, motherhood intervened and gave me time and distance from the experiences I wanted to capture on paper."

With the completion, in 1969, of *Santacqua*, her first stage play, she finally combines both writing and theatre into a single career. Two years later, she writes *Jewish Strawberries* and *Trying*, both one-act plays. In 1972 *Canadian Gothic* and *American Modern*, also short plays, are premiered as a double bill by the Manhattan Theatre Club in New York. A

success, the plays receive numerous subsequent productions throughout North America both on stage and radio. Her first novel, *Reflections on a Mountain Summer*, is published in 1974. The book is especially well-received in England where it is eventually serialized on the BBC.

In 1975, *Artichoke*, her second full-length play, opens at the Long Wharf Theatre, in New Haven, Connecticut, with Coleen Dewhurst in the leading role. Like much of her other work, the play is based on memories of a prairie childhood and explores the relationship between past deeds and the present behavior of the characters involved. Numerous productions of *Artichoke* and the double bill *Canadian Gothic/American Modern* make her one of the most frequently-produced playwrights during 1976 in the United States. That same year, she and her husband are divorced after 17 years of marriage.

The following year, she is asked by the Manitoba Theatre Centre in Winnipeg to do a stage version of her short story *At the King Edward Hotel*. This play, under the new title *The Last Chalice*, is premiered by M.T.C. and is subsequently optioned for Broadway. She has also written two screen plays, *Woman Wanted* and *Surfacing* (an adaptation of the novel by Margaret Atwood), as well as *Midnight Clear*, a film version of Ernest Joselovitz's drama *Hagar's Children*, completed in 1978.

Now an American citizen, she is an Associate Fellow of Jonathan Edwards College at Yale University, a member of New Haven's Centre for Independent Study and makes her home in Guilford, Connecticut. Her papers form part of the University of Calgary's Canadian Authors Manuscripts Collection.

Stage Writing

Santacqua: three acts; written in 1969; unpublished; first produced by the Herbert Berghof Playwrights Unit, New York, 1969, under the direction of Austin Pendleton.

Jewish Strawberries: one-act; written in 1971; unpublished; first produced by Wayne State University Workshop, Detroit, Michigan, 1971.

Trying: one-act; written in 1971; unpublished; first produced by Wayne State University Workshop, 1971.

Canadian Gothic: one-act; accompanies *American Modern* as a program of two one-act plays; written in 1972; first published along with *American Modern* by Dramatists' Play Service, New York, 1977; subsequently published on its own in the Chilton Book Company anthology, *Best Short Plays of 1978*; first produced by Manhattan Theatre Club, New York, 1972, under the direction of Austin Pendleton; subsequently produced by Berkeley Stage Company, Berkeley, California, 1974, under the direction of Robert W. Goldsby; Centaur Theatre, Montreal, 1975, under the direction of William Davis; Manitoba Theatre Centre's Warehouse, 1976, under the direction of Eric Steiner; The Belfry, Victoria, 1977, under the direction of Don Shipley; the Phoenix Theatre, New York 1976, under the direction of Daniel Freudenberger; adapted for radio, 1974; first broadcast by CBC, 1974; subsequently broadcast on its own in Ireland, 1976, by Radio Telefis Eireann; broadcast, 1979, in United States, through Earplay.

American Modern: one-act; accompanies *Canadian Gothic* as a program of two one-act plays; written in 1972; first published along with *Canadian Gothic* by Dramatists' Play Service, New York, 1977: first produced by Manhattan Theatre Club, New York, in 1972, under the direction of Austin Pendleton; subsequently produced by Berkeley Stage Company, 1974, under the direction of Robert W. Goldsby; Centaur Theatre, 1975, under the direction of William Davis; Manitoba Theatre Centre's Warehouse, 1976, under the direction of Eric Steiner; The Belfry, 1977, under the direction of Don Shipley; the Phoenix Theatre, New York, 1976, under the direction of Daniel Freudenberger; adapted for radio, 1974; first broadcast by CBC, 1974; subsequently broadcast on its own through Earplay, St. Paul, Minnesota, 1978.

Artichoke: full-length; written in 1975; first published by Dramatists Play Service, New York, 1979; first produced by Long Wharf Theatre, New Haven, Connecticut, 1975, under the direction of Arvin Brown starring Colleen Dewhurst; subsequently produced by Tarragon Theatre, Toronto, 1976, under the direction of Bill Glassco; Centaur Theatre, Montreal, 1977, under the direction of Elsa Bolam; Berkeley Stage Company, Berkeley, 1977; Alley Theatre, Houston, 1979, under the direction of Beth Sanford; Manhattan Theatre Club, New York, 1979, under the direction of Lynne Meadow; adapted for television and first produced by CBC in 1979.

The Last Chalice: full-length; written in 1977; unpublished; commissioned and first produced by Manitoba Theatre Centre, 1977, under the direction of Arif Hasnain.

Miscellaneous

Reflections on a Mountain Summer: a novel; written in 1974; first published by Alfred A. Knopf, New York and simultaneously by McClelland and Stewart, Toronto, 1974; published by Macmillan, London, England, 1975; serialized as a 10-part program and broadcast on BCC's *Woman's Hour*; optioned by Lorimar Productions, Hollywood, California, 1979, for feature film; screenplay to be written by Joanna M. Glass.

At the King Edward Hotel: short story; written in 1975; first published by St. Martin's Press, New York and Macmillan, London, England, in *Winter's Tales 22*, 1976.

Surfacing (adaptation of Margaret Atwood's novel): screenplay; written in 1975; unproduced.

Woman Wanted: screenplay; written in 1976; unproduced.

Midnight Clear (adaptation of play *Hagar's Children* by Ernest Joselovitz): screenplay; written in 1978; unproduced.

In Progress

To Grandmother's House We Go: full-length play; set in Connecticut; to be written with grants award by the National Endowment for the Arts, Washington, D.C.

Two Short Stories

Tom Grainger

Born 1921, in Lancashire, England. He leaves school at the age of 14 and begins working as a "scavenger" in a cotton mill. This is followed by a succession of low-paying, dead-end jobs interrupted by a six-year term in the Royal Air Force. He emigrates to Canada in 1956 and a year later is married. Self-educated, his first published work, a short story entitled *Not for Zenocrate Alone*, appears in the literary journal *Prism* in 1960.

In 1964 he tries his hand at playwriting and wins the 1964 National Playwriting Seminar, in London, Ontario, with *Daft Dream Aydin*. The same year, his play, *The Action Tonight*, wins the annual playwriting competition sponsored by the Ottawa Little Theatre. Awarded a fellowship to the Yale School of Drama in 1965, he studies playwriting under John Gassner. After some time, in New York, he returns to Canada in 1970 and settles in Vancouver. That year, two of his plays, *The Helper* and *In Arizona the Air is Clean*, take first and third prize in the Centennial Playwriting Competition sponsored by the Playhouse Theatre Company.

In 1973, several of his plays are produced by CBC Radio, Vancouver. A year later, his play, *The Injured*, wins the first annual Clifford E. Lee Playwriting Award. Concerned with social injustice and the

Vancouver Sun

plight of the 'little man', his plays begin to gain recognition in the United States, Germany and Britain. After a New Play Centre production in 1975, his *Down There* is staged at the Octagon Theatre, Bolton, England.

In a chapter on his work in the book *Stage Voices* (Doubleday, 1978) he writes, "If there is one quality that can lift the saddened heart, the quality is innocence. As the educators and the media manipulators make inroads on our young, this quality is becoming as hard to find as clean air in a quiet place. The decay and near-disappearance of blushing is a symptom of a grave spiritual sickness if to bring back the blush we must also call back the fig leaf, then let us lay in a goodly stock before those crafty boys in the futures market get wind of our need." Married, he and his wife presently make their home in Vancouver.

Stage writing

Daft Dream Adyin: three acts; written in 1963; first published by Chilton Book Company, New York, 1969, in *Best Short Plays*, edited by Stanley Richards; subsequently published by Avon Books, New York and Toronto, 1970; unproduced; winner of the 1964 National Playwriting Seminar, London, Ontario.

The Action Tonight: one act; written in 1964; first published in *Prism*, volume IV, number three, winter 1965; first produced by Ottawa Little Theatre, 1965; adapted for radio and produced by CBC in 1973; winner of the 1964 Ottawa Little Theatre Playwriting Competition.

The Last of Abraham Schurmann: one act; written in 1968; unpublished; first produced by Savage God, Vancouver, 1969, under the direction of John Juliani.

In Arizona the Air is Clean: one act; written in 1969; unpublished; typescript reproduction available from the New Play Centre; unproduced; adapted for radio; first produced by CBC Radio, Vancouver, 1970; winner of third prize in 1970 Centennial Playwriting Competition sponsored by Playhouse Theatre Company, Vancouver.

The Helper: one act; written in 1969; first published by Fineglow Press, Toronto, and New Play Centre, 1975, in *West Coast Plays*; first produced by New Play Centre, 1975; winner of first prize in the 1970 Centennial Playwriting Competition sponsored by Playhouse Theatre Company.

The Kill: one act; written in 1970; published by Ottawa Little Theatre, 1969, in *Ranking*

Play Series II; typescript reproduction available from New Play Centre; first workshopped by New Play Centre, Vancouver in 1971, under the direction of John Juliani.

The Agreement: one act; unpublished; typescript reproduction available from New Play Centre; unproduced.

The Great Grunbaum: one act; written in 1973; unpublished; typescript reproduction available from New Play Centre, Vancouver; first produced by New Play Centre, 1974, under the direction of Jim McQueen.

The Man from Wulfshausen: one act; unpublished; typescript reproduction available from New Play Centre; unproduced.

Down There: three acts; written in 1974; unpublished; first produced by New Play Centre, 1974; subsequently produced by Octagon Theatre, Bolton, England, 1975.

The Injured: three-act drama; written in 1974; first published by Playwrights Co-op, Toronto, 1976; typescript reproduction available from New Play Centre; first produced under direction of Howard Dallin by Studio Theatre, Edmonton, 1975; winner of first annual Clifford E. Lee Playwriting Award, 1974.

In Agony: full-length; adaptation of Miroslav Krleza's *U Agoni ju*; unpublished; first produced by Metro Theatre, Vancouver, 1976.

Roundabout: three acts; written in 1976; unpublished; typescript reproduction available from New Play Centre; first produced by New Play Centre, 1976, under the direction of Robert Graham.

The Exile: two acts; written in 1977; unpublished; unproduced.

The Sounding: full-length; written in 1977; unpublished; unproduced.

Miscellaneous

Not for Zenocrate Alone: short story; written in 1959; first published in *Prism*, Fall, 1960.

Wouldn't it Frost You: radio play; written in 1963; first produced by BBC Radio, London, England, 1964.

Secondary sources

Section on Tom Grainger included in *Stage Voices*, ed. by Geraldine Anthony, Doubley, 1978.

Warren Graves

Born February 5, 1933, in London, England. Father a policeman. His first clear memories, he says, are of "...being evacuated at the age of seven, returning to London to enjoy 'the Blitz', doodlebugs and V2's and then being evacuated again at 11 (after it was all over) because my new school was still evacuated." His first literary endeavours are letters home to his mother written while an evacuee ("...a practice that I continue these 40 years later"). As a member of a boy scout theatrical troupe, he also develops an interest in acting.

After leaving school at the age of 16 in order to earn a living, he continues his education through voracious reading in public libraries. Required to spend two years in the service, at the age of 18 he enlists in the Royal Air Force. On returning to civilian life in 1952, he begins 11 years in a ladies clothing retail shop in London's Oxford Street.

His spare time is spent trying to get work in radio, television, theatre, and with magazines. He has moderate success with magazines and is able to get some work on BBC Radio.

In 1963, now a married man with two small daughters, he decides that his future lies outside England and ladies clothing. He and his wife consider New Zealand, but eventually decide to move to Calgary where he works first for Eaton's and then as a life insurance salesman. He later moves his family to Edmonton where he joins the

Alberta Government Publicity Bureau. His job involves the preparation of publications and travelling exhibitions.

At the same time, he becomes active in the Walterdale Playhouse, Edmonton's community theatre. It is here that "...I really learned 'the business' by doing it all." He directs both his own plays and those of other dramatists, as well as acting in productions of Joe Orton's *What the Butler Saw* and *The Girl in the Freudian Slip*. His first play, *Yes Dear*, a comedy, as is much of his other work, is produced at the Playhouse in 1966. During that year he becomes vice-president and artistic director of the theatre.

During this same period he begins writing radio and television scripts for the CBC's Alberta Schools Broadcasts. In 1967, his wife gives birth to a son ("...by way of a Centennial project"). Also in 1967 he is awarded the Alberta Centennial Medal. After a year as secretary to the Lieutenant Governor, he continues with the Alberta Government as a Clerk Assistant to the Legislature.

In 1974, he leaves the Legislature to join the newly-formed Alberta Educational Communications Corporation as an in-house writer. By 1976, this group has become "...highly organized, bureaucratized and compartmentalized." He feels that "...I had no alternative but to step out into the chilly, isolated world of the Freelance." He also continues to act, playing in three melodramas produced by Edmonton's Citadel Theatre in 1978. Still a resident of Edmonton, he continues writing for radio, television and the stage.

Stage Writing

Yes Dear: one act; written in 1966; first published by Samuel French, Canada, in 1967; first produced by Walterdale Playhouse, Edmonton, 1966, under the direction of the author; winner of the first annual Edmonton Journal Literary Award, 1966.

Love in a Greenhouse: three acts; written in 1967; unpublished; first produced by Walterdale Playhouse, Edmonton, 1967, under the direction of the author; winner of the second prize in Alberta's Centennial Playwriting Competition, 1977.

The Hand that Cradles the Rock: two acts; written in 1968; first published by Playwrights Co-op, Toronto, 1972; first produced by Backdoor Theatre, Toronto, 1972, under the direction of Gino Marracco; subsequently produced by Sunshine Theatre, Kelowna, British Columbia, in 1978, under the direction of Ita D'Arcy; winner of the second prize in the Alberta Playwriting Competition, 1969.

The Mumberly Inheritance, or, His Substance Frittered: two acts; written in

1971; first published by Playwrights Co-op, Toronto, 1971; first produced by Walterdale Playhouse at the Citadel Theatre, 1971, under the direction of the author; subsequently produced by the Charlottetown Festival in 1978 under the direction of Donald Grant.

The Proper Perspective: one act; written in 1971; first published by Borealis Press, Ottawa, 1974, in *Contemporary Canadian Drama*, edited by Joseph Shaver; subsequently published by Playwrights Co-op, 1978, in the same volume as *Who's Looking After the Atlantic?*; first produced by Carleton University, Ottawa, 1974, under the direction of Joseph Shaver, subsequently produced by Lunch Time Theatre, Charlottetown, 1976, under the direction of Leigha Leigh Brown; winner of the first prize in the Ottawa Little Theatre Playwriting Competition, 1972.

Who's Looking After the Atlantic?: one act; written in 1972; first published with *The Proper Perspective* by Playwrights Co-op, Toronto, 1978; rewritten for television and first produced by ITV, Edmonton, 1978, under the direction of Keith Digby.

Chief Shaking Spear Rides Again, or, The Taming of the Sioux: two acts; written in 1974; first published by Playwrights Co-op, Toronto, 1975; first produced by Walterdale Playhouse at the Citadel Theatre, 1974, under the direction of the author.

Goodbye Cruel World: three acts; written in 1978; unpublished; first produced by the author at the Citadel Theatre, 1978, under the direction of Ron Wigmore; subsequently revised for television and produced by ITV, Edmonton, 1978, under the direction of John Blanchard.

Scrooge (based on the story by Charles Dickens): two acts; written in 1978; first published by Playwrights Co-op, Toronto, 1979; first produced by Theatre 3, Edmonton, 1978, under the direction of Keith Digby; subsequently revised for television and produced by ITV, Edmonton, 1979, under the direction of John Blanchard and Joan Kirsch.

Mors Draculae: three acts; written in 1979; first published by Playwrights Canada, 1980; first produced by Stage West, Edmonton, under the direction of Bill Fisher, 1979.

Beauty and the Beast: two acts; written in 1979; first published by Playwrights Canada, 1980; first produced by Theatre 3, Edmonton, 1979, under the direction of Keith Digby.

Radio Writing

Man of Letters: two 30-minute segments; written in 1977; first produced by CBC Radio, Calgary, 1978, for regional broadcast.

Ride on the Bus: 30 minutes; written in 1977; first produced by CBC Radio, Calgary, for regional broadcast, 1978.

Time Out: 60 minutes; written in 1978; first produced by CBC Radio, Edmonton, 1978, for national broadcast.

Television Writing

Bill Before the House: 30 minutes; written in 1972; first produced by CBC's Alberta Schools Broadcasts, Edmonton, 1972, for regional broadcast; winner of an Ohio State Award and the Jury Prize, Osaka Film Festival, Japan.

Dial 9 to Get Out: 30 minutes; written in 1973; first produced by CBC's Alberta Schools Broadcasts, Edmonton, 1973, for regional broadcast.

Father Lacombe: 30 minutes; written in 1974; first produced by CBC's Alberta Schools Broadcasts, Edmonton, 1974, for regional broadcast; winner of an Ohio State Award.

Fort Edmonton - Fort Macleod - Crowfoot: three 30-minute segments; written between 1974 and 1977; first produced by CBC's Alberta Schools Broadcasts, Edmonton, between 1974 and 1977, for regional broadcast.

Sex'n Stuff: 30 minutes; written in 1975; first produced by CBC's Alberta Schools Broadcasts, Edmonton, 1975, for regional broadcast; winner of the Gold Plaque for Educational Film at the Chicago International Film Festival, 1976.

Western Bush Pilot: three 30-minute segments; written in 1975; unproduced; lodged with the Canadian National Archives as historic reference material.

Country Joy: six 30-minute episodes; written in 1979; first produced by CBC, Edmonton, for network broadcast, under the direction of Don McCrae and Mark Schoenberg.

Parliamentary Process: five 15-minute and two 30-minute episodes; written in 1978; first produced by Tinsel and Sham Productions for the Alberta Department of Education under the direction of Nick Bakyta.

Macpherson: six 60-minute episodes (miniseries); written in 1979; first produced by ITV, Edmonton, for national and international distribution; executive producer, Joan Krisch.

In Progress

History of Parliament: a five-part series for the Alberta Schools Broadcasts.

Country Joy: part of the writing team for 22 episodes of a new CBC program.

Series on Parliamentary Procedure: a 12-part series for educational radio.

Alberta Song: 90-minute musical for the Alberta Government's Festival of the Arts, 1980.

The Spy and the Pianist: radio drama; CBC, Edmonton; producer, Lawrie Seligman.

Seat of Learning: 30-minute film; University of Alberta; producer, Ken Pappes.

Robert Gurik

Born November 16, 1932, in France, of
Hungarian parents. Receives his primary
and secondary education in Paris.
Emigrates to Montreal in 1951 where he
enrols as a student of applied science at the
University of Montreal. After graduating,
he studies engineering at Montreal
Polytech, receiving his diploma in 1957. For
the next 15 years, he supports himself by
working as an engineer for various
companies in and around Montreal. In
1963, Théâtre de la Mangragore, which he
founds, produces his first play, *Le Chant du
poète*. Over the next three years, he writes
Les Portes, Api 2967, Les Louis d'Or and
one novel, *Spirales*. In 1965, he and five
others found the *Centre d'essai des auteurs
dramatiques*, an organization dedicated to
the promotion of Quebec playwriting. Also
active in the amateur theatre movement, he
serves on the board of directors of
*Association Canadienne du théâtre
d'amateurs*. In 1966, he meets costume and
scenic designer, Renée Noiseaux, who
directs the first production of his play *Api
2967* at Théâtre du Gesu. The two later
marry. In 1967, he wins a Massey Award
for his "modern fable", *Le Pendu*, and is
named Quebec's theatre man of the year. A
second Massey Award, for his play *Les
Louis d'Or*, follows in 1969. In 1972, he
decides to leave engineering altogether in
order to write full-time and in 1974 he
begins teaching French literature at the
University of Montreal. In 1975, his
screenplay *Les Vautours* is entered in the
Cannes Film Festival. Fluent in French,
English and Hungarian, and now holding
Canadian citizenship, he currently lives in
Montreal with his wife and their two
children.

Stage Writing

Le Chant du poète: one-act satire; written in
1963; first published in *Les Cahiers de
L'ACTA*, Volume 1, Number 4, 1963; first
produced by Théâtre de la Mangragore,
Montreal, in 1963.

63: short play; written in 1963; first
published by Leméac, Montreal, 1974,
along with *Play Ball, Un plus un égale zéro,
Phèdre, La Sainte et le truand, Le Trou,* and
Le Signe du cancer in a volume entitled *Sept
courtes pièces*; unpublished.

Les Portes: one act; written in 1965;
unpublished; first produced at Place Ville
Marie, Montreal, in 1965, under the
direction of B. Lapierre.

Api 2967: a multi-media science fiction; first
written as a two-act play in 1966;
unpublished; first produced at Théâtre du
Gésu for the Festival d'Art dramatique,
Montreal, 1966, directed by Renée
Noiseaux under the title *Api or not Api, voilà
la question*, subsequently revised and
retitled *Api 2967* in 1967; first published by
Factum Inc. in 1966; subsequently
published by Leméac in 1971 in the same
volume as *Api 2967* and *La Palissade*; first
produced by Théâtre de l'Egrégore, 1967,
under the direction of Roland Laroche;
subsequently produced at the Venice
Biennale by the Company Gerreau-
Fermetti, 1969; by Théâtre de la Cité, Paris,
1969; by Cie la Grande Roue, Sherbrooke,
Quebec, 1974; La Grande Roue,

Sherbrooke, 1975; adapted for television and first produced by Hollandaise, Holland, 1973; revised and translated into English by Marc F. Gelinas as *Api 2967* and published by Playwrights Co-op, Toronto in 1973; subsequently published by Talonbooks, Vancouver, in 1974.

Les Louis d'Or: two acts; written in 1966; first published in *Théâtre Vivant*, Number 1, 1966; first produced at Expo '67, Montreal, under the direction of P. Saulnier; winner of the 1969 Massey Award for the Best Canadian Play.

La Palissade: two acts; written in 1966; revised in 1970; first published by Leméac in 1971; first produced by Collège Militaire, St. Jean, Quebec, in 1973.

Le Pendu: two-act "modern fable"; written in 1967; first published by Factum Inc. in 1967; subsequently published by Leméac in 1970; first produced at Théâtre du Gésu for the Festival d'Art dramatique in 1967 under the direction of Roland Laroche; subsequently produced in Paris, in 1968; Théâtre de l'Egrégore in 1968; adapted for radio; first produced by Radio-Canada in 1970; adapted for television; produced by O.R.T.F., France, in 1971; translated by Philip London and Laurence Bérard as *The Hanged Man*; first published by New Press, Toronto, in *New Drama 4*, 1972; first produced in English at the Centennial Drama Festival in St. John's, Newfoundland, in 1967; winner of the Massey Award for Best Canadian Play of 1967.

Hamlet, prince du Québec: two-act satire; written in 1968; first published by Editions de l'Homme, 1968; first produced by Théâtre de l'Escale, 1968, under the direction of Roland Laroche; translated into English the same year by Marc F. Gelinas; unpublished; first produced in English by London Little Theatre, London, Ontario, in 1978.

A coeur ouvert: tragi-comedy; written in 1969; first published by Leméac in 1969; first produced by Compagnie de Quat'Sous, Montreal, in 1969, under the direction of

Yves Gelinas; translated into English by Marc F. Gelinas as *Hearts*; unproduced.

Allo, Police! (with Jean-Pierre Morin): one act; written in 1970; first published by Leméac in 1974; first produced at the Théâtre du Gésu in 1970 under the direction of Claude Deslandes.

Les Fourberies de Scapin (adaptation of the play by Molière): full-length; written in 1970; unpublished; first produced by Collège Lionel-Groulx, Ste. Thérèse, Quebec, in 1970, under the direction of Jean-Luc Bastien.

Echec à la Reine: full-length; written in 1971; unpublished; first produced by an amateur company in 1971.

Play Ball: full-length; written in 1971; first published by Leméac in 1974 along with *63, Un plus un égale zéro, Phèdre, La Sainte et le truand, Le Trou* and *Le Signe du cancer* in a volume entitled *Sept courtes pièces*; first produced by Théâtre Populaire du Québec in 1971, under the direction of Jean-Luc Bastien; subsequently produced by Théâtre d'Austheure, 1976.

"0": full-length; written in 1971; unpublished; first produced by Collège Lionel-Groulx, 1971, under the direction of Jean-Luc Bastien.

J'écoute: one act; part of a trilogy entitled *Les Tas de sièges*, along with *Face à face* and *D'un séant à l'autre* written in 1971; first published by Leméac in 1971; first produced as part of trilogy in Ste-Foy, Quebec, in 1972, under the direction of F. Villemure; subsequently produced by Festival de Megantic, 1973; adapted for television; first produced by O.R.T.F., France, 1974.

Face à face: one act; part of a trilogy along with *J'écoute* and *D'un séant à l'autre*; written in 1971; first published by Leméac in 1971; first produced as part of trilogy in Ste-Foy, Quebec, in 1972, under the direction of F. Villemure; subsequently produced at Festival de Megantic, 1973; produce separately by Fête du Patrimonie, Chateauguay, Quebec, in 1978; produced separately by Théâtre cooperatif, Paris, France, 1976, under the direction of F. Guillet; adapted for television; produced by O.R.T.F., France.

D'un séant à l'autre: one act; part of a trilogy, along with *J'écoute* and *Face à face*, written in 1971; first published by Leméac in 1971; new version entitled *Un plus un égale zéro* published by Leméac in 1974 along with *63, Play Ball, Phèdre, La Sainte et le truand, Le Trou* and *Le Signe du cancer* in a volume entitled *Sept courtes pièces*; first produced separately by Troupe des Arlequins, Montreal, in 1971; subsequently produced along with *J'écoute* and *Face à face* in Ste-Roy, Quebec, 1972, under the direction of F. Villemure; subsequently produced, as trilogy, by Festival de Megantic, 1973; produced on its own by Théâtre d'Astheure, 1976; adapted for radio; produced separately by CBC, Montreal, 1977; adapted for television; produced as part of trilogy by O.R.T.F., France

Le Procès de Jean-Baptiste M.: full-length; written in 1972; first published by Leméac in 1972; produced by Théâtre du Nouveau Monde, Montreal, in 1972, under the direction of Roland Laroche; subsequently produced by Théâtre du Bois de Boulogne, Quebec, 1975; Theatre 13, Paris, 1976; and in 1977 by TEP, Paris; translated into English by Allan Van Meer as *The Trial of Jean-Baptiste M*; first published by Talonbooks, Vancouver, 1974; first produced by Globe Theatre, Regina, under the title *The Trial of Mr. What's His Name* in 1974, under the direction of Roland Laroche; subsequently produced by City Stage, Vancouver, 1978.

Le Champion: two-part play; written in 1973; first published by Leméac in 1977; unproduced.

Sept courtes pieces: seven sketches including *Phèdre, La Sainte et le Truand, Un plus un égale zéro, 63, Le Signe du Cancer, Play ball, Le Trou*; written in 1973; first published by Leméac in 1974; first produced by La Troupe des huits, Plessiville, Quebec, 1974. Plessiville, Quebec, 1974.

Le Tabernacle a trois etages: two acts; written in 1972; first published by Leméac 1972; first produced in Ste-Foy, 1973, under the direction of F. Villemure; subsequently produced by Théâtre de la Cité in 1973, under the direction of D. Lanuette.

La Sainte et le truand: short play written in 1973 in collaboration with theatre students at l'Université du Québec; first published by Leméac in 1974 along with *63, Play Ball, Un plus un égale zéro, Phèdre, Le Trou* and *Le Signe du cancer* in a volume entitled *Sept courtes pièces*; first produced by l'Université du Québec under the direction of Gilbert Lepage.

Phèdre: dramatic monologue; written in 1973; first published by Leméac in 1974 along with *63, Play Ball, Un plus un égale zéro, Le Trou* and *Le Signe du cancer* in a volume entitled *Sept courtes pièces*; unproduced.

Lénine: two-part play; written in 1974; first published by Leméac in 1975; first produced by Théâtre de l'Arc en Ciel.

Un plus un: one act; written in 1975; unpublished; first produced by Troupe des huits, Plessiville, 1975.

Gurik en morceaux: one act; written in 1976; unpublished; first produced by Centre d'essai des auteurs dramatiques at the University of Montreal, 1976.

La baie des Jacques: full-length; written in 1976; first published by Leméac in 1978; first produced by Collège Lionel-Groulx in 1976.

Hocus Pocus: written in 1977; unpublished; first produced by Troupe des Beaux Cossins at the National Library, 1977.

Miscellaneous

Portrait: television script; written in 1973; first produced by Radio-Canada for Quebec broadcast.

Le Signe du cancer: radio script; written in 1973; published by Leméac in 1974 along with *63, Play Ball, Un plus un égale zéro, Phèdre, La Sainte et le truand* and *Le Trou* in a volume entitled *Sept courtes pièces*.

Le Trou: radio script; written in 1973; published by Leméac in 1974 along with *63, Play Ball, Un plus un égale zéro, Phèdre, La Sainte et le truand* and *Le Signe du cancer* in a volume entitled *Sept courtes pièces*.

Pâques: television script; written in 1974; first produced by Radio-Canada for Quebec broadcast.

Les Vautours: film script; written in 1974; Canadian submission to the Cannes Film Festival in 1975.

J'ai le gout de t'embrasser (with Jean-Pierre Morin): film script; written in 1976.

Spirales: novel; written in 1965; first published by Holt, Rinehart and Winston, 1966.

Herschel Hardin

Born August 17, 1936, in Vegreville, Alberta, a small town 60 miles south of Edmonton. A "Mackenzie King child," as he says, he describes his background as "essentially egalitarian and multi-ethnic." At 18 he moves to Ontario to study philosophy at Queen's University. While a student, he sees his first play — the Canadian Players production of *Peer Gynt* starring Bruno Gerussi. After graduating with a B.A. in 1958, he spends two years travelling in Europe. Returning to Canada and in search of "a city environment," he decides to settle in Vancouver. Two years later he writes *The Great Wave of Civilization*, a play about the effect of the liquor trade on the Blackfoot Indians. Married by this time, he devotes himself full-time to writing, helped in great measure by his wife's financial support. After another brief period in Europe, he returns to Canada but continues to find playwriting unprofitable. "I didn't seem to have any record of employment until 1967. It is embarrassing when I have to fill out unemployment forms." His second play, *School for Swindle*, completed in 1965, is an adaptation of the *Threepenny Opera* by Bertolt Brecht who, along with Shakespeare and Büchner, Hardin feels is a major influence on his dramatic work.

In 1967, he writes a drama about the economic destruction of the North, *Esker Mike and His Wife, Agiluk*, which he sends

Glen E. Erickson

to the New York theatre journal, *The Drama Review*. In 1969, *TDR* publishes the play. It is read by Toronto director Ken Gass who produces it in 1971. That same year he tells the *Globe and Mail*, "I have always felt strongly about Canadian themes. Never that they were second best. Consequently I've never felt it a duty to write plays on Canadian subjects. It would never occur to me to write a play about Joan of Arc. If I were Shakespeare I would never set *Hamlet* in Denmark."

By 1974, he loses interest in the theatre and turns to free-lance writing on economics and subjects relating to broadcasting. That same year, he completes a book-length study on Canadian economics, *A Nation Unaware*, which is published by the Vancouver house, J.J. Douglas. Still working as a free-lance journalist, he writes both political and economic commentary for several newspapers including the *Toronto Star* as well as working for the CBC as a bilingual critic on national affairs. He lives in West Vancouver with his wife (a professional gardener), and their two daughters.

Stage Writing

The Great Wave of Civilization: three-act drama; written in 1962; first published in 1976 by Talonbooks, Vancouver; first produced by Festival Lennoxville in 1976 under the direction of Paul Thompson; the play is winner of the Alberta Centennial Playwriting Prize.

School for Swindle: full-length adaptation of Bertolt Brecht's *Threepenny Opera*; written in 1965; unpublished; unproduced.

Esker Mike and His Wife, Agiluk: long one-act drama; written in 1967; first published in 1969 by *The Drama Review* and by Playwrights Co-op in 1973; subsequently by Talonbooks, Vancouver, in 1973; first produced by Factory Theatre Lab, Toronto, in 1971, under the direction of Maruti Achanta and subsequently by Troupe, Vancouver, in London, Toronto, Winnipeg, Ottawa and New York under the direction of Jon Bankson; by Factory Theatre Lab in 1972 under the direction of Eric Steiner.

William Lyon Mackenzie, Part 1: written in 1968; unpublished; unproduced.

Miscellaneous

A Nation Unaware: a study of Canadian economics; published in 1974 by J.J. Douglas, Vancouver.

Lezley Havard

Born September 8, 1944, in England. A theatre enthusiast since childhood, by age 16 she is travelling the country, working as an actress and stage manager. Soon afterwards she marries a theatre colleague, Bernard Havard. At the age of 19 she and her husband, accompanied by their first child, tour Australia with various theatre companies.

Moving to Canada in 1965, they travel from city to city, working in most of the regional theatres throughout the country. As well as acting, Ms. Harvard assists backstage with everything from lighting to set construction. While in Toronto she directs a play at Young People's Theatre.

In 1975 she turns from directing to writing plays. *Jill*, her first dramatic work, wins the Clifford E. Lee Playwriting Award the following year. *Victims*, her second effort, wins an award in the 1976 Women's Year Competition sponsored by the Playwrights Co-op.

She presently lives in Atlanta, Georgia, with her husband, an administrator at the Alliance Theater, and their three children.

Stage Writing

Jill: two acts; written in 1975; unpublished; first produced by the Citadel Theatre, Edmonton, 1977, under the direction of Sheldon Larry; subsequently produced by Festival Lennoxville, 1977, under the direction of Richard Ouzounian; produced as *Hide and Seek* on Broadway in 1980 under the direction of Melvin Bernhart and starring Elizabeth Ashley; winner of the 1976 Clifford E. Lee Playwriting Competition.

Victims: three one-act plays; written in 1976; first published by Playwrights Co-op, Toronto, 1977, in *Women Write for the Theatre*, volume four; first produced by the Alliance Theatre, Atlanta, 1977, under the direction of Fred Chappell; winner of a 1977 Women Write for the Theatre Award.

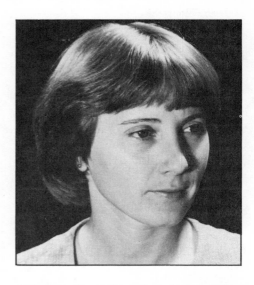

Only Yesterday: full-length; written in 1976; unpublished; unproduced.

In the Name of the Father: full-length; written in 1979; unpublished; first produced by Atlanta New Play Project in 1979 under the direction of Fred Chappell; subsequently produced by Alliance Theatre, Atlanta in 1980 under the direction of Fred Chappell.

In Progress

Murder Is a Stranger: a full-length murder mystery for the stage.

Tom Hendry

Born in Winnipeg, June 7, 1929, of Scottish and Irish parents. Father a CNR foreman; mother "a spinning mill, storyteller, waitress, chocolate dipper and forelady." He grows up in Norwood, an English-language ghetto in French-speaking St. Boniface. After graduating from Kelvin Technical High School, Winnipeg, in 1947, he enrols as a student in the Faculty of Arts at the University of Manitoba, only to be expelled in December of the same year. He switches to Accounting but maintains his interest in theatre by working as an actor and director at the Winnipeg Little Theatre and in productions mounted by the Accountancy Faculty. At the same time, he begins to work for the CBC both as an actor and writer of documentaries and short stories. He plays the part of Buddy Jackson in the early radio serial *The Jacksons and their Neighbours* and has various roles in television directed by John Hirsch, Felix Lazarus and Don Browne-Wilkinson. He is also a member of John Hirsch's Muddiwater Puppet Company.

Ellen Tolmie

Theatre continues to be his hobby, even after he begins his practice as a chartered accountant in 1955. His first play, *Do You Remember?*, originally seen on television, is produced for the stage in 1957 by the Winnipeg Summer Theatre Association. Also in 1957, he and John Hirsch found Theatre 77 in Winnipeg. After one semi-professional season, Theatre 77 merges with the Winnipeg Little Theatre to become the Manitoba Theatre Centre. In 1958 he takes over the job of producer at Winnipeg's Rainbow Stage. Two years later, having decided to devote all his time to theatre, he sells the accounting firm of Hendry and Evans.

In 1961, after "three non-subsidized, break-even seasons" with Rainbow Stage, he returns to the Manitoba Theatre Centre where two of his plays, *Trapped* and *All About Us*, are produced. In the same year, the first of his three children is born. A Canada Council Award to study theatre outside the country allows him to travel extensively in Europe and the United States during 1963. Returning to Canada in 1964,

he reorganizes Toronto's Canadian Players which then produces his revue *All About Us*. Due to his efforts, Jean Roberts and Marigold Charlesworth become the company's manager and artistic director. Also in 1964, he becomes the first full-time secretary-general of the Canadian Theatre Centre (ITI), a position he holds for five years.

In 1967, he organizes *Colloquium '67: The Design of Theatres*, a meeting of well-known theatre people and architects from across Europe and the United States, held at Expo '67 in Montreal. The same year, he receives the Centennial Medal for his contribution to Canadian theatre.

In 1969, while literary manager of the Stratford Festival, his "disposable opera," *Satyricon*, is produced at the Festival's Avon Theatre under the direction of John Hirsch. Also in 1969, a stage version of his radio play *Fifteen Miles of Broken Glass* is produced by Toronto's Central Players. A year later, the play wins the Lieutenant-Governor's Medal. He leaves the Stratford Festival in the summer of 1970 and the following year helps to found both Playwrights Co-op and Toronto Free Theatre, two organizations deeply involved in improving the level of Canadian content in Canadian theatres. Toronto Free produces his three plays: *How Are Things With the Walking Wounded?*, *Gravediggers of 1942* and *Byron*. In 1974, he is instrumental in the creation of a new Playwrights Colony at the Banff School of Fine Arts and heads the school's playwriting program for two years. Several of his plays — including *Naked at the Opera*, *A Memory of Eden*, *Confidence* and *Apart from Everything is Anything the Matter?* — are workshopped at Banff during this period.

In 1976, he begins writing for CBC television's *Royal Suite* and *King of Kensington* series. His association with *King of Kensington* continues for three years.

He is currently president of Toronto Free Theatre, chairman of the Playwrights Co-op, and a member of the editorial board of the magazine, *Canadian Forum*. He lives in Toronto with his wife, Judith Carr Hendry (manager of the Toronto Free Theatre) and their three children.

Stage Writing

Do You Remember?: originally written in 1954 as a 30-minute television script and broadcast by CBC Winnipeg in 1954, produced and directed by John Hirsch; subsequently re-written for the stage as a musical revue with music by Neil Harris; unpublished; first produced by Rainbow Stage, Winnipeg, in 1957, under the direction of John Hirsch.

Trapped!: two-act comedy-thriller for children; written in 1960; unpublished; first produced by Manitoba Theatre Centre, Winnipeg, 1961, under the direction of John Hirsch.

All About Us: a revue with music by Allan Laing and extra material by Len Peterson; written in 1963-1964; unpublished; first produced during 1964 and 1965 by Manitoba Theatre Centre and Canadian Players Foundation in Winnipeg on a cross-country tour, directed by John Hirsch.

Fifteen Miles of Broken Glass: originally written in 1965 as a 90-minute television script; subsequently adapted in 1968 to a 60-minute radio script; rewritten in 1969 as

a two-act comedy-drama for the stage; first published by Playwrights Co-op, Toronto, in 1972; subsequently published by Talonbooks, Vancouver, in 1975; first produced for the CBC-TV series *Festival* in 1966 and re-broadcast in 1967, under the direction of John Hirsch; subsequently broadcast on radio for *CBC Showcase*, in 1968, directed by Esse W. Ljungh; subsequently produced on stage by Central Players, Toronto, in 1969, and remounted in 1971, under the direction of Martin Kinch; subsequently produced on the stage by Pier One Theatre, Halifax, and Alberta Theatre Projects, Calgary; winner of the 1970 Lieutenant-Governor's medal.

Satyricon: "a disposable opera" with music by Stanley Silverman; written in 1968; unpublished; first produced by Stratford Festival at Avon Theatre in 1969, under the direction of John Hirsch.

Doctor Selavy's Magic Theatre (created by Richard Foreman from the Hendry-Silverman songs for **Satyricon**): one-act masque; unpublished; first produced at Lennox Art Center, Lennox, Massachusetts, in 1971, under the direction of Lyn Austine and Oliver Smith; subsequently produced at the Mercer-O'Casey Theater, New York, in 1972, and at Oxford Playhouse, England, by *ETC*, 1978, under the direction of Naomi Caldicott; album based on original production put out by United Artists.

That Boy, Call Him Back: one act; written in 1970; first published in 1974 by *Performing Arts Magazine*, Toronto; first produced by Factory Theatre Lab Workshop, Toronto, 1971.

Blue Leaves: a short play; written in 1971; unpublished; unproduced.

The Harbor at Porto Del Oro: a short play; written in 1972; unpublished; unproduced.

Masquerade: a short play; written in 1972; unpublished; unproduced.

The One That Got Away: a short play; written in 1972; unpublished; unproduced.

Time Machine: a short play; written in 1972; unpublished; unproduced.

Seance: one act; written in 1972; unpublished; unproduced.

You Smell Good to Me: one act; written in 1972; first published by Playwrights Co-op along with *The Missionary Position* in a volume entitled *Friends and Lovers* in 1972; first produced by Smellgood Productions, at Theatre-in-the-Dell, Toronto, in 1972, directed by David Gustafson; subsequently workshopped at Factory Theatre Lab, Toronto, 1972.

How Are Things with the Walking Wounded?: drama in three scenes; written in 1972; first published in 1972 by Playwrights Co-op; first produced by Toronto Free Theatre, 1972, directed by Martin Kinch.

The Missionary Position: one act; written in 1972; first published by Playwrights Co-op along with *You Smell Good to Me* in a volume entitled *Friends and Lovers*, in 1972; unproduced.

Gravediggers of 1942: two-act musical; music by Steven Jack; written in 1973; first published by Playwrights Co-op in 1973; subsequently published by *Canadian Theatre Review*, Toronto, Summer 1977; first produced by Toronto Free Theatre in 1973, under the direction of Eric Steiner; subsequently produced by Penguin Theatre, Ottawa, 1978, directed by Ian F. Carkner.

Aces Wild: "a vaudeville with music"; extra music by Steven Jack; written in 1972; unpublished; first produced by Creation Two in Hamilton and Toronto, under the direction of the author.

Naked at the Opera: a comedy in four scenes; written in 1974; unpublished; first in 1974 under the direction of Joyce Doolittle.

Apart from Everything Is Anything the Matter?: two-act comedy; written in 1975; unpublished; first workshopped at Banff School of Fine Arts in 1975.

A Memory of Eden: three-act drama; written in 1975; unpublished; first workshopped at Banff School of Fine Arts in 1975, under the direction of Douglas Riske.

Byron: "a play with songs"; lyrics by Lord Byron, music by Steven Jack; written in 1976; unpublished; first produced by Toronto Free Theatre in 1976, under the direction of Martin Kinch.

Confidence: a thriller; written in 1976; unpublished; first workshopped at Banff Playwrights Colony, Alberta, in 1976, under the direction of William Lane.

Seance II: one-act drama; written in 1977; first published by *Quarry Magazine*, Winter 1978-79; unproduced.

Miscellaneous

Wolf, Adolph and Benito, The Steps Behind Her, Sea and Sky: short stories for radio; written and broadcast by CBC between 1951 and 1959.

Box Car Ballet, A City in White, House Divided: 30-minute film documentaries written in 1956; produced by CBC-Winnipeg in 1956, under the direction of Felix Lazarus.

The Anniversary (an adaptation of the Anton Chekhov story): 30-minute television script; written in 1964; first produced by CBC-TV in 1965 for broadcast, under the direction of John Hirsch.

A National Focus for Theatre in the Context of Theatrical Development in the National Capital Region: report to the Theatre Foundation of Ottawa; written in 1966; unpublished.

Last Man on Horseback: 60 minutes; written in 1968; unpublished; first produced for *CBC Showcase* in 1969, under the direction of Esse W. Ljungh.

Private Places (with Ron Kelly): feature film script; written in 1976; unproduced.

Royal Suite: three episodes; written in 1976; produced by CBC-TV in 1976 for national broadcast; directed by Sheldon Larry and Ron Kelly.

King of Kensington: two episodes written in 1976; three episodes written in 1977; broadcast nationally by CBC-TV, Toronto, in 1976 and 1977; directed by Sheldon Larry, Gary Plaxton and George Bloomfield.

Please Say You're Real: 30-minute television script; written in 1978; first produced by CBC-Winnipeg, 1978.

Little Judge Big Mouth: 30-minute film script; written in 1978; first produced by CBC-Winnipeg, 1978.

In Progress

Farr Away: a novel.

King of Kensington: occasional episodes for CBC-TV series.

Toronto the Good: a musical; music by Paul Hoffert.

Your Place or Mine?: a comedy-drama.

Ann Henry

Born August 7, 1914, in Winnipeg. Father a whaler from the Shetland Isles; he later becomes an evangelist and still later a social activist. He is a leader in the Winnipeg general strike of 1919. He runs for the House of Commons during the 1920's. When she is four, her mother is sent to a mental hospital and remains there until her death 29 years later. Like thousands during the Depression, she is forced to leave school after grade 10 since her family cannot afford the necessary textbooks. Although she can neither swim nor dive, her first job after leaving school is as a high diver with a water show attached to a travelling carnival. An older sister dies in 1932 at the age of 20 due to a mistake on the part of a hospital intern.

Married in 1935, she moves to La Riviere, a small village outside Winnipeg. Here her two sons and daughter are born. After continual absences, which cause the family both hardship and actual hunger, her husband deserts, leaving her to raise the children alone. She supports her family by doing a variety of odd jobs including farm labour, cleaning barns and plucking chickens. Having been evicted and finding work hard to come by, she and the children hitch-hike to Winnipeg, where, almost destitute, they sleep in the railway station, bus depot and the immigration building which is being used as an emergency shelter for the homeless. Eventually she lands a job as a sales clerk in the Hudson's Bay Company Store and wins a long fight with City Hall for the right to rent low-income housing. After working for a time as the private secretary to the chief engineer of an aircraft plant, although she can neither type nor take shorthand, she becomes a reporter for the *Winnipeg Citizen* and later the *Winnipeg Tribune.*

The first woman to cover the police beat, the law courts and the provincial legislature, she becomes a weekly and later a daily columnist as well as drama editor and critic. "When I left, three people, so help me, took my job—two reporters and a librarian."

During the 1950's and 1960's she writes for magazines, radio and television and is also a frequent participant in game shows and panel discussions. During this period she wins a Hollywood writing prize and first prize in a fiction contest run by *Maclean's Magazine.* After marrying again in 1964, she begins to write for the stage. Her first play, *Lulu Street,* is produced in 1967 at the Manitoba Theatre Centre.

A widow since 1975, she currently lives in Winnipeg with her daughter and four grandchildren.

Stage Writing

Lulu Street: three-act drama; written between 1966 and 1967; first published by Playwrights Co-op, Toronto, 1975, and subsequently by Talonbooks, 1975; first produced by the Manitoba Theatre Centre in March, 1967 under the direction of Edward Gilbert; subsequently produced at various regional theatres across Canada including Festival Lennoxville (directed by John Hirsch); adapted for radio; produced by CBC for national broadcast; adapted for television; produced by CBC for national broadcast.

All The Men On The Moon Are Irish: two-act drama for children; first produced by the Voyageur School at the Manitoba Warehouse Theatre under the direction of Loa Henry.

Radio Writing

Isabel: 30 minutes; written in 1978; produced by CBC for regional broadcast.

Travels With Aunt Jane: 30 minutes; written in 1977-78; produced by CBC for national broadcast.

Miscellaneous

Laugh Baby, Laugh: autobiography; written in 1966; published by McClelland and Stewart, Toronto in 1967.

It's All Free On The Outside: novel; written in 1974; published by McClelland and Stewart in 1975.

In Progress

Shut Up and Eat Your Mud (working title): comedy with songs; begun in 1974.

John Herbert

Born John Brundage on October 13, 1926, in Toronto. Father a professional baseball player and coach; mother teaches science, art and English literature in a Toronto high school. Between the ages of 8 and 14, he takes lessons in painting at the Art Gallery of Ontario. An early interest in theatre leads him to write, what he calls, a marsh-melodrama (a script in which he plays the female lead) entitled *They Died With Their Boots On* in 1942. He leaves school a year later, at the age of 17, for a job as a commercial artist with the advertising department of Eaton's in Toronto.

In 1946, according to Herbert, a local street gang beats him up for being "a sissy". The police charge *him*, however, with gross indecency. He flees to Chicago but is arrested seven weeks later. The result is six months in a reformatory in Guelph and it is from this experience that his best-known play, *Fortune and Men's Eyes*, is based. "The Experience", he says later, "was a crash course in self-discovery." On his release, he travels throughout Canada and the United States working at various jobs — waiter, labourer, carnival spieler and commercial artist. He returns to Toronto once during this period to spend a year studying life drawing and portraiture at the Ontario College of Art. In 1955, back in Toronto permanently, he begins to train seriously for a career in the theatre. A student at the New Play Society School from 1955 until 1958, he studies acting, directing, fencing, lighting and stage management. In 1958, he takes classes as well at both the Volkoff Ballet School and the National Ballet School.

In 1960, he becomes artistic director of Toronto's Adventure Theatre. *Private Club* and *A Household God*, the first of his plays to reach the stage, are produced by this company in 1962. Later the same year, he leaves Adventure Theatre to become artistic director of the New Venture Players, a position he holds until 1965 when he begins his own company, the 35-seat Garret Theatre at 529 Yonge Street. During these years, he completes several plays including

Iris McCaig

Fortune and Men's Eyes, written in 1963, for which he is awarded—but turns down— the Dominion Drama Festival's Massey Prize. Throughout the 60's and into the early 70's, the Garret produces a great deal of new work and many young theatre people — Ken Gass among them — pass through the theatre. In 1975, *Fortune and Men's Eyes*, already seen off-Broadway and already made into a film, which Herbert subsequently disowns, is finally given a professional production by Toronto's Phoenix Theatre and the play wins that year's Chalmers Outstanding Play Award.

Herbert, however, remains bitter about the Canadian theatre scene and what he feels is the lack of recognition he and his work have received. "People here have no respect for theatres," he tells one interviewer, "and it has no meaning for their lives . . . Toronto is just a heavy, gray, hypocrisy." Following the closing of the Garret in 1976, he spends much time travelling in Europe, seeing productions of his play, and working in London and Paris. He says later that he personally subsidized the Garret by nearly $20,000. Angry and outspoken throughout his life, he once said that he "naturally identifies with the destruction that's given. I had my destruction when I was 19. I just can't forget it and what it did to me." He begins to teach writing at the Three Schools of Art, a position which he holds through the present. Currently resident in Toronto, he is an associate editor of *Onion*, a bi-monthly arts newspaper, for which he writes regularly.

Stage Writing

They Died With Their Boots On: a one-act "marsh-melodrama"; written in 1942; unpublished; first produced by Taylor Stratten Camp, Canoe Lake, Algonquin Park, Ontario, 1942.

A Household God: one act; written between 1960 and 1961; unpublished; first produced by the New Venture Players at the Bohemian Embassy Coffee House, Toronto, 1962, under the direction of the author.

Private Club: one act; written between 1960 and 1961; unpublished; first produced by the New Venture Players at the Bohemian Embassy Coffee House, Toronto, 1962, under the direction of the author.

A Lady of Camelias (adapted from A. Dumas fils' *La Dame aux camelias):* written in 1962; unpublished; first produced by the New Venture Players at the Victoria Auditorium, Toronto, 1964, under the direction of the author.

Pearl Divers: one act; written in 1962; first published in an anthology of Herbert's plays, *Some Angry Summer Songs,* by Talonbooks, 1977; first produced by Forest Hill Chamber Theatre, Toronto, 1974, under the direction of the author.

Fortune and Men's Eyes: two-act drama; written in 1963; first published by Grove Press, New York, 1967; published in French by Leméac, Montreal, in 1971, in translation by René Dionne; published by Penguin, London, in *Open Space Plays*, 1974; first produced as a workshop at the Stratford Festival in 1965; subsequently produced by The Actor's Playhouse, New York, 1967, under the direction of Mitchell

Nestor; Phoenix Theatre, Toronto, 1975, under the direction of Graham Harley; the play has received several major productions around the world and has had three New York revivals; the 1975 Phoenix Theatre production won the Chalmers Outstanding Play Award; adapted as a film script, 1969, and produced by MGM, Cinamex International, and the Canadian Film Development Corporation, 1971, under the direction of Harvey Hart.

World of Woyzeck: Adapted from the Büchner play; written in 1963; unpublished; first produced by the Garret Theatre, Toronto, 1969, under the direction of the author.

Beer Room: one act; written in 1966; first published in an anthology of Herbert's plays, *Some Angry Summer Songs,* by Talonbooks, 1977; first produced by Factory Theatre Lab, Toronto, 1970, under the direction of Ian Mcdowell; subsequently produced by Forest Hill Chamber Theatre, Toronto, in 1974, under the direction of the author.

Born of Medusa's Blood: three acts; written in 1966; unpublished; first produced by Medusa Inc. at Theatre-in-Camera, Toronto, 1973, under the direction of the author.

Close Friends: one act; written in 1966; first published in an anthology of Herbert's plays, *Some Angry Summer Songs,* by Talonbooks, 1977; first produced at the Festival of Underground Theatre, 1970, under the direction of Ken Gass; subsequently produced by Forest Hill Chamber Theatre, in 1974, under the direction of the author; produced by the Phoenix Theatre, Toronto, 1976, under the direction of the author.

Closer to Cleveland: written in 1967; unpublished; unproduced.

Omphale and the Hero: three acts; written in 1972; first published by the *Canadian Theatre Review* (*CTR* 3) in 1974; first produced by the Forest Hill Chamber Theatre, Toronto, 1974, under the direction of the author.

The Dinosaurs: one act; written in 1973; first published in an anthology of Herbert's plays, *Some Angry Summer Songs*, by Talonbooks, 1977; first produced by the Forest Hill Chamber Theatre, Toronto, 1974, under the direction of the author.

The Token Star: three-act comedy; written in 1979; unpublished; first produced by Poor Alex Theatre, Toronto, in 1980.

Miscellaneous

Belinda Wright and Jelko Yuresha: a ballet biography, published by Kaye Bellman, London, 1972.

The House That Jack Built: a novel, serialized in *Onion*, Toronto, 1975-1976. Several short stories and articles in *York Memo, Unity, Saturday Night, Village Voice, Variety, Performing Arts, Glitter, Onion,* and the *Globe and Mail* and others.

In Progress

The Elephants' Graveyard: a three-act drama.

The Real Mrs. Reynard: a three-act comedy.

The Token Star: a three-act comedy.

The Power of Paper Dolls: a three-act drama.

Queen City Blues: a film script.

The Devil's Church: a novel.

Secondary Sources

Section on Herbert included in *Stage Voices* (Geraldine Anthony, ed.), Doubleday, 1978, pp. 166-206.

Michael Hollingsworth

Born February 5, 1950, in Swansea, Wales. Father an economist; mother a nurse. The family moves to Toronto in 1956 where he receives his schooling. Finding school "too slow" he leaves after grade 12 and continues his education through extensive reading. His passion for theatre (which begins "...in the usual dimly lit closets, keyholes and bongo clubs") is further developed by his involvement with rock and roll bands and, in particular, by his attendance at a 1965 Rolling Stones concert in Toronto which further demonstrates to him the theatrical potential of rock music.

In 1972, his first play, *Strawberry Fields*, a play dealing with contemporary violence, is produced by Factory Theatre Lab. A year later, his next play, *Clear Light*, is closed by the Metropolitan Toronto Police Department's Morality Squad after 12

Bobbe Besold

performances at Toronto Free Theatre. During 1975, he works with experimental theatre director John Juliani while enrolled as a graduate theatre student at York University. As part of his work at York, he plays a "hippie" janitor in Eric Nicol's comedy, *Citizens of Calais*. Leaving York before completing his degree, he begins to develop an interest in combining video with theatre and rock. This leads to a collaboration with the Hummer Talent Cartel, a feminist political theatre group, and to the founding of the Video Cabaret Theatre of Science of which he is currently artistic co-director. A founding member of the punk-rock band, The Government, which is featured in many productions by Video Cabaret, he describes himself today as "the world's tallest free-standing rock playwright."

In 1980, he tells *CTR*: "It strikes me that theatre has to deal with two of the greatest consciousness-shapers of this and coming decades. To be able to examine why we are what we are, and what we will become. I feel that music and television have to be included in this new form." He currently makes his home in Toronto.

Stage Writing

Strawberry Fields: long one-act drama about contemporary violence; written in 1972; first published by Playwrights Co-op, Toronto, in 1973; subsequently published in *The Factory Theatre Lab Anthology* by Talonbooks, Vancouver, in 1974; first produced by Factory Theatre Lab, Toronto, in 1973, under the direction of Paul Bettis; subsequently produced by Factory Theatre Lab, Toronto, in 1976 as a rock-drama under the title *Fields*, and directed by the author.

Clear Light: three-act drama; written in 1973; first published by Playwrights Co-op, Toronto, in 1973; subsequently published by Coach House Press, Toronto, in 1973; first produced by Toronto Free Theatre, Toronto, in 1973, under the direction of Martin Kinch.

Cheap Thrills: two acts; written between 1974 and 1975; unpublished; first produced

by Theatre Passe Muraille, Toronto, in 1977, under the direction of the author.

White Noise: long one-act; written in 1976; unpublished; first produced by New Theatre, Toronto, in 1977, under the direction of Clarke Rogers.

Punc Rok: one act; written in 1977; unpublished; first produced by Theatre Passe Muraille, Toronto, in 1977, under the direction of the author.

Broken Record: two acts; written between 1977 and 1978; unpublished; unproduced.

Electric Eye: one-act video drama; written between 1977 and 1978; unpublished; first produced by Video-Cabaret Theatre of Science at A Space, Toronto, in 1978, under the direction of the author; subsequently shown at Factory Theatre Lab, Toronto, The Performance Garage, New York, and The Kitchen, New York, all in 1978.

Trans World: one-act comedy-drama about a Howard Hughes figure; written in 1978; first published by Playwrights Co-op, Toronto, in 1979; first produced by Toronto Free Theatre, Toronto, in 1978, under the direction of Bill Lane.

1984 (a video cabaret adaptation of the novel by George Orwell): long one-act using two live performers, seventeen televisions and a punk rock band; written in 1979, since re-written; unpublished; first produced by Video Cabaret Theatre of Science and Theatre Passe Muraille, Toronto, in 1979, under the direction of Michael Hollingsworth.

In Progress

A screen play dealing with the game of chess.

A rock-video translation of George Orwell's *Brave New World*.

Secondary Sources

Interview in *Canadian Theatre Review*, Winter 1980 (*CTR* 25).

Patricia Joudry

Born October 18, 1921, in Spirit River, Alberta. The family moves to Montreal in 1925. While attending high school she writes and acts in her own plays as well as taking part in productions by Dorothy Davis' Children's Theatre. After small acting roles on CBC Radio in Montreal she moves to Toronto in 1940 where she continues to work for the network as both an actress and playwright. From 1940 to 1943 she writes and stars in the situation comedy *Penny's Diary*. In 1945, drawn by a starting salary of $25,000 she moves to New York as co-author of *The Aldrich Family*. Returning to Canada in 1949, she resumes acting as well as writing for CBC Radio. In 1951 and 1952 she writes and stars in the situation comedy *Affectionately, Jenny*. Between 1951 and 1956, six of her one-hour radio dramas are produced by the CBC for the series *Stage*. CBC also produces five of her one-hour television dramas between 1953 and 1961.

Peggy Merseredu

Teach Me How to Cry, perhaps her best-known stage play, is successfully produced off-Broadway in 1955. Movie rights are purchased by Universal-International studios for $25,000 and in 1956 it is named Best Play in the annual Dominion Drama Festival. A year later she shares the 'Woman of the Year' award with Gabrielle Roy as Canada's outstanding woman in literature and art.

Also in 1957 she moves to London, England with John Steele, her second husband. The next year, *Teach Me How to Cry* is the first all-Canadian production to run in London's West End. She makes headlines when Warner Brothers purchases the movie rights to her stage play *Semi-Detached* for $250,000. In 1960, however, the play closes on Broadway after three performances. While in England, she experiences a period of religious delusion. The entry on her in *Canadian Who's Who 1961-'63* indicates that "since 1961, (she) discovered that she had psychic powers and that she was transmitting plays direct from the Spirit World". During this time she believes herself to be the recipient of 18 full-length plays and 12 TV plays "transmitted"

by the late G.B. Shaw. These experiences are described in her autobiography *Spirit River to Angels' Roost and Religions I Have Loved and Left*.

Her health restored through Jungian analysis, she wins two fellowships to continue her writing at the MacDowell Colony in New Hampshire. Following her return to Canada in 1973, McClelland and Stewart publishes her novel *The Dweller on the Threshold*. Divorced from her first husband Delman Dinsdale in 1952 and from John Steele in 1975, she has two daughters from her first marriage and three from her second. Still an active writer, she now makes her home on a farm in Quebec.

Stage Writing

The Stranger in My House: a one-act play produced in Toronto.

Teach Me How to Cry: a three-act drama first published by Dramatists Play Service, New York, in 1955. Republished in *Canada's Lost Plays: Women Pioneers*, by CTR Publications in 1979; first produced off-Broadway at the Theatre deLys April 5, 1955 for a six-week run; first Canadian production staged by the University of Toronto Alumnae Dramatic Club at Hart House Theatre March 13 and 14, 1956 directed by Leon Major. Production wins the D.D.F. best play award in 1956. Play produced in London West End for five weeks in July 16, 1958 under the title *Noon Has No Shadows* with an all-Canadian cast directed by Leon Major. Film version of play released by Empire-Universal Studios as "The Restless Years" in 1958. Adapted as a 60-minute radio drama. First produced by Andrew Allan on CBC Stage, April 19, 1953; re-broadcast May 21, 1961. Adapted as a 60-minute television drama. First produced by Henry Kaplan on CBC Theatre, Oct. 31, 1953.

The Sand Castle: a three-act drama produced by Margo Jones at the Margo Jones Theatre in Dallas, Texas in 1955. Adapted as a 60-minute television drama. First produced by Henry Kaplan on CBC G.M. Presents, April 12, 1955. Broadcast on U.S. network in 1958.

Three Rings for Michelle: a three-act drama distributed in playscript form by Dramatists Play Service, New York, in 1960. First produced by Joudry and John Steele at the Avenue Theatre, Toronto, Nov. 15, 1956.

Walk Alone Together: a comedy. $1,000 second prize winner in 1959 Stratford Festival-*Globe and Mail* Playwriting Competition. Produced at the Duke of York's Theatre in London West End in June 1960 after a four week road tour as *Will You Walk a Little Faster?*

Semi-Detached: a three-act drama written in 1959. Produced by Philip Rose at the Martin Beck Theatre on Broadway March 10, 1960 after a month-long pre-Broadway tour.

The Song of Louise in the Morning: a long one-act domestic drama published by Dramatists Play Service, New York, in 1960. Amateur productions.

Valerie: a comedy staged by Bernard Braden in London in 1961. Adapted as a 60-minute television drama. First produced

by Basil Coleman on CBC Playdate, Oct. 18, 1961.

The Man With the Perfect Wife: a comedy produced at the Royal Poinciana Playhouse, Palm Beach, Florida, March 22, 1965.

Think Again: a three-act satirical comedy begun in 1969. Published in the *Canadian Theatre Review*, No. 23, Summer 1979.

Now: a science fiction multi-media drama written in 1970 while at the MacDowell Colony.

I Ching: a two-act drama written in 1971.

My Lady Shiva: a two-act dramatization of her novel *The Dweller on the Threshold* begun in 1973.

Radio Plays

Going Up Please: a comedy produced by Rupert Caplan over CBC radio, Montreal in 1939.

Penny's Diary: a 30-minute weekly situation comedy series broadcast nationally by the CBC from 1940 to 1943.

The Aldrich Family: co-author from 1945 to 1949 of the 30-minute situation comedy series heard on NBC and CBS.

Forsaking All Others: a 30-minute romance produced by Andrew Allan on CBC Buckingham Theatre, May 3, 1950.

The Luckiest Guy: a 30-minute romantic drama produced on CBC Summer Stage, June 4, 1950.

Listen! He's Proposing: a 30-minute comedy romance produced on CBC Buckingham Theatre, June 7, 1950.

By Any Other Name: produced on CBC Winnipeg Drama, August 17, 1950.

An Inspector Calls: an adaptation of the text by J.B. Priestley. Produced on CBC Ford Theatre, Oct. 6, 1950.

The Storm: produced on CBC Winnipeg Drama, Sept. 21, 1950 and on CBC Prairie Playhouse, Oct. 22, 1953. Unpublished manuscript copy available at Concordia University radio drama collection.

Intermission: a 60-minute drama produced by Andrew Allan on CBC Stage, Jan. 28, 1951.

The Apple Tree: a 60-minute adaptation produced on CBC Ford Theatre, March 30, 1951.

Eve Does Her Durndest: a 30-minute comedy produced on CBC Summer Fallow, June 18, 1951.

Affectionately, Jenny: a 30-minute CBC weekly situation comedy series broadcast from July 1 to Sept. 23, 1951 and Feb. 25 to June 30, 1952. Unpublished manuscript copy available at Concordia University radio drama collection.

The Examiner: produced on CBC Vancouver Theatre, July 6, 1951 and on CBC Pacific Playhouse, Dec. 16, 1956. Unpublished manuscript copy available at Concordia University radio drama collection.

The Monster: produced on CBC Vancouver Theatre, August 31, 1951 and on CBC Pacific Playhouse, Jan. 31 and March 2, 1958. Unpublished manuscript copy available at Concordia University radio drama collection.

Winter Farrow: a 30-minute comedy produced on CBC Summer Fallow, Oct. 8, 1951.

No Highway: produced on CBC Ford Theatre, March 28, 1952.

The Land Is Your Inheritance: a 30-minute drama produced on CBC Summer Fallow, April 28, 1952.

Visit to the City: a 30-minute comedy produced on CBC Summer Fare, Sept. 5, 1952.

Pig in the Parlor: a 30-minute comedy produced on CBC Summer Fallow, Sept. 29, 1952.

The Auction Sale: a 30-minute drama produced on CBC Summer Fallow, Oct. 13, 1952.

Mother is Watching: a 60-minute drama produced by Andrew Allan on CBC Stage, Nov. 23, 1952. Unpublished manuscript copy available at Concordia University radio drama collection.

Lace On Her Petticoat: produced on CBC Ford Theatre, Dec. 12, 1952.

Happy Is the Day: a 60-minute comedy drama produced by Andrew Allan on CBC Stage, Dec. 14, 1952.

Anne of Green Gables: Thirteen 30-minute episodes based on Lucy Maud Montgomery's novel broadcast on the CBC from Jan. 2, 1953 to Jan. 8, 1954.

Thatcher Place: a 60-minute comedy-drama produced by Andrew Allan on CBC Stage, March 29, 1953. Unpublished manuscript copy available at Concordia University radio drama collection.

Taking Stock: a 30-minute play produced on CBC Summer Fallow, April 19, 1954.

The Landrace Lands Again: a 30-minute play produced on CBC Summer Fallow, May 24, 1954.

Corrida: a 30-minute drama produced on CBC Vancouver Theatre, Sept. 10, 1954 and Feb. 15, 1957. Unpublished manuscript copy available at Concordia University radio drama collection.

Anne of Avonlea: 30-minute dramatizations based on Lucy Maud Montgomery's novel broadcast on the CBC from Sept. 24 to Dec. 24, 1954.

The Hermit: a 30-minute play produced on CBC Summer Fallow, Oct. 25, 1954.

Child of the Cliffs: a 60-minute drama produced by Esse W. Lljung on CBC Stage, Jan. 15, 1956. Unpublished manuscript copy available at Concordia University radio drama collection.

The Arrival of Anne: produced on CBC Wednesday Night, June 12, 1957.

Bitter Gold: a drama produced on CBC Drama in Sound, June 10, 1958.

Miscellaneous

The Painted Blind: a 60-minute domestic drama produced by Henry Kaplan on CBC G.M. Theatre, Feb. 14, 1956.

A Woman's Point of View: a 30-minute romantic drama produced by Ronald Weyman on CBC On Camera, July 8, 1957.

The Immortal Rose: a 60-minute TV drama written in 1958. Unproduced.

The Song of Louise in the Morning: a domestic drama produced on BBC-TV and CBS Television Workshop in 1960.

Gift of Truth: produced on CBC-TV, May 1961.

Something Old, Something New: a 60-minute drama produced by Harvey Hart on CBC G.M. Presents, June 11, 1961.

The Dweller on the Threshold: a novel published by McClelland and Stewart in 1973.

And the Children Played: autobiographical account published by Tundra Books in 1975.

Betty Lambert

Born August 29, 1933, in Calgary. Father a bread salesman and carpenter; mother a cleaning lady. She receives both her primary and secondary education in Calgary. Her first poem is published when she is 13. This is followed by a prize-winning short story at age 17 and a summer in the creative writing program at the Banff School of Fine Arts.

Having received a B.A. in Philosophy from the University of British Columbia, she travels extensively through England, France and Mexico, and obtains a Canada Council grant to study ancient Greek theatre at Epidaurus. During this time, she represents Canada at a meeting of the International Association of Theatre for Children and Young People in France. On returning to Canada, she begins to write plays for radio and television, over 30 of which are produced by CBC beginning in 1958. Her first work for the stage, a children's play entitled *The Riddle Machine*,

is produced by Vancouver's Holiday Theatre, in 1967. After a national tour, it plays at Expo '67 in Montreal and enjoys frequent productions throughout the United States as well as a staging by Belgium's National Jeudtheater.

In 1975, Vancouver's New Play Centre presents her sex comedy, *Sqrieux-de-Dieu*. This production tours the country the following year. Currently an associate professor of English at Simon Fraser University, she is divorced and makes her home in Burnaby.

Stage Writing

The Riddle Machine: two acts; written in 1966; first published in *Contemporary Children's Theatre*, by Avon Equinox, New York, in 1974; first produced by Holiday Theatre, Vancouver, in 1966, under the direction of Robert Sherrin; subsequently produced and toured by Holiday Theatre, Vancouver, in 1966, under the direction of Joy Coghill; also produced by Jack and Jill Theater, Chicago, Pittsburgh Playhouse, Pittsburgh, and by the National Jeudtheater, Belgium.

Song of the Serpent: full length children's play; written in 1967; first published by Playwrights Co-op, Toronto, 1973; first produced by Holiday Theatre, Vancouver, 1967, under the direction of Jane Heyman; subsequently produced and toured by Holiday Theatre, Vancouver, 1967, under the direction of Margaret Foulkes.

The Good of the Sun: one act; written in 1968; first published by *West Coast Review*, Vancouver, in 1975; first produced by CBC Radio, Vancouver, in 1969, for national broadcast; subsequently produced by the University of Victoria at MacPherson Theatre, Victoria, 1970.

The Visitor: full-length; written in 1969; unpublished; first produced by Playhouse Theatre, Vancouver, in 1970, under the direction of Joy Coghill.

World, World Go Away: two-act children's play; written in 1970; unpublished; first produced by Holiday Theatre, Vancouver, in 1970, under the direction of Ray Michal.

Sqrieux-de-Dieu: two-act sex comedy; written in 1975; first published by

Playwrights Co-op, Toronto, 1975; subsequently published by Talonbooks, Vancouver, 1976; first produced by New Play Centre at the Vancouver East Cultural Centre, 1975, under the direction of Richard Ouzounian; subsequently produced by Festival Lennoxville, 1976, under the direction of Richard Ouzounian, in 1977, Festival Lennoxville produced the show again with the same director and a different cast; this production toured Eastern Canada and was shown at the National Arts Centre, Ottawa.

Clouds of Glory: two acts; philosophical comedy; written in 1978-79; published by Playwrights Canada, 1979; first produced by the New Play Centre, Vancouver, 1979, under the direction of Richard Ouzounian; subsequently produced by Festival Lennoxville, 1979, under the direction of Richard Ouzounian.

Radio Writing

The Lady Upstairs: 30 minutes; written in 1957; first produced by CBC Radio, in 1958, for national broadcast.

The Sea Wall: 90 minutes; written in 1961; first produced by CBC Radio, 1962, for national broadcast.

Falconer's Island: 60 minutes; written in 1965; first produced by CBC Radio, 1966, for national broadcast.

Once Burnt, Twice Shy: 90 minutes; written in 1964; typescript reproduction available from the New Play Centre, Vancouver; first produced by CBC Radio, 1965, for national broadcast; subsequently produced by CBC Radio, 1973, for national broadcast.

Grasshopper Hill: written in 1979; first produced by CBC Radio, in 1979.

Television Writing

The following is a selection from numerous television scripts broadcast both nationally and regionally by CBC, and other television stations.

Prescription for Love: written in 1964; first produced by CTV, Vancouver, in 1965, for regional broadcast.

Return of a Hero: 60 minutes; written in 1967; first produced by CBC Vancouver.

When the Bough Breaks: written in 1970; first produced by CBC, Montreal, in 1971.

The Infinite Worlds of Maybe: written in 1975; first produced by CBC, 1976, for national broadcast; subsequently produced by CBC, in 1977 and 1978, for national broadcast.

Brooke: 60 minutes; written in 1977; first produced by CBC, Toronto, in 1978, for national broadcast.

Nobody Knows I'm Here: 30 minutes; written in 1977; first produced by CBC, Vancouver, in 1978, for regional broadcast.

Miscellaneous

Crossings: a novel; written in 1979; first published by Pulp Press, Vancouver; subsequently published by Viking Press, 1980.

In Progress

Fire and Ice: a play.

Rod Langley

Born in Perth, Australia in 1942, one of two children. Mother an accountant. While he is still a child, the family moves to Cunderin, where his mother opens a library. He and his twin brother leave school after grade eight. Both, however, continue their education through extensive reading in their mother's library. Returning to Perth at age 16, he works first in an office and then as a cowboy, rounding up wild cattle for a slaughterhouse.

In 1960, he leaves Australia for Vancouver where he works at various jobs before travelling east to Montreal. While a mature student at Sir George Williams University he writes *Allegro*, his first one-act play, which is produced there. After receiving a B.A., he marries and moves to Vancouver where he earns a Master's degree at the University of British Columbia. In 1967, his second play, *The Station*, is premiered at UBC's Frederic Wood Theatre, with subsequent productions in Toronto, Paris and London. His first full-length play, *The Veterans*, completed two years later, is produced at Vancouver's Arts Club Theatre.

Glen E. Erickson

On commission from Regina's Globe Theatre, he writes *Tales From a Prairie Drifter*, a play about the Metis uprisings led by Louis Riel. After the initial production by the Globe in 1973, the script is adapted and made into a television film by the CBC and the National Film Board. *Bethune*, his second drama, portrays the maverick Canadian doctor who served during the civil wars in Spain and China. Impressed by the CBC radio production of *Bethune*, the Globe Theatre and Montreal's Centaur Theatre jointly commission a stage version of the play which is premiered in Regina in 1974 and subsequently produced in Vancouver, Montreal, and Edmonton. In 1976, CBC asks him to adapt the script into a television drama to star Donald Sutherland. When the CBC decides to abandon his play in favor of a script by an American writer, he is supported by ACTRA in his attempt to stop the broadcast. The American version of *Bethune* is finally aired in 1978.

He currently makes his home in Lantzville, British Columbia.

Stage Writing

Allegro: one-act; written in 1962; unpublished; first produced at Sir George Williams University, Montreal, 1963.

The Station: one-act; written in 1967; first published by Playwrights Co-op, Toronto, 1972; first produced by Frederick Wood Theatre, Vancouver, 1967; subsequently produced by Theatre Passe Muraille, Toronto, 1974, under the direction of Hrant Alianak; subsequently produced in London, England and at Theatre l'Absidiole in Paris, France.

The Veterans: three acts; written in 1969; unpublished; first produced by the Arts Club Theatre, Vancouver, 1969.

Tales from a Prairie Drifter: two acts; written in 1972; first published by Playwrights Co-op, 1974; first produced/commissioned by Globe Theatre, Regina, 1973, under the direction of Ken Kramer; adapted as a film script under the new title, *This Riel Business*; filmed by National Film Board, 1978, and produced on television by CBC and the National Film Board, 1979.

Bethune: 120-minute radio script; written in 1973; subsequently rewritten as a three-act stage play in 1974; first published by Talonbooks, Vancouver, 1975; commissioned and produced by Globe Theatre, Regina, 1974, under the direction of Robert Sime; subsequently produced by City Stage, Vancouver, 1975, under the direction of Ray Michal; by the Centaur Theatre, Montreal, 1975, under the direction of George Plawski; by the Citadel Theatre, Edmonton, 1977, under the direction of Keith Digby; commissioned by CBC to write television version; unproduced; subsequently produced by BBC Radio, London, England, 1978.

Jacques Languirand

Born May 1, 1931, in Montreal. Receives his secondary education at Collège Saint-Croix and Collège Saint-Laurent where he studies classics. While at Collège Saint-Laurent, he is active in Les Compagnons de Saint-Laurent, the school drama society.

In 1949, at the age of 19, he travels to Paris to study theatre with Charles Dullin, Michel Vitold and Etienne Decroux. While in Paris, he meets many of the leading writers and artists of the day and comes under the influence of the ideas of Albert Camus and Jean-Paul Sartre.

Returning to Canada in 1953, he finds a job with Radio-Telediffusion français and later works for Arts Spectacles, both in Montreal, In 1956, he completes his first play, *Les insolités*, a comedy in the absurdist vein. The play wins first prize in the 1956 Western Quebec Drama Festival and in the finals of the Dominion Drama Festival later that year. The play is greatly praised by festival judges. After the festival, *Les insolités* is staged by the Compagnie de Montréal at Montreal's Théâtre d'Anjou, under Languirand's direction. When interviewed about the play, he says it is the product of experiments with automatic writing and the spontaneous association of words. His usual theme—the problems and anxieties of 20th century man—as well as his interest in formal innovation remain consistent throughout his career.

In 1956, he opens Théâtre de Dix Heures, a cabaret theatre in Montreal. Here he produces the works of Beckett, Jean Genet, and in 1957, his own play *Le roi ivre*. The works attract only modest audiences. In 1962 he is awarded the Governor General's Prize for *Le dictionnaire insolité*. In 1963, his play, *Les violons d' automne,* enjoys a three-week run in Paris, an honour infrequently accorded plays from Quebec at that time. In the same year, his only novel, *Tout compte fait, ou l'Eugène*, is published also in Paris.

From 1964 to 1966, he serves as artistic director and writer-in-residence at Théâtre du Nouveau Monde in Montreal, teaches at the National Theatre School, McGill University and Université Laval. He spends

Kéro

time as well working as an audio-visual and multi-media designer and supervises the designs for a major multi-media exhibition at Expo '67. In the late 60s, he works for a time as a director for the National Film Board. He also translates into French some of the work of Marshall McLuhan. In 1969, his multi-media play *Man, Inc.* opens the new St. Lawrence Centre Theatre in Toronto. During the mid-70s, he turns to radio in Montreal and becomes widely-known as host of a musical talk show. Married, he continues today to make his home in Montreal.

Stage Writing

Les insolités: three-act comedy; written in 1955; first published by Cercle du Livre de France, Montreal, 1962, in the same volume as *Les violons d' automne*; first produced at the Western Quebec Drama Festival in 1956 under the direction of the author; subsequently produced by Compagnie de Montréal, Montreal, 1956, under the direction of the author; winner of the first prize at the Western Quebec Drama Festival, 1956.

105

Hamlet: full-length adaptation; written in 1956; first published by Editions du Jour, Montreal, 1957; unproduced.

Le roi ivre: full-length; written in 1956; first published in *Voix et image du pays* by Presses de l'Université du Québec, Montreal, 1970; first produced by Théâtre de Dix Heures, Montreal, 1957, under the direction of the author.

Diogène: one-act fantasy; written in 1957; first published in *La barre du jour* (Vol. I, Nos. 3, 4, 5), 1965; first produced at Percé Art Centre, Gaspé, 1958, under the direction of Louis-Georges Carrier.

Le gibet: three-act comedy; written in 1957; first published by Cercle du Livre de France, 1960; first produced by Comédie-Canadienne, Montreal, 1958, under the direction of Louis-Georges Carrier; subsequently produced in English at the Stratford Festival's Avon Theatre.

Les grands départs: three-act comedy; written in 1957; first published by Cercle du Livre de France, 1958; subsequently published by Editions de Renouveau pedagogique, Montreal, 1970; adapted for television; produced by Radio-Canada, 1957; original stage version produced at Percé Art Centre, 1958.

Les Violons d' automne: three acts; written in 1960; first published by Cercle du Livre de France, 1962, in the same volume as *Les insolités*; first produced by Théâtre Club, Montreal, 1961, under the direction of Jan Doat; subsequently produced in Paris, 1963.

Klondyke: two acts; written in 1964; first published by Cercle du Livre de France, 1970, in same volume as *Québec et l'Americanité;* first produced by Théâtre du Nouveau Monde, Montreal, 1965, at the Commonwealth Festival, London, England, under the direction of Jean Gascon.

Les cloissons: one act; written in 1964; first published in *Ecrits du Canada français*, Volume 22, 1966; first produced by Théâtre de la Place, Montreal, 1965.

Man, Inc. (L'âge de Pierre): full-length multi-media musical; written in 1969; unpublished; chosen to open the new St. Lawrence Centre Theatre in Toronto in 1970 in a production directed by the author with multi-dimensional stage designs by Ralph Alswang, music by Norm Symonds, and starring Don Francks.

Miscellaneous

Le dictionnaire insolité: humorous essays; written in 1961; published by Editions du Jour, Montreal, 1962; winner of the 1962 Governor General's Prize.

Tout compte fait, ou l'Eugène: novel; written in 1962; published by Editions Denoël, Paris, 1963.

Le Québec et l'Americanité: a study; written in 1969; first published by Cercle du Livre de France, 1970, in same volume as *Klondyke.*

Secondary Sources

Berube, Renald, "Jacques Languirand, Le Klondyke et l'Americanite" in *Livres et auteurs québécois*, 1971, pp. 86-96.

"Les grands départs de J. Languiarand, ou la mise a l'epreuve de la parole", in *Voix et image du pays*, volume II, published by Cahiers de Sainte-Marie, Montreal, 1969, pp. 63-76.

Godin, Jean-Cleo, et Mailhot, Laurent, in *Théâtre québecois*, Editions HMH, Montreal, 1970, pp. 173-190.

Roy Hewitson, Lucille, "Jacques Languirand de la nostalgie à l'impuissance" in *Etudes françaises*, Vol. V, No. 2, 1969, pp. 207-216.

John Lazarus

Born December 24, 1947, in Montreal. Father an insurance executive; mother an artist. After studying at McGill University, he is accepted into the acting program at the National Theatre School, Montreal. Graduating in 1969, he then works as an actor, appearing at the Stratford Festival, touring with children's companies in British Columbia and Manitoba, performing in numerous CBC radio and television shows as well as in "one really low budget movie." He also conducts acting workshops in and around Vancouver.

In 1970, he turns to playwriting and is awarded second prize in the British Columbia Centennial Playwriting Competition of that year for *Mad King Andrew*, a play for children. His next effort, *Chester, You Owe My Bird an Apology*, takes first place in the 1971 National Playwriting Competition sponsored by *Performing Arts Magazine*. A broadcaster and scriptwriter for CHQM radio, Vancouver, and Vancouver Co-op Radio from 1973 to 1977, he is also hired by CBC radio in 1974 to do freelance "arts" broadcasts. At the same time he conducts a series of workshops in playwriting and radio production, as well as writing and producing educational, audio-visual programs for schools and government departments.

In 1975, he receives the first of two playwriting grants from the Canada Council and begins teaching playwriting at Vancouver Community College. A year later, his play *Midas* wins "Honourable Mention" in the Clifford E. Lee Playwriting Competition.

In 1979, he tells the *Canadian Theatre Review*, "You work for years to achieve certain satisfactions from your work. By the time you learn to achieve those things, the process of working for them has changed so that those things are no longer the things you want. But now you have them and you don't know what else to want. That's scary—but stimulating and liberating." Married and the father of two daughters, he currently makes his home in Vancouver.

Nola Erhardt

Stage Writing

Mad King Andrew: one-act play for children; unpublished; unproduced; second prize in the 1970 British Columbia Centennial Playwriting Competition.

Chester, You Owe My Bird an Apology: one-act comedy; written in 1971; first published by Playwrights Co-op, Toronto, in 1972; subsequently published in 1975, by Playwrights Co-op in same volume as *Babel Rap*; subsequently published by Commcept, Vancouver, 1978, in *Transitions Transitions 1: Short Plays*; first produced by West Vancouver Little Theatre Guild, Vancouver, 1972, under the direction of the author; adapted for radio; produced by CBC, Vancouver, 1973, for regional broadcast; winner of the 1971 National Playwriting Competition sponsored by *Performing Arts Magazine*.

Babel Rap: one-act comedy; written in 1972; first published by Playwrights Co-op in 1972; subsequently published by Playwrights Co-op, 1975, in same volume as *Chester, You Owe My Bird an Apology*; subsequently published by Playwrights Co-op in *Five Canadian Plays*, 1978; first produced by Troupe, Vancouver, 1972, under the direction of the author and Jon Bankson; subsequently produced by City Stage, Vancouver, 1972, under the direction of Ray Michal; by Factory Theatre Lab, Toronto, 1974, under the direction of Marcella Lustig; produced by Citadel Too, Edmonton, 1975, under the direction of Scott Swan; adapted for radio; produced by CBC Vancouver, 1972, for regional broadcast; adapted for television; produced by CBC Edmonton, 1974, for national broadcast.

Encroaching Chaos: one-act; written in 1973; unpublished; first produced by Troupe, 1973, under the direction of Jon Bankson; adapted for radio; produced under the title *Helios* by CBC Vancouver 1977, for national broadcast.

A Cold Beer with a Warm Friend: one-act; written in 1973; unpublished; first produced by Troupe, 1973, under the direction of Jon Bankson.

How We Killed the Moose: one-act; written in 1974; unpublished; first produced by New Play Centre, Vancouver, 1975, under the direction of Jane Heyman; adapted for radio; produced by CBC Vancouver, 1975, for regional broadcast.

You Remind Me Of: one-act; unpublished; unproduced.

Midas: two acts; written in 1976; unpublished; first produced by Tamahnous Theatre and New Play Centre, Vancouver, 1977, under the direction of Jackie Crossland; winner of "Honourable Mention" in Clifford E. Lee Playwriting Competition, 1976.

Where Now, Captain Cook?: two-act musical; music by Joan Beeow; written in 1978; unpublished; first produced by Kaleidoscope Theatre, Vancouver, 1978, under the direction of Kathryn Shaw.

Puppets: seven-minute 'curtain raiser'; written in 1978; unpublished; first produced at Tamahnous "Writers' Show", 1978, under the direction of Suzie Payne; subsequently toured by Tamahnous.

Marks on Paper: one-act play about "adult illiteracy"; written in 1979 on commission by Northern Lights College, British Columbia; unpublished; first produced by

Chinook Touring Theatre, Fort St. John, British Columbia, 1979; subsequently toured through other parts of British Columbia.

Radio Writing

Four Propositions: 30 minutes; written in 1970; first produced by CBC Vancouver, 1971, for regional broadcast.

Greek Myths: three 30-minute plays; written in 1971; first produced by CBC Vancouver for regional broadcast in 1971.

I Hear You've Been Involved in Dirty Jokes: 30 minutes; written in 1971; first produced by CBC Vancouver, for regional broadcast, 1971.

Dollar on the Sidewalk: 20 minutes; written in 1977; first produced by CBC Vancouver (on a double bill with *Half an Inch Closer*) for regional broadcast.

Half an Inch Closer: 10 minutes; written in 1977; first produced by CBC, Vancouver (on a double bill with *Dollar on the Sidewalk*) for regional broadcast.

Several dozen plays, satires and other fiction written for and broadcast by Vancouver Co-op Radio since 1973; 100 pieces of original material produced by CBC Radio.

Miscellaneous

Backyard Theatre: "a kid's activity book"; written in 1973; first published by Cedar House, Vancouver, 1973; subsequently published by Young Readers' Press, New York, under the title *Classroom Theatre*, in 1974.

In Progress

Dreaming and Duelling: two-act stage play; "Two close friends, high school fencing students, become involved in a fantasy of their own making, and attempt to duel to the death with sharpened foils."

Secondary Sources

Short essay by Lazarus included in *Transitions 1: Short Plays*, Commcept, 1978, pp. 265-267.

Roland Lepage

Born October 31, 1928, in Quebec City. Father an accountant. Studies the classic at Petit Séminaire de Québec, graduating with a B.A. in 1947. He continues his studies at Université Laval where he completes his Master's degree at the age of 21. At this time he also studies painting at Ecole des Beaux-Arts and takes music lessons. He becomes interested in the theatre and begins to act with Comédiens de al Nef, a company directed by Pierre Boucher. After playing in many of the company's productions, he decides to puruse an acting career and sets out for France in 1949 to study acting in Bordeaux. While there, he performs with the Théâtre d'Essai and the Grand-Théâtre de Bordeaux. His acting takes him through southwestern France where he plays various roles from Molière to commedia dell'arte.

Bob Cunningham

He returns to Quebec in 1951 and, along with Pierre Boucher and Paul Hébert, founds Les Comédiens de Québec, a company in which he plays in many classical plays. He also begins to act on the radio, and is hired to teach diction at the Petit-Séminaire de Québec. After two years, he returns to France, this time to Paris, where he studies acting with Maurice Escande and Beatrix Dussane at the Comédie Française. He continues to act in France, most often at the Studio des Champs-Elysèes, and also to travel through Italy and England. Three years later, he returns to Montreal "ready to get to know my own country" and establishes a solid acting career, playing at various theatres in the city, and also performing on various television series. Through his work on two children's shows, *Ping et Pong* and *Sang et Or*, a producer asks him to write for a new children's series. He winds up writing 32 episodes for the series *Marcus* which is produced by Radio-Canada in 1962 and '63. For the next nine years, he writes for several other children's series including *Coeurs aux Poings, Marie-Quatre-Poches, La Ribouldigue,* and *Nic et Pic*, and also plays leading parts on two of the programs. *Les Pères Noel*, his first stage work, is also a children's play and is produced by Théâtre

du Rideau Vert in 1968. The following year, he writes another children's play, *Le Gros-Doudoud de Paillasson*, for the same theatre, and a third play for young audiences, *La Toilette de Gala*, which is produced by Théâtre pour Enfants de Québec. At this same time, he is also hired by the French section of National Theatre School to teach diction and theatre history. It is through his connection with the acting school that he is asked to do an adaptation of an Italian Renaissance play, *L'Alphabet des habitants*, which he completes in 1972. The adaptation makes use of Quebecois culture and slang. Premiered by the National Theatre School in 1972, it is re-mounted three years later. His next play, *Le Champ des morts*, is based on the poetry of Edgar Lee Masters, and is premiered by the National Theatre School in 1973.

His third full-length play, *Le Temps d'une vie* is written in 1973 and the play becomes immensely popular in Quebec. In 1977, *Le Temps* is taken to France where it is performed at the renowned *Festival d'Avignon*. In 1978, Lepage himself returns to the stage in his new play, *La Complainte des Hivers Rouges*, produced by the Théâtre du Trident in Quebec City. The company then re-mounts *Le Temps* and takes it on a European tour, again with Lepage starring. Later that year, the play's success spreads to English-Canada when the Tarragon Theatre in Toronto produces it in a translation by Sheila Fischman. The play wins the 1978 Chalmers Award for an Outstanding Canadian Play.

From his home in a renovated mansion in old Quebec City, he continues to divide his time today between acting on radio, television and the stage, and writing plays.

Stage Writing

Les Pères Noel: one-act children's play; written in 1968; unpublished; first produced by Théâtre du Rideau Vert, Montreal, in 1968, under the direction of André Pagé.

La Toilette de Gala: one-act children's play; written in 1969; first produced by Théâtre pour Enfants de Québec, Quebec City, in 1969, under the direction of Marc Legault.

Le Gros-Doudou de Paillasson: one-act children's play; written in 1969; unpublished; first produced by Théâtre du Rideau Vert in 1969, under the direction of André Pagé.

L'Alphabet des habitants (adaptation of an Italian Renaissance play): written in 1972; unpublished; first produced by National Theatre School, Montreal, in 1972, under the direction of Giovanni Pole; re-mounted by National Theatre School in 1975.

Le Champs des morts (based on Edgar Lee Master's *Spoon River Anthology*): written in 1973; unpublished; first produced by National Theatre School, Montreal, in 1973, under the direction of Jean-Pierre Ronfard; re-mounted by National Theatre School in 1978; subsequently produced by Montreal Conservatory in 1978; Théâtre Lionel-Groulx, Ste. Thérèse, Quebec, in 1978.

Le Temps d'une vie: a drama of rural Quebec in eight scenes; written in 1973; first published by Leméac, Montreal, in 1974; first produced by National Theatre School in 1974, under the direction of André Pagé; subsequently produced by Théâtre

d'Aujourd'hui, Montreal, in 1975, under the direction of André Pagé; Théâtre du Trident, Quebec City, Quebec, in 1977, under the direction of Normand Chouinard; Théâtre Populaire du Québec, Montreal, in 1977, under the direction of André Pagé; Théâtre d'Aujourd'hui, Montreal, in 1977 under the direction of André Pagé; subsequently taken on a provincial tour; at the Festival d'Avignon, France, in 1977; Théâtre Populaire in Montreal in 1978; subsequently taken on a tour of France and Belgium, starring Roland Lepage; translated into English by Sheila Fischman in 1978 as *In a Lifetime*; first produced by Tarragon Theatre, Toronto, in 1978, under the direction of Bill Glassco; winner of Chalmers Award in 1978 for an Outstanding Canadian Play.

La Complainte des hivers rouges: full-length; written in 1974; first published by Leméac in 1974; first produced by the National Theatre School in 1974, under the direction of Michelle Rossignol; subsequently produced by Théâtre du Monument National, Montreal, in 1974, under the direction of Michelle Rossignol; produced by Théâtre du Trident, Quebec City, in 1978, under the direction of Michelle Rossignol; starring Roland Lepage.

La Pétaudière: satirical musical comedy; music by André Angelini; written in 1974; first published by Leméac in 1975; first produced by National Theatre School in 1974, under the direction of André Pagé; subsequently produced by Théâtre du Monument National, in 1974, under the direction of André Pagé; produced by Théâtre sans Nom, Montreal, in 1976, under the direction of Réjean Wagner.

La Folle du Quartier-Latin (Quebecois version of Giraudoux's *Madwoman of Chaillot*): two-act comedy; written in 1976; unpublished; first produced by Théâtre du Trident in 1976, under the direction of Paul Hébert.

Miscellaneous

Marcus: 32 television scripts for children; written in 1962; produced by Radio-

Canada, Montreal, from 1962 to 1963; national broadcast.

Coeurs aux poings: eight 30-minute television scripts for program for young audiences; written in 1963; produced by Radio-Canada, Montreal, from 1963 to 1964; national broadcast.

Marie-Quatre-Poches: 24 30-minute television scripts for children; written between 1966 and 1968; produced by Radio-Canada, Montreal, from 1966 to 1968; national broadcast.

La Ribouldingue: 52 30-minute television scripts for children; written between 1967 and 1970; produced by Radio-Canada, Montreal, from 1967 to 1970; national broadcast.

Nic et Pic: four 30-minute television scripts for children; written in 1971; produced by Radio-Canada, Montreal, in 1972; national broadcast.

Qu'il me soit fait selon votre parole: a full-length film script; written between 1975 and 1977; unproduced.

Antonine Maillet

Born May 10, 1929, of an Acadian family in Bouctouche ("the heart of Acadia"), New Brunswick. While still a child, she becomes keenly interested in Acadian history and literature, a subject which is reflected in most of her subsequent writings in both the novel and dramatic form. Her earliest sketches are produced for her family and friends on the veranda of her home. She does her university work at the University of Moncton and, for a time, at the University of Montreal, receiving her B.A. from the former institution in 1950. In 1958, the same year that she receives her M.A. in Literature from Moncton, she has her play, *Poire-Acre*, produced at a local festival and it wins first prize.

She spends part of 1963 and 1964 living in Paris on a Canada Council Bursary (she spends another year in Paris in 1969-1970) and later begins teaching at Notre-Dame d'Acadie in Moncton, at Jesuit College in Quebec, at Laval, and at the University of Montreal. During this same time, she continues writing and manages to sell a 16-part radio series to CBC, Montreal. The series, in the form of monologues, tells of the life of an Acadian "concierge", her problems, her successes, her views of the world. The script, originally written in 1968 and produced during 1969, is published by

Guy Dubois

Leméac in 1971 and begins attracting attention from potential stage producers. In 1972, two years after receiving her doctorate from the University of Laval, the stage version of this series, *La Sagouine*, is produced at Montreal's Théâtre du Rideau Vert with Viola Léger in the title role. Its success is immediate and the play begins touring across Quebec, into other parts of Canada (in both English and French) and,

111

in 1976, plays in Paris to enthusiastic reviews. By 1979, *La Sagouine* has been played nearly a thousand times. That same year, her novel *Pélagie-la-Charette*, wins the Prix Goncourt of France, the first work by a non-European writer ever to do so. ("Winning the Goncourt," she tells the *Toronto Star*, "won't change my desire to be true to life and to my countrymen...It's as if somebody writing in Chaucer's English were to win the Nobel Prize for literature.")

She currently makes her home in Montreal though she still maintains a summer home in Bouctouche ("a lighthouse...to which my nephew, who's an architect, attached a house.")

Stage Writing

Entr'Acte: written in 1957; unpublished; produced at the Dominion Drama Festival.

Poire-Acre: one act; written in 1958; unpublished; produced in Moncton in an amateur production; wins first prize in the Dominion Drama Festival.

Bulles de savon: one act; written in 1959; unpublished; produced at a local amateur festival.

Les Jeux d'enfants sont faits: one act; written in 1960; unpublished; produced at the Dominion Drama Festival.

Les Crasseux: one act; written in 1968; first published in *Théâtre Vivant* No. V, 1968, and in the same year by Holt, Rinehart and Winston; subsequently published by Leméac, Montreal, 1973; first produced by La Compagnie Jean Duceppe, Montreal, in 1974, under the direction of Paul Hébert.

La Sagouine: first written as a 16-part radio series in 1970-71; produced by Radio-Canada in 1970-71; published by Leméac, Montreal, in 1971 and subsequently by Grasset, Paris, 1976; produced on stage at Théâtre du Rideau Vert, Montreal, in 1972, with Viola Léger in the title role; subsequently produced with Viola Léger in the role for tours of Quebec, across Canada, and in Europe (the play is produced in Paris in 1976, and in 1978 at the Avignon Festival); in 1979, it is translated into English by Luis de Cespedes, published by Simon and Pierre, and produced at the Saidye Bronfman Centre in Montreal, under the direction of Ronald Irving, and at Toronto's Théâtre du P'tit Bonheur; by 1979, the production has been played in both French and English more than 1,000 times; a finalist in the 1979 Chalmers Competition for Outstanding Play of the Year.

Mariaàgélas: full-length; written in 1972; unpublished; first produced by Théâtre du Rideau Vert in 1973 under the direction of Roland Laroche.

Gapi et Sullivan: full-length; written in 1973; first published by Leméac, 1976; unproduced.

Evangéline Deusse: full-length; written in 1973; first published by Leméac, 1975; subsequently published by Grasset, Paris, 1975; first produced at Théâtre du Rideau Vert, 1976, under the direction of Yvette Brind'Amour with Viola Léger in the title role.

Emmanuel-à-Joseph-à-Dâvit: full length; written in 1975; first produced by Théâtre du Rideau Vert, Montreal, in 1978 under the direction of Yvette Brind'Amour.

Gapi: full-length; written in 1975; first published by Leméac, 1976; first produced by Théâtre du Rideau Vert in 1976 under the direction of Yvette Brind'Amour with Gilles Pelletier as Gapi; produced at the National Arts Centre, Ottawa, 1977, under the direction of Yvette Brind'Amour with Gilles Pelletier in the title role.

La Veuve enragée: full-length; written in 1976; first published by Leméac, 1977, with an introduction by Jacques Ferron; first produced at Théâtre du Rideau Vert in December 1977, under the direction of Yvette Brind'Amour with Viola Léger in the title role.

Le Bourgeois gentleman: full-length; written in 1977; first published by Leméac, 1978; produced by Théâtre du Rideau Vert, Montreal, in 1978, under the direction of Paul Buissonneau.

Miscellaneous

Pointe-aux-Coques: novel; written in 1957; first published by Fidés; subsequently published by Leméac, 1972; winner of Champlain Prize, 1960.

On a mangé la dune: novel; written in 1961; first published by Beauchemin, Montreal, 1962; subsequently published by Leméac in 1977.

Rabelais et les traditions populaires en Acadie: doctoral thesis; published by Les Presses de l'Université Laval, 1971.

Par derrière chez mon père: short stories; first published by Leméac, 1972.

Don l'Orignal: an Acadian novel; first published by Leméac, 1972; winner of Governor General's Award, 1972.

L'Acadie pour quasiment rien: "tourist guide" in collaboration with Rita Scalabrini; first published by Leméac, 1973.

Mariaàgélas: novel; first published by Leméac, Montreal, 1973; subsequently by Grasset, Paris, 1975; winner of City of Montreal Grand Prix, 1973, Prix des Volcans, Paris, 1975, and Prix France-Canada, 1975.

Emmanuel-à-Joseph-à-Dâvit: novel; first published by Leméac, 1975.

Les Cordes-de-bois: novel; published by Leméac, Montreal, and by Grasset, Paris, 1977; winner of Prix des Quatre Jurys, 1978.

Pélagie-la-Charrette: novel; written in 1978; published by Grasset and by Leméac, 1979; to be published in English by Doubleday in 1980; winner of the Prix Goncourt, 1979.

Des McAnuff

Born in Toronto in 1953. His first dramatic works, *Urbania* and *The Champion*, musicals for which he writes both music and lyrics, are produced at Toronto's Woburn Collegiate in 1971 and 1972. In 1972, he enrols in a writers' workshop at York University and the following year studies theatre at Ryerson Polytechnical Institute. In 1973 he writes *Leave It to Beaver Is Dead*, first produced at Toronto's Glen Morris Studio Theatre. The play wins a playwriting contest co-sponsored by Factory Theatre Lab and the Canadian Council of Christians and Jews and, in 1975, is re-mounted as part of the first season at the new Theatre Second Floor.

In 1974, he becomes assistant artistic director at Toronto Free Theatre which produces his next two plays, *Troll* and *The Pits*. He later composes music for Michael

John Mahler

Ondaatje's *Collected Works of Billy the Kid* and serves as musical director for the production, both at Toronto Free Theatre and later at the Manitoba Theatre Centre. A co-founder of the Choke Sisters Mock Rock Band in 1975, he writes material for and performs with the group. That year, as artistic director of the Mother Earth Theatre, he directs a production of his own, *Trash*. In 1976, he co-founds the Green Thumb Theatre which produces his musical version of *The Bacchae*. He also directs his own version of *Faustus* at the Annex Theatre.

Moving to New York City in 1976, he directs a production of *Crazy Locomotive*, by the Polish dramatist Witkiewicz, at the Chelsea Theater. This production wins three Obie Awards. When the Chelsea Theater company moves out of its off-Broadway space in the Brooklyn Academy of Music, he and three friends establish the Dodger Theater on the vacant premises. As associate director of this theatre, he directs Barry Keefe's *Gimme Shelter* in 1978. The following year, New York's *Soho News* singles him out for two Soho Arts Awards: for director of the year (for *Leave It to Beaver Is Dead* and *Gimme Shelter*) and author of the best off-Broadway play of the year, the latter for *Leave It to Beaver Is Dead*. In 1980, he directs Keefe's *It's A Mad World, My Masters*, for Toronto Arts Productions.

A member of Playwrights Canada and Canadian Actors' Equity, he continues to write and direct plays in New York.

Stage Writing

Urbania: a sci-fi rock musical; book, lyrics and music written in 1970; unpublished; first produced by Woburn Collegiate Institute, in 1971, under the direction of the author and John Wilcox; subsequently produced at the Poor Alex Theatre, Toronto, in 1971, under the direction of the author.

The Champion: book, music and lyrics written in 1971; unpublished; first produced by Woburn Collegiate Institute, in 1972, under the direction of Ken Whittaker.

Silent Edward: a children's musical; book, lyrics and music written in 1972; unpublished; first produced by Studio Theatre, Hamilton Place, 1973, under the direction of David Harris; subsequently produced by Young People's Theatre in 1974, under the direction of Martin Kinch; produced by Citadel-on-Wheels, Edmonton, in 1976, under the direction of Keith Digby.

A Lime in the Morning: book, lyrics and music written in 1973; unpublished; first produced by Shelter Theatre Workshop, in 1974, under the direction of Larry Davis and Des McAnuff; subsequently produced by Toronto Centre for the Arts in 1974, under the direction of Alex Dimitriev.

Troll: full-length; written in 1973; unpublished; first produced by Toronto Free Theatre in 1974, under the direction of Martin Kinch.

The Pits (with John Palmer): full-length; written in 1974; unpublished; first produced by Toronto Free Theatre in 1975, under the direction of John Palmer.

Trash (with Larry Davis): a rock musical; written in 1974; unpublished; first produced by Mother Earth Theatre at Harbourfront Theatre, Toronto, in 1975, under the direction of the author.

Leave It to Beaver Is Dead: two acts; written in 1973; first published by Playwrights Co-op in 1976; first produced by Hart House Theatre at the Glen Morris Studio, Toronto, in 1973, under the direction of Wayne Fairhead; subsequently produced by Factory Theatre Lab, Toronto, for Playwrights Workshop series in 1974; produced by Theatre Second Floor, Toronto, in 1975, under the direction of Paul Bettis; winner of *Soho News* Arts Award for Best Off-Broadway Play, 1979.

The Choke Sisters: theatrical rock musical written in 1974; unpublished; unproduced.

Faustus (with Ross Douglas, adapted from the play by Christopher Marlowe): book, music and lyrics written in 1975; unpublished; first produced by Theatre Passe Muraille, Toronto, in 1976, under the direction of Andrea Ciel Smith; subsequently produced at the Annex Theatre, Toronto, and taken on a tour of Ontario schools under the direction of the author.

The Bacchae (with Larry Davis, Evelyn Datl, David Kosub; based on the play by Euripides): book, lyrics and music written in 1976; unpublished; first produced by Green Thumb Theatre, Toronto, in 1976.

Stage Directing

Newsstand: 1974; workshop at Toronto Free Theatre.

Trash: 1975; production at Mother Earth Theatre, Toronto.

Crazy Locomotive: (Witkiewicz); 1976; production at Chelsea Theater, New York.

Gimme Shelter: (Barry Keefe); 1978; production at Dodger Theater, New York.

Leave It to Beaver Is Dead: 1978; production at the Public Theater, New York.

Bottle in Holeville: 1979; production at Dodger Theater, New York.

It's a Mad World, My Masters: (Barry Keefe); 1980; production at St. Lawrence Centre (Toronto Arts Productions), Toronto.

Miscellaneous

Kids: television script; written in 1974; first produced by CBC in 1975.

Secondary Sources

Extended interview in *CTR* 27 (Summer 1980).

Ken Mitchell

Born on 13 December 1940 in Moose Jaw, Saskatchewan. Spends his early life and adolescence in and around the family farm. In 1961 he decides to spend a year in England. When he returns, he enrols in the English program in the University of Saskatchewan where he is awarded a Bachelor of Arts degree in 1965. While at the University, he begins to have his short stories published in various Canadian magazines and journals and some are read on CBC radio. At this same time, he begins writing radio plays for CBC and these are broadcast on both the regional and national networks. In 1967, he is awarded an M.A. in English by the University of Saskatchewan and later that year he joins the English Department at the University of Regina as a faculty member. In 1970, he writes his first stage play, *Heroes*, which

Bruce Pendlebury

wins first prize in a playwriting competition in Ottawa. He later spends time travelling in Britain, Holland and Greece. Shortly thereafter he tries his hand at acting and performs at folk festivals with the country and western band, Humphrey and the Dumptrucks, with whom he writes the musical *Cruel Tears.* In 1978, his play, *The Shipbuilder,* wins first prize in the University of Regina Drama Department's playwriting competition. He remains on the faculty in the English Department teaching courses in Canadian Literature and Creative Writing. He spends part of 1979-'80 in Scotland on a Canada-Scotland writers' exchange and in 1980 is invited to teach in China.

Stage Writing

Heroes: one-act; written between 1970 and 1971; first published by the Playwrights Co-op (Toronto) in 1973 and subsequently in a Playwrights Co-op collection entitled *Five Canadian Plays,* 1978; first produced by Surrey University, Guildford, England, 1972; in 1975 produced by Regina's Globe Theatre under the direction of Esse W. Ljungh.

Pleasant Street: one-act black comedy; written in 1971; unpublished; first produced by Saskatoon's 25th Street House Theatre (1972) under the direction of Stan McGaffin.

This Train: one-act tragi-comedy; written in 1972; first published by *Performing Arts in Canada* (1973) and later that year by Playwrights Co-op; first produced by Tarragon Theatre (Toronto) in 1973 under the direction of Steve Whistance-Smith; subsequently produced by Regina's Globe Theatre (1975), under the direction of Esse W. Ljungh; produced by Northern Light Theatre (Edmonton, 1976), under the direction of Scott Swan; and on CBC Radio in 1973 and CBC Television in 1977.

Cruel Tears (in collaboration with Humphrey and the Dumptrucks): three-act country opera; written between 1974 and 1975; first published by Pile of Bones Publishing (Regina, 1976) and subsequently by Talonbooks (Vancouver, 1977); first

produced by Persephone Theatre (Saskatoon, 1975) and directed by Brian Richmond; subsequently adapted for CBC Radio production, 1976; presented at the Vancouver Festival Habitat and Montreal Cultural Olympics in 1976; taken on national tour of 16 cities in 1977.

The Medicine Line: one-act outdoor drama; written in 1974; first published by the Saskatchewan Department of Culture and Youth, 1974; first produced by the community of Moose Jaw in the summer of 1976 under the direction of Robert Clinton; remounted by the same group in the summer of 1977.

Genesis: two-act historical epic; written in 1975; unpublished; first produced by the Merely Players for a tour of Saskatchewan under the direction of Robert Clinton (1975).

Showdown at Sand Valley: one act; written between 1968 and 1975; first published by Gage Publishers in *Cues and Entrances* (1977); first produced by the Merely Players for a tour of Saskatchewan under the direction of Robert Clinton (1975).

The Shipbuilder: full-length drama for voices and percussion; written between 1976 and 1978; first published by *Canadian Theatre Review* (*CTR 21*) January 1979; first produced by the University of Regina Drama Department (1978) and directed by Gabriel Prendergast; winner of the University of Regina Drama Department's playwriting competition.

Davin: The Politician: three-act drama; written between 1975 and 1978; first published by NeWest Press in 1979; first produced by the Globe Theatre and the city of Regina (1978) under the direction of Myra Benson; remounted by the same group later that year.

Radio Plays

Sand Valley Centennial: 30 minutes; written in 1966; produced by CBC, Regina, in 1967 for regional broadcast.

A Very Loving Person: 60 minutes; written in 1967; produced by CBC, Winnipeg, in 1967 for national broadcast.

The Bloodless Battle of White Forehead: 30 minutes; written in 1967; produced by CBC, Regina, in 1967 for regional broadcast.

Peter Danchuck: 30 minutes; written in 1968; produced by CBC, Calgary, in 1968 for both regional and national broadcast.

Showdown at Sand Valley: 30 minutes; written in 1968; produced by CBC, Regina, in 1968 for regional broadcast.

The Medicine Line: 30 minutes; written in 1969; produced by CBC in 1970 for national broadcast.

The Meadowlark Caper: a series of five 30-minute segments; written in 1970; produced by CBC, Calgary, in 1971 for national broadcast; second national broadcast in 1972.

Isn't It a Lovely Day?: 60 minutes; produced by CBC, Calgary, in 1971 for national broadcast.

The Bald Eagle: 60 minutes; written in 1975; produced by CBC, Calgary, in 1976 for national broadcast.

Cruel Tears: 90 minutes; written in 1976; produced by CBC, Regina, in 1976 for national broadcast.

Miscellaneous

Song of Wandering Riley: 90-minute screenplay; written in 1968 for National Film Board, Montreal; unproduced.

Striker: 30-minute screenplay; written between 1975 and 1976; produced by the National Film Board, 1977.

Channel Two: 30-minute television script; commissioned by CBC in 1974; unproduced.

This Train: 60-minute television script; written in 1976; produced by CBC for regional broadcast in 1977.

Everybody Gets Something Here: short stories; written between 1964 and 1976; first published by Macmillan of Canada, Toronto, 1977.

Wandering Rafferty: a novel; written between 1968 and 1971; first published by Macmillan of Canada, Toronto, 1972; subsequently published in paperback by General Publishing, Toronto, 1975.

The Meadowlark Connection: a Saskatchewan spy thriller; written in 1973; first published by Pile of Bones Publishing, Regina, in 1975.

Horizon, Writings of the Canadian Prairie: an anthology of regional literature compiled and edited between 1975 and 1976; published by Oxford University Press, Toronto, 1977.

Numerous poems and short stories published in *Canadian Fiction Magazine, Fiddlehead, Saturday Night, Canadian Forum, Prism International, NeWest Review* and the *Journal of Canadian Fiction.*

In Progress

The Con Man: a novel; to be published by Talonbooks, Vancouver.

Ancient History: poetry; to be published by Prairie Books Modern Press.

Sinclair Ross: criticism; to be published by McClelland and Stewart in 1980.

Mavor Moore

Born James Mavor Moore on March 8, 1919, one of three sons of Francis John Moore, an Anglican minister, and Dora Mavor Moore, a pioneer in the development of Canadian theatre. The family's interest in cultural affairs originates with his maternal grandfather, James Mavor, an economist with many contacts in world artistic circles. His parents separate when he is nine years old. He receives his early education at the University of Toronto Schools. He produces his first play at 10 in a corner of Deer Park Library, turns to playwriting a year later and at age 14 makes his professional acting debut in a radio serial for children.

In 1936, he enrols as a student of English at the University of Toronto. To finance his studies, he works for CBC Radio as both an actor and writer. Because of this and his involvement in a multitude of campus activities ("I was all over the place . . . I was into everything, particularly plays, needless to say, but, also I was president of the philosophical society and God knows what else") he fails his second year. Switching to Philosophy with an English option he completes his degree in 1941 at the head of his year.

While a student, he appears in many productions at Hart House Theatre, and, in 1938, is the first U. of T. undergraduate to direct the winning entry in the University's drama festival. He is also a leading member of the Village Players, an amateur company founded by his mother to tour Shakespeare to Ontario high schools. In the late 1930s, the Players begin to produce the works of other playwrights (including the first Canadian productions of Lorca and Brecht) in a renovated barn on the Moore property. In 1940, he makes his professional stage debut with the John Holden Players, a weekly stock company in Bala, Ontario.

After graduating from University in 1941, he becomes CBC Radio's youngest producer, eventually directing such national feature productions as *Carry On Canada, This Canada,* and the Victory Bond series *Highlights for Today.* Two years later,

he leaves the CBC to serve as an infantryman in the Canadian army. After training in Canada he is shipped to England where he spends the rest of the war as a captain in army intelligence. In 1943 he marries Darwina Faessler.

In 1945 he is appointed Chief Producer of the CBC's new International (short-wave) Service in Montreal, moves to Vancouver as Producer for the CBC's Pacific region. Back in Toronto in the latter part of 1946, he helps his mother establish the New Play Society, a professional theatre company for which he is variously actor, writer and director. The following year he produces the first *Spring Thaw*, a topical revue which quickly becomes the country's most popular theatrical event, and is produced annually for the next two decades. At the same time he begins to teach acting at Lorne Greene's Academy of Radio Arts and continues as a free-lance writer and actor for CBC Radio. From 1946 onwards he spends many summers in New York as Executive Producer of radio and film for the United Nations Information Division. In 1947, 1949 and 1957 he wins Peabody Awards for his programs on the role of the U.N. The first of his four daughters is born in 1947. In 1948, his first stage play, *Who's*

Who, is produced by the New Play Society.

Deeply involved in the development of Canadian television, he serves as the CBC's chief television producer from 1950 to 1953 ("...my job was divided into three the day I left") and then, in 1954, as Assistant Television Program Director. His musical adaptation of Voltaire's *Candide* is produced by CBC Radio in 1952 under the title *The Best of All Possible Worlds* and produced on stage in 1956 as *The Optimist.* As well, in 1954, he begins to write a musical based on the short stories of Stephen Leacock. Two versions of this work are produced by the CBC: *The Hero of Mariposa* is heard as part of the radio series *Wednesday Night*, followed a few months later by the television play *Sunshine Town,* presented in 1957 on stage in London, Toronto and Montreal.

Involved in the foundation of the Stratford Festival in 1953, he is made a member of the Festival's board and later a senator. In 1954, he joins the acting company at Stratford.

From 1958 through the early 1960s, he is both an actor and director at Toronto's Crest Theatre. He also mounts occasional productions for the Canadian Opera Company and the Canadian Players. This same year, he begins a two-year stint as drama critic for the *Toronto Telegram*, though continuing to write and perform for television.

In 1964 he is appointed artistic director of the Charlottetown Festival, a position he holds for the next four years. His translation of Gratien Gélinas' *Yesterday the Children Were Dancing* is produced in Charlottetown in 1967. The same year, he collaborates with composer Harry Somers and librettist Jacques Languirand on the opera *Louis Riel*, staged by the Canadian Opera Company, and is awarded a Centennial Medal for his co-chairmanship of the national Centennial Conference. Divorced by this time, he marries writer Phyllis Grosskurth in 1968. A year later, his musical adaptation of *Johnny Belinda* is staged at Charlottetown.

From 1965 onwards, he concentrates on planning the new St. Lawrence Centre and, on its completion in late 1969, becomes its first general director. *The Awkward Stage*, his study of theatre in Ontario, is published

the same year, when he also receives an honorary D.Litt. from York University.

Resigning his position at the St. Lawrence Centre in 1970, he accepts a teaching position in the Theatre Department at York University. In 1973 he is awarded the Order of Canada. In 1974 he is appointed to the Canada Council and becomes a member of the Editorial Advisory Board of the *Canadian Theatre Review*. In 1975, he is asked to serve on the Executive Committee of the Canada Council. Two years later he becomes the first chairman of the newly-formed Guild of Canadian Playwrights, and in 1979 he becomes Chairman of the Canada Council, the first artist to be so appointed.

In 1979 also, his comic opera *Abracadabra*, with composer Harry Freedman, premieres at the West Coast Courtenay Festival, and in 1980 his musical version of *Fauntleroy* (music by Johnny Burke) appears at the Charlottetown Festival. He currently lives in Toronto.

Stage Writing

Who's Who: full length; written in 1947; unpublished; first produced by New Play Society, Toronto, 1948.

Sunshine Town: a musical based on Stephen Leacock's *Sunshine Sketches of a Little Town;* originally written as a radio script (see Radio Plays); unpublished; first produced by CBC-TV in 1954; adapted for the stage and produced by the New Play Society in 1957; produced at Charlottetown Festival in 1968.

The Best of All Possible Worlds: a musical based on Voltaire's *Candide;* originally written as a radio script (see Radio Plays); rewritten for the stage; unpublished; first produced by the New Play Society in 1956, as *The Optimist*. CBC-TV version in 1974.

The Ottawa Man (based on Gogol's play, *The Inspector General)*: originally written as a television script; unpublished; first produced by CBC-TV in 1958; adapted for the stage and first produced by Crest Theatre, Toronto, in 1961 under the direction of the author; subsequently produced by Charlottetown Festival in

1967 under the direction of the author; produced by Festival Lennoxville in 1972 under the direction of Frances Hyland.

Louis Riel (with Jacques Languirand and Harry Somers): full-length opera; written in 1966; unpublished; first produced by Canadian Opera Company at O'Keefe Centre, Toronto, and Place des Arts in Montreal in 1967; produced again by Canadian Opera Company in Ottawa and Washington in 1975.

Johnny Belinda: musical based on Elmer Harris' play: written in 1968; unpublished; first produced by Charlottetown Festival in 1969 under the direction of Alan Lund; subsequently re-mounted by Charlottetown Festival in 1975; adapted for television and first produced by CBC, 1976.

Getting In: one act; written in 1972 for CBC-TV; stage version first published by Samuel French, New York and Toronto in 1973; stage version unproduced.

The Pile: one act; written in 1972 for CBC radio; stage version first published by Simon and Pierre, Toronto, in *A Collection of Canadian Plays,* Volume II, in 1973; stage version unproduced.

Inside Out: one act; written in 1972; first published by Simon and Pierre, Toronto, in *A Collection of Canadian Plays,* Volume II, in 1973; unproduced.

The Argument: one act; written 1973 for BBC-TV, London; stage version published in *Performing Arts*, 1974.

The Store: one act; written for CBC-TV in 1972; stage version first published by Simon and Pierre, Toronto in *A Collection of Canadian Plays,* Volume II, in 1973; stage version unproduced.

Customs: one act; written in 1973 for radio (U.S. Earplay); stage version first published by Gage Publishing in *Cues and Entrances* in 1977.

Abracadabra: one act opera (composer Harry Freedman); written in 1978; first produced 1979 by Courtenay Youth Music Festival, B.C.; unpublished.

Love and Politics: full-length musical based on Nicholas Flood Davin's *The Fair Grit*; written in 1979; unpublished; first produced by the Press Theatre, St. Catharines, in 1979.

Fauntleroy: full-length musical version of the novel by Frances Hodgson Burnett; music by Johnny Burke; unpublished; first produced by Charlottetown Festival, in 1980 under the direction of Alan Lund.

Radio Writing

More than 100 plays produced by CBC and BBC and broadcast in Canada, the United States, Britain, and Europe, including the following:

The Hero of Mariposa (based on Stephen Leacock's *Sunshine Sketches of a Little Town*): written in 1953; unpublished; first produced by CBC Radio in 1954 for *Wednesday Night* series; subsequently adapted for television and stage (see Stage Writing).

The Best of All Possible Worlds: (based on Voltaire's *Candide*): written in 1952; unpublished; first produced by CBC Radio in 1952; rewritten in 1954 and produced by CBC Radio, under the title *The Optimist*, as part of the series *Wednesday Night*; subsequently adapted for TV and stage (see stage (Stage Writing).

The Optimist (based on Voltaire's *Candide):* written in 1953; unpublished; first produced by CBC Radio in 1954 for *Wednesday Night* series; subsequently adapted for TV and state (see Stage Writing).

Come Away, Come Away: written for CBC radio, 1972; CBC-TV 1973; published by Methuen in *Encounter: Canadian Drama in Four Media,* 1973, ed. Eugene Benson.

Television Writing

More than 50 television plays produced by CBC, BBC, and other networks, including the following:

Catch a Falling Star: written in 1956; first produced by CBC in 1957.

The Well: written in 1960; first produced by CBC in 1961.

The Man Who Caught Bullets: written in 1961; first produced by CBC in 1962.

The Roncarelli Affair (based on F.R. Scott's papers): written 1974 for CBC; published by Macmillan in *The Play's the Thing,* 1975; produced by CBC-TV in 1974.

Miscellaneous

The Arts in Canada: chapters on theatre, radio and television; first published by Macmillan, Toronto in 1958.

And What Do You Do?: poetry; first published by Dent, Toronto, in 1960.

Yesterday the Children Were Dancing (translation of Gratien Gélinas' play): first published by Clarke Irwin in 1967; first produced by Charlottetown Festival in 1967 under the direction of the translator; produced by CBC television for *Festival* in 1968.

Man, Inc. (translation of Jacques Languirand's play): written in 1969; unpublished; first produced by the St. Lawrence Centre Theatre Company in 1970.

The Awkward Stage: The Ontario Theatre Study: edited by Mavor Moore; first published by Methuen, Toronto in 1969.

Four Canadian Playwrights: essays; first published by Holt, Rinehart and Winston, Toronto, 1973.

Essays and critical articles on the arts and theatre and drama, published in *Saturday Night, Manchester Guardian, Canadian Forum, Performing Arts, Opera Canada, Canadian Theatre Review, Maclean's, Vanguard, Toronto Star, Toronto Globe and Mail, University of Toronto Quarterly, Canadian Literature,* etc.

Numerous songs for *Spring Thaw* composed between 1947 and 1966, as well as the lyrics for *The Hero of Mariposa* and for *The Best of All Possible Worlds.*

Arthur Murphy

Born February 8, 1906, in the coal-mining town of Dominion, Nova Scotia. While a student at Dalhousie University, he becomes interested in theatre through the activities of the University's Drama Workshop and the regular visits by stock companies from both the United States and England. A short-story writer in his spare time, he soon switches to playwriting in the hopes of developing a better ear for dialogue. Although active in campus productions as a director and actor, he decides, upon graduating from Dalhousie in 1926, to become a doctor. ("I considered becoming a full-time dramatist very seriously...If at 25 I'd had the bit of success I have now, I sometimes think I would have, but it's difficult to say. I don't know what I would have done.")

Entering into medical practice in 1930, he beings to write radio programs as a hobby. In the mid-40s, his daughter, Joanne, moves to New York to study acting.

Having established himself by the 50s as a radio dramatist, he is asked to write scripts for the Ben Casey "medical" television series, earning him the epithet "The doctor who prescribes for Ben Casey". He continues his medical practice, however, and later does surgical studies at the Montreal General Hospital.

Back in Halifax in the early 60s, he is active in the creation of the Neptune Theatre, where several of his plays are produced. He also serves as its founding Board president. During this period, he becomes associate professor of surgery at Dalhousie University and serves on the staff of both Victoria General Hospital and the Halifax Infirmary. In addition, he writes for medical journals in both Canada and abroad and serves as playwright-in-residence at Dalhousie University. In 1967, he and several other well-known writers, including W.O. Mitchell, Robertson Davies, Eric Nicol and Yves Theriault, collaborate on *The Centennial Play*, a dramatic celebration of Canada's first century as a nation. A year later, he leaves medicine to serve as chairman of the board of the Universities Grants Commission of

Nova Scotia. He is the recipient of an L.L.D. from St. Francis Xavier University and an honourary membership in the Guild of Canadian Playwrights. Married, he is the father of three children and continues to make his home in Halifax.

Stage Writing

The Breadwinner: full-length comedy about a "young wife who works to put her husband through college but would rather have a baby"; written in 1966; unpublished; first produced by Rothsay Players, Rothsay, New Brunswick, in 1967 under the direction of Storer Boome.

The Centennial Play: full-length; written in 1966 in collaboration with Robertson Davies, W.O. Mitchell, Eric Nicol and Yves Theriault; unpublished; first produced by Ottawa Little Theatre in association with Canadian Festival of the Arts, 1967, under the direction of Peter Boretski.

The First Falls on Monday: a two-act look at "what happened in the week before confederation in 1867"; written in 1966; first published by University of Toronto

Press in 1972; first produced by Kawartha Summer Theatre, Lindsay, Ontario in 1967 under the direction of Ted Follows; adapted for radio and subsequently produced by CBC.

The Sleeping Bag: a full-length play about a shy, withdrawn woman marooned in the Arctic; written in 1966; unpublished; first produced by Neptune Theatre, Halifax, in 1966 under the direction of Leon Major; remounted by Neptune Theatre in 1967 for a national tour.

Thy Sons Command: a two-act play about "the conflict between neighbours, an aristocratic French wine grower and a blunt English cattle raiser. The younger people, without pedigree, carry the story"; written in 1966; unpublished; first produced by

Hamilton Players, Hamilton, Ontario, in 1967; winner of a 1967 Centennial Project Award for playwriting.

Miscellaneous

The Story of Medicine: "a 'popular' history"; written in 1945; first published by Ryerson Press, Toronto, in 1954.

Articles published in various national and international medical journals.

In Progress

To the Editor and **Sir, the Acquisitor:** two stage plays.

John Murrell

Born October 15, 1945 in the United States. He grows up in rural Alberta, completes his formal education at the University of Calgary (where he majors in Drama), and teaches public school for five years. Finding that most of the plays in prescribed school textbooks are dated as well as non-Canadian, he begins to write new plays, some on Canadian subjects, which he then produces with his students. Local theatres begin to become aware of his work and by 1973 his plays are receiving frequent productions. Eventually moving to Calgary, he gains further experience as a director, actor and writer, primarily in children's theatre.

His writing, however, remains essentially a hobby until his play *Power in the Blood* wins the 1975 Clifford E. Lee Playwriting Award. That year, he becomes writer-in-residence for Alberta Theatre Projects. For the ATP company, he writes *A Great Noise, A Great Light* (about William "Bible Bill" Aberhart and the beginnings of the Social Credit Party in the West), and *Waiting*

for the Parade (about five Calgary women waiting out the Second World War). As writer-in-residence, he also begins tutoring other young playwrights and assists in the planning of future ATP productions. It is at this point that he is finally able to concentrate exclusively on his own writing. As he tells the *Calgary Herald*, "I realized that people were starting to think of me as a playwright, rather than as a teacher or a director. I had to make the decision whether or not to really dedicate myself to writing. After a great deal of thought, I decided that this was what I wanted to do more than anything else."

In 1976, his first play not written on commission, *Memoir*, about the 19th century actress Sarah Bernhardt, wins first prize in the University of Saskatchewan Playwriting Competition. This play is produced at the Guelph Spring Festival in 1977, with the celebrated Irish actress Siobhan McKenna as Bernhardt. In 1978, he is appointed an associate director of the Stratford Festival, where he is asked to produce a new translation of Chekhov's *Uncle Vanya* which "will make the humour of the original accessible to English speaking audiences." As he knows only a few hundred words of Russian, he completes the project with the help of a Russian-speaking friend and several dictionaries. The translation is successfully produced at Stratford in 1978. The same year, he undertakes a translation of Machiavelli's *Mandragola* which later plays to packed houses at Theatre Calgary. His translation of Racine's rarely-produced *Bajazet* is commissioned and done at Toronto's Tarragon Theatre in 1979. Though *Bajazet* is not a critical success, two of his earlier plays—*Memoir* and *Waiting for the Parade*—are widely produced the same year. *Memoir* is played in Europe, the United States and South America while *Waiting for the Parade* is produced in London and New York.

Currently living in Calgary, he is married and the father of one daughter.

Stage Writing

Haydn's Head: full-length drama "about the bizarre but factual adventures of the composer Haydn's skull after his death"; written in 1970; winner of the 1971 Alberta Playwriting Competition; unpublished; first produced in an amateur production in Edmonton, 1973, under the direction of Don Pimm.

Power in the Blood: full-length drama "about a crisis in the life of a female evangelist"; written in 1972; winner of the Clifford E. Lee Playwriting Competition in 1975; unpublished; first produced in Edmonton, 1975, under the direction of Michael Forrest; subsequently produced by Persephone Theatre, Saskatoon, in 1977, under the direction of Howard Dallin.

Arena: full-length comedy "about group psychotherapy"; written in 1974; unpublished; first produced at the Pleiades Theatre, Calgary, in 1975, under the direction of Kenneth Dyba.

Teaser: full-length farce "about pornographic movie-making"; written with Kenneth Dyba in 1975; unpublished; first produced at the Pleiades Theatre, Calgary, in 1975, under the direction of Kenneth Dyba.

A Great Noise, A Great Light: full-length drama "about William 'Bible Bill' Aberhart and the 'Dirty Thirties' in Alberta"; written in 1976, unpublished; first produced by Alberta Theatre Projects, Calgary, in 1976, under the direction of Brian Rintoul.

Waiting for the Parade: full-length play "about five Calgary women during the Second World War"; written in 1977; unpublished; first produced by Alberta Theatre Projects, Calgary, in 1977, under the direction of Douglas Riske; subsequently produced by Northern Light Theatre, Edmonton, in 1978, under the direction of Scott Swan; at Tarragon Theatre, Toronto, in 1979, under the direction of Eric Steiner; by the National Arts Centre (both on tour and in repertory) 1979, under the direction of David Hemblen; and in London at the Lyric Hammersmith Theatre starring Fiona Reid, 1979; finalist for the 1979 Chalmers Best Play Award.

Memoir: full-length play "about the last days of actress Sarah Bernhardt"; written in 1974; first published by Avon Books, New York, 1978; first produced at the Guelph Spring Festival, 1977, under the direction of Eric Salmon; subsequently produced at the National Arts Centre, Ottawa, 1978, under the direction of John Wood, and at the Olympia Theatre in Dublin, Ireland, 1977, under the direction of William Chappell. The Irish production was later transferred to the Ambassador's Theatre in London's West End, 1978; winner of the 1976 University of Saskatchewan Playwriting Competition.

Uncle Vanya: a translation of the play by Anton Chekhov; completed in 1978; first published by Theatrebooks, Toronto, 1978; first produced at the Stratford Festival in 1978, under the direction of Robin Phillips and Urjo Kareda; subsequently produced by the Globe Theatre, Regina, 1978, under the direction of Myra Benson.

124

Mandragola: a translation of the play by Niccolo Machiavelli; completed in 1978; unpublished; first produced at Theatre Calgary, 1978, under the direction of Rick McNair.

Bajazet: a translation of the play by Jean Racine; completed in 1979; unpublished; first produced at Tarragon Theatre, Toronto, in 1979, under the direction of Henry Tarvainen.

In Progress

Parma: a play based on John Ford's *'Tis Pity She's A Whore*; scheduled for production at the Stratford Festival in 1981.

The Seagull: a translation of the play by Anton Chekhov; scheduled for production at the Stratford Festival in 1980.

James Nichol

Born May 29, 1940, in Toronto. Father a commercial artist. He grows up in the small town of Paris, Ontario where, at age 19, he begins to write plays. *The Back Room,* an early script entered in the annual playwriting competition run by the Ottawa Little Theatre, is returned to him with words of advice and encouragement scrawled at the bottom of one of the pages. The next year, he wins honourable mention for *Miss Hawkins.*

After high school, he spends two "useless" years at the University of Toronto, first in engineering and then in arts (". . . and then I decided to get a real education, and got married"). After leaving university, he takes a job as a supervisor in the cost accounting department of a Toronto insurance company. At the same time, he studies playwriting with Eli Rill, under whose guidance he writes *Sweet Home Sweet* in 1965. Through the experimental Playwrights Studio, he is able, for the first time, to see his work performed on stage.

At the age of 25, he returns to Paris where he supports himself and his family by working as a salesman for the same insurance company he had been employed by in Toronto. He continues to write in his spare time, turning his memories of childhood in Paris into a steady stream of plays for television, radio and the stage.

"I've invented my own Paris mythology," he says, "which resembles less and less the actual town and its people. I'm usually writing about past things out of my boyhood."

In 1966, he sells an hour-long drama to CBC radio. An association with CBC producers George Jonas and Robert Weaver, begun at the same time, leads to further productions of his work. Three years later, he receives a $3,500 grant from the Canada Council and is finally able to leave the insurance business. He writes a full-length radio drama entitled, *The House on Chestnut Street.*

As well as regular productions by the CBC, his works are also aired in England, Ireland, Australia and the United States. In 1970, his play, *Tub,* wins several awards at the Ontario Festival of One-Act Plays. In 1973, his radio play, *A Sense of Property,* wins an award from the Union of European Broadcasters. In 1976, he becomes playwright-in-residence at the National Arts Centre. *Sainte-Marie Among the Hurons,* written during his year in Ottawa, is produced by the Centre in 1977. He currently lives in Toronto with his wife, Judi, and their three sons.

Stage Writing

Sweet Home Sweet: two acts; written in 1965; unpublished; first produced by Playwrights Studio, Toronto, in 1965; subsequently produced by Second Stage, Halifax, 1972, under the direction of Robert Reid.

The Book of Solomon Spring: two acts; written in 1967; unpublished; first produced by Factory Theatre Lab, Toronto, 1972, under the direction of David Gustafson.

The House on Chestnut Street: originally written as a radio drama in 1969; first published by Macmillan of Canada, Toronto, 1972, in the anthology *Isolation in Canadian Literature*; subsequently published as a stage play by the Playwrights Co-op, Toronto, 1972; first produced by CBC Radio, Toronto, 1969, for national broadcast; first produced on stage by Theatre Calgary, 1972, under the direction of Joel Miller.

Tub: one act; written in 1969; first published by Playwrights Co-op, 1972; first workshopped at Stratford Festival in 1969, under the direction of Powys Thomas; subsequently produced by the Mini-Theatre, London, Ontario; winner of numerous awards at the Ontario Festival of One-Act Plays, 1970.

Sainte-Marie Among the Hurons: two acts; written in 1972; first published by Playwrights Co-op, 1977; first produced by Theatre London, 1974, under the direction of Heinar Piller.

Gwendoline: two-act drama; written in 1978; first published by Playwrights Co-op, 1978; first produced by Blyth Summer Festival, Blyth, Ontario, 1978, under the direction of James Roy.

Child: full-length; written in 1978; first published by Playwrights Canada, 1979; first produced by Blyth Summer Festival, 1979 under the direction of James Roy.

Radio Writing

Among the major plays—

Feast of the Dead: 90 minutes; written in 1970; first produced by CBC Radio, Toronto, in 1970 for national broadcast.

Purr: 60 minutes; written in 1972; first published in *Exile*, Toronto, 1972; first produced by CBC Radio, Toronto, in 1972 for national broadcast.

A Kingforks Mythology: five interrelated 60-minute plays; written in 1972; first produced by CBC Radio, Toronto, in 1976 for national broadcast; one of this series, *A Sense of Property*, was winner of the Union of European Broadcasters Play Award, 1973.

The Life of Friedrich Neitzsche: a series of five 30-minute plays; written in 1978; first produced by CBC Radio, Toronto, in 1978 for national broadcast.

Picasso and His Women: a series of five 30-minute plays; written in 1979; first produced by CBC Radio, Toronto, in 1979 for national broadcast.

Television Writing

Among the major plays —

The Negative Reward of Non-Achievement: 30 minutes; written in 1966; first produced by CBC-TV, Montreal, in 1968 for regional broadcast.

The Ballad of Willie and Rose: 30 minutes; written in 1971; first produced by CBC-TV, Toronto, in 1971 for national broadcast.

The Cutty Stool: 30 minutes; written in 1971; first produced by CBC-TV Toronto in 1971 for national broadcast.

Hold That Line!: 30 minutes; written in 1971; first produced by Westinghouse, Los Angeles, in 1972.

The Betrayal: 60 minutes; written in 1974; first produced by CBC-TV, Toronto, in 1975 for national broadcast.

In Progress

Murder at Blenheim Swamp: a full-length stage play.

The Murder of Maggie Sykes: feature film screenplay.

Nova Scotia Brothers: 90-minute television drama.

The Life and Death of Steve Biko: 60-minute radio drama.

Eric Nicol

Born on December 28, 1919, in Kingston, Ontario, of English parents. Father an accountant. Family moves to Vancouver and he later attends the University of British Columbia where he graduates with a B.A. in French, in 1941. After graduation, he spends three years in the RCAF as ground crew. Returning to U.B.C. after the war, he continues his French studies, obtaining his M.A. in 1948. That same year, his first book, *Sense and Nonsense*, is published by Ryerson Press. Shortly after, he travels to Paris and audits classes at the Sorbonne. In 1951, he moves to London, England where he begins writing radio and television comedy for the BBC. On his return to Canada, he finds work as a syndicated columnist for the Vancouver *Province*, and continues to write radio and television scripts, on a free-lance basis, for the CBC.

In the mid-60's, he begins trying his hand at writing stage plays and one of his first works, *Like Father Like Fun*, opens on Broadway (retitled *A Minor Adjustment*) in 1967. The play is not a success (it only lasts one night) and he writes a book on the

experience, *A Scar Is Born*. By the late 1970's he has completed some 20 radio plays and over a dozen television scripts — all produced by either the BBC or the CBC. As a novelist and humourist, he has written some 20 books including three that win the Leacock Medal for Humour — *Roving I*,

Shall We Join the Ladies?, and Girdle Me a Globe. In 1975, his play, Citizens of Calais, is done at Toronto's York University and Nicol spends time there as playwright-in-residence. He describes himself publicly as "an anarchist in theory; a liberal in practice." The father of three, he presently lives in Vancouver.

Stage Writing

Like Father, Like Fun: two-act comedy; written in 1966; first published by Talonbooks, Vancouver, 1975; subsequently reprinted by Talonbooks in Three Plays by Eric Nicol in 1975; first produced by the Playhouse Theatre Company, Vancouver, 1966, under the direction of Malcolm Black; subsequently produced at the Royal Alexandra, Toronto, and later at the Brooks Atkinson Theatre, New York under the title A Minor Adjustment, starring Austin Willis and William Redfield, directed by Henry Kaplan, 1967.

Beware the Quickly Who: two-act play "for children aged 7-10"; written in 1967; first published by Playwrights Co-op, 1973; first produced by the Holiday Theatre, Vancouver, 1967, directed by Joy Coghill.

The Centennial Play: full-length; written in 1960 with Robertson Davies, W.O. Mitchell, Arthur Murphy and Yves Theriault; unpublished; first produced by Ottawa Little Theatre in association with the Canadian Festival of the Arts, Ottawa, in 1967 under the direction of Peter Boretski.

The Clam Made a Face: one-act "participation play for very young children, based on West Coast Indian legends"; written in 1968; first published in 1972 by New Press/Firebrand; subsequently published by Simon and Pierre, Toronto, in 1975; first produced by the Holiday Theatre, 1968, under the direction of Ray Michal; subsequently produced by Young People's Theatre, Toronto, and taken on a tour of Ontario in 1971-'72; presented at the International Children's Theatre Festival, Montreal, 1972; toured by Theatre New Brunswick, 1979.

The Fourth Monkey: two-act comedy set in the Gulf Islands of British Columbia; written in 1968; first published in 1975 by Talonbooks; subsequently reprinted by Talonbooks in Three Plays by Eric Nicol in 1975; first produced by the Playhouse Theatre Company, Vancouver, 1968, under the direction of Malcolm Black.

Pillar of Sand: two-act "parable of the irrational — the religious stylite of Byzantium as seen through the eyes of the blow-your-minders"; written in 1972; first published by Talonbooks, 1975; subsequently published by Talonbooks in Three Plays by Eric Nicol in 1975; first produced by the Playhouse Theatre Company, 1973, under the direction of Malcolm Black.

Citizens of Calais: two-act comedy about a professional director and his problems staging an historical epic with an amateur company; written in 1975, first published in Canadian Theatre Review, summer, 1975, (CTR 7); first produced at York University, Toronto, in a student production directed by Malcolm Black with Toronto playwright Michael Hollingsworth in the cast.

Free at Last!: two-act "contemporary comedy"; written in 1978; unpublished; first produced by New Play Centre, Vancouver, and Theatre New Brunswick, 1980.

Radio Writing

A selected list by the author.

Love Is a Wanton: 30 minutes; written in 1951; unpublished; first produced by CBC, Vancouver, for national broadcast in 1952.

Uncle Lush: 30 minutes; written in 1952; unpublished; first produced by CBC, Vancouver, for national broadcast in 1952.

It's All in the Mind: 30 minutes; written in 1962; unpublished; first produced by CBC, Vancouver, in 1962 for national broadcast.

Once More, From the Top: 60 minutes; written in 1974; unpublished; first produced by the CBC *Stage* series, Toronto, in 1975 for national broadcast.

Miscellaneous

A selected list by the author.

Instant Ivy: 60-minute television script; written in 1966; produced by CBC, Toronto, national broadcast for the *Show of the Week* series.

Spud Murphy's Hill: 30-minute television script; written in 1968; produced by CBC, Vancouver, for national broadcast.

The Man from Inner Space: 60-minute television script; written in 1973; first produced by CBC, Toronto, for national broadcast on *The Play's the Thing* series, in 1974.

Among his many books and collections of columns from the Vancouver *Province* are:
Sense and Nonsense (1948, Ryerson).
Roving I (1950, Ryerson, winner of the Stephen Leacock Medal for Humour).

Twice Over Lightly (1953, Ryerson).
Shall We Join the Ladies? (1955, Ryerson, winner of the Leacock Medal for Humour).
Girdle Me a Globe (1957, Ryerson, winner of the Leacock Medal for Humour).
Say, Uncle (1961, Harper and Row).
A Herd of Yaks (1962, Ryerson).
Russia, Anyone (1963, Harper and Row).
Space Age, Go Home! (1964, Ryerson).
An Uninhibited History of Canada (1965, Musson).
100 Years of What? (1966, Ryerson).
In Darkest Domestica (1967, Ryerson).
A Scar Is Born (1968, Ryerson).
Vancouver (1970, Doubleday).
Don't Move (1971, McClelland and Stewart).
Still a Nicol (1972, McGraw-Hill, Ryerson).
One Man's Media (1973, Holt, Rinehart and Winston).
Letters to My Son (1974, Macmillan of Canada).
There's a Lot of It Going Around (1975, Doubleday).
Canada Cancelled Because of Lack of Interest (1977, Hurtig).
The Joy of Hockey (1978, Hurtig).

John Palmer

Born in Sydney, Nova Scotia, in 1940. Family moves to Ottawa during his childhood where he receives both his primary and secondary education. While still in high school, he begins to direct, write and act in plays. After a year of pre-med training at Queen's University, Kingston, he returns to Ottawa to study English at Carleton University where he is active in campus productions as both a writer and a director. In 1965 and again in 1966, his work wins prizes in the Canadian University Drama League Playwriting Competition. At the same time, he directs plays at Ottawa's Le Hibou Theatre and Stratford's Black Swan Coffee House and

then spends a year as artistic director of the Little Vic Theatre, also in Stratford. In 1967 and 1968 he works in Glasgow, Scotland as an actor and director at the Citizen's Theatre and The Close Theatre under a training program sponsored by the Community Programs Branch of the Ontario Ministry of Education.

On his return to Canada, he is appointed artistic director of the Woodstock Little Theatre. With Martin Kinch, he founds the Canadian Place Theatre in Stratford in 1968. A year later, his play, *Memories for My Brother, Part One,* is co-produced in Stratford by the Canadian Place and Theatre Passe Muraille under his direction.

In 1970, he directs a production of Henrik Ibsen's *A Doll's House* in Ottawa which is then presented as part of the St. Lawrence Centre's *Festival of Underground Plays* later the same year. In 1971, he starts a two-year term as dramaturge at Toronto's Factory Theatre Lab.

A co-founder and former literary manager of Toronto Free Theatre, he serves as the theatre's associate director in 1976 and 1977. He tells the *Toronto Star* in 1977, "What we have to do now is lay the groundwork for the next 100 years . . . to allow the Canadian people to see themselves through their nation's art." His articles on theatre have appeared in various publications including *Performing Arts in Canada,* and *Canadian Forum.* A founding member of Playwrights Co-op, he has lived for various periods in New York. He currently makes his home in Toronto.

Stage Writing

I'm Going to Pin My Medal on the Girl I Left Behind: full-length; written in 1964; unpublished; first produced at Carleton University, Ottawa, 1965; subsequently produced at Yale University.

Visions: of an Unseemly Youth: full-length; written in 1965; unpublished; first produced by Little Vic Theatre, Stratford, 1966, under the direction of the author; subsequently produced by Le Hibou Theatre.

Confessions of a Necrophile or Never Laugh When a Hearse Goes By: full-length; written in 1965; unpublished; first produced by Little Vic Theatre, 1966, under the direction of the author.

Memories for My Brother, Part I: 20 scenes; written in 1967; first published by Playwrights Co-op, Toronto, 1972; first produced by Canadian Place Theatre and Theatre Passe Muraille in Stratford, 1969, under the direction of Martin Kinch.

Out to Breakfast: full-length; written in 1969; unpublished; first produced by Theatre Passe Muraille, 1971, under the direction of John Palmer.

A Touch of God in the Golden Age: three acts; written in 1970; first published by Playwrights Co-op, 1972; first produced by Factory Theatre Lab, Toronto, 1971, under the direction of Martin Kinch.

Bland Hysteria: two acts; written in 1970; first published by Playwrights Co-op, 1972; first produced by St. Lawrence Centre, Toronto and Theatre Aquarius, Ottawa, 1971, under the direction of the author; revised as *The Great Canadian Beaver Conspiracy* and produced by St. Lawrence Centre, 1971; subsequently produced under this title by Theatre Aquarius, 1972, under the direction of Peter Mandina.

Memories for My Brother, Part II: full-length; written in 1970; unpublished; first produced by St. Lawrence Centre, 1972, under the direction of Henry Tarvainen.

The End: two acts; written in 1971; first published by Playwrights Co-op, 1972; first produced by Toronto Free Theatre, 1972, under the direction of Martin Kinch.

The Pits: full-length; written in 1974 with Des McAnuff; unpublished; first produced by Toronto Free Theatre, 1975, under the direction of the author.

Henrik Ibsen on the Necessity of Producing Norwegian Drama: one-act; written in 1975; first published by *Canadian Theatre Review,* Spring 1977 (*CTR* 14); subsequently published by Playwrights Co-op in 1978; first produced by Factory Theatre Lab, 1976, under the direction of Martin Kinch as part of the Factory's Festival of Short Plays; adapted for radio and produced by CBC, Toronto, in 1976.

Miscellaneous Writing

"Canadian Playwright Crisis — The Twelfth Hour": article; written in 1960; published in *Performing Arts in Canada,* Fall 1961.

"The Man Behind the News": short story; written in 1972; published in *Canadian Forum,* 1973.

Monkeys in the Attic: film script; written in 1972; produced by KT Productions,

Toronto, 1973, under the direction of Morley Markson.

Sabrina Jones: television script; written in 1975; produced by CBC, Toronto, 1976.

"Notes on a Production of Tango": article; published in *Drama at Calgary,* Volume III, No. 3.

Rich Kids: film script; written in 1977; produced by Stephen Chesley Associates, Toronto, 1978.

Stage directing

Memories For My Brother, Part I (John Palmer): produced by Theatre Passe Muraille, Toronto, 1969.

Out to Breakfast (John Palmer): produced by Theatre Passe Muraille, 1971.

Bland Hysteria (John Palmer): produced by St. Lawrence Centre, 1971.

Charles Manson aka Jesus Christ (Fabian Jennings and Allan Rae): produced by Theatre Passe Muraille, 1972.

Hope (Larry Fineberg): produced by Toronto Free Theatre, 1973.

Moby Dick: produced by Factory Theatre Lab, 1973.

The Tooth of Crime: (Sam Shepard): produced by Centaur Theatre, Montreal, 1974.

The Pits: (John Palmer): produced by Toronto Free Theatre, 1975.

The False Messiah (Rick Salutin): produced by Theatre Passe Muraille, 1975.

No Deposit, No Return (Bob Wallace): produced by WSDG, off-off Broadway.

Money (Rick Salutin): produced by Young People's Theatre, Toronto, 1976.

Hotel Paradiso (Feydeau): produced by Toronto Arts Productions, 1976.

Out to Brunch (collective creation): produced by Factory Theatre Lab, 1976 as part of the Festival of Short Plays.

Me? (Martin Kinch): produced by Toronto Free Theatre, 1977.

Gossip (George F. Walker): produced by Toronto Free Theatre, 1977.

Stephen Petch

Born in Vancouver in 1952. Family moves to Ontario during his childhood. His first plays, written while he is still in high school, are produced by the Kitchener Little Theatre. He graduates from the University of Waterloo in 1972 as a psychology major. The same year, he writes *The General*, his first significant play. *The General* is produced a year later by the Backdoor Theatre Company for the Toronto Multi-Cultural Theatre Festival. His next play,

Passages, is workshopped at Toronto's Factory Theatre Lab in 1974. The play is also a finalist in the 1975 Clifford E. Lee Playwriting Competition.

From 1974 to 1976, he travels in Turkey, Greece and Mexico. On returning to Canada, he begins to work with Toronto's Theatre Second Floor which premieres his next two plays—*Turkish Delight* and *Aftershock* (a collective creation). In 1979, *Sight Unseen* is produced by the Tarragon

Theatre, Toronto, followed a few months later by *Victoria* at the Stratford Festival's Third Stage. Unmarried, he currently makes his home in Victoria, British Columbia.

Stage Writing

The General: one act; written in 1972; first published by Playwrights Co-op, Toronto, 1973; subsequently published by Playwrights Co-op, 1974, in *Now in Paperback, Canadian Playwrights of the 1970's*; first workshopped at Factory Theatre Lab, Toronto, in 1972; produced for the Multi-Cultural Theatre Festival by Backdoor Theatre Company, Toronto, 1973, under the direction of Gino Marocco.

Passage: two acts; written in 1973; first published by Playwrights Co-op, 1974; first workshopped by Factory Theatre Lab, Toronto, 1974, under the direction of Patricia Carol Brown.

Turkish Delight: two acts; written in 1975; first published by Playwrights Co-op, 1975; first produced by Theatre Second Floor, Toronto, 1976, under the direction of Paul Bettis.

Aftershock, A Murder Mystery: full-length, collectively created; written in 1975; unpublished; first produced by Theatre Second Floor, 1976, under the direction of Paul Bettis.

Sight Unseen: full-length drama; written in 1977-78; first published by Playwrights Co-op, 1979; first produced by Tarragon Theatre, Toronto, 1979, under the direction of Jack Blum.

Victoria: full-length; written in 1978-1979; first published by Playwrights Canada in 1979; first produced by Stratford Festival's Third Stage, 1979, under the direction of Kathryn Shaw.

Len Peterson

Born in Regina in 1917, the only son of Scandinavian parents. A child of the Depression, he is educated at Kitchener Public School and Scott Collegiate. A talented athlete, he excels at many sports including wrestling. After high school, he enrols in a general arts program at Regina's Luther College. Disillusioned, he then switches to mathematics and science at Northwestern University, Chicago, where he begins to write plays. Encouraged by his professors to write, he moves to Toronto in 1939 in the hopes of making it a full-time career.

That year, after several rejections, he sells his first play to CBC Radio for $25. Over the next few years several of his scripts are produced by Esse Ljungh and Andrew Allan who, at the time, are working for the CBC in Western Canada. With the start of World War II, he enlists in the Canadian Army but continues to submit plays and short stories to CBC and to various magazines. While in the service, his writing talent so impresses his commanding officer that he is offered a job in Ottawa writing documentaries about the war and life in the army.

In 1944, Andrew Allan, now head of drama at CBC, asks him to join a small group of Toronto-based writers in preparing scripts for the new *Stage* series. This group, which includes Lister Sinclair, Joseph Schull, Hugh Kemp, Tommy Tweed, Ted Allan and Alan King, is responsible for the majority of the scripts produced for the series during its 12 years on the air. Writing an average of one script every two weeks, he produces hundreds of radio plays during the next decade. Among them are *Burlap Bags, Maybe in a Thousand Years, They're All Afraid* and *Joe Katona.* Dealing with controversial topics such as racism and social inequality, many of the scripts anger both audiences and CBC officials who feel that plays produced by the network should emphasize the positive aspects of life in Canada. In spite of this criticism, *Burlap Bags* and *They're All Afraid* receive the Ohio State Award for radio drama, beating competition from the major American networks.

In 1951, he is instrumental in founding the Jupiter Theatre in Toronto. Over a period of three years the theatre produces 16 plays, many of which are previously unproduced in North America, before being forced to close in 1954 because of a $10,000 deficit. Two years later he helps to found the Canadian Theatre Centre, a branch of the International Theatre Institute, with which he is associated for many years, and is president of the organization when it disbands in 1974. After a trip to the Arctic, financed by CBC, he writes *The Great Hunger*, a play about Eskimo life, produced in 1960. That same year, his well-known radio play, *Burlap Bags*, is produced by Toronto Workshop Productions. In 1961, his play *Joe Katona* wins the prestigious Columbus Award for radio drama. The play is later adapted for television and then rewritten as a novel. Commissioned by the Canadian Players, his stage play, *All About Us* tours the country in 1962.

During the next eight years, he concentrates on writing for radio, returning to the stage with *Almighty Voice*, first produced by Young People's Theatre, Toronto, in 1970. His next stage play, *Women in the Attic*, is premiered by Regina's Globe Theatre the following year. In 1972, Toronto Workshop Productions commissions him to write *The Working Man*, a play celebrating the centenary of the Canadian workers' movement. A founding member of Playwrights Co-op in 1973, he continues today to write plays for stage, radio and television. He and his wife, Iris, make their home in Toronto.

Stage Writing

Burlap Bags: one-act drama; originally written for radio in 1946; first published by Playwrights Co-op, Toronto in 1972; first produced for national broadcast by CBC Radio for *Stage* series 1946; subsequently broadcast by CBC Radio as part of celebrations for 21st anniversary of the *Stage* series in 1965; adapted for the stage in 1960; first produced by Toronto Workshop Productions in 1960 under the direction of George Luscombe.

The Great Hunger: three-act drama written in 1958; first published by Book Society of Canada in 1967; first produced by Arts Theatre, Toronto in 1960 under the direction of Leo Orenstein; subsequently produced by Globe Theatre, Regina, in 1976 under the direction of Frank Norris.

All About Us: full-length play written in 1963; unpublished; first produced by Canadian Players for a national tour in 1963 under the direction of John Hirsch.

Women in the Attic: three-act drama; written on a commission from the Globe Theatre in 1971; first published by Playwrights Co-op in 1972; first produced under the title *The Queen Street Scrolls* by the Globe, Regina, in 1971 under the direction of Kenneth Kramer.

The Workingman: full-length play; written in 1972; unpublished; commissioned and first produced by Toronto Workshop Productions in 1972 under the direction of George Luscombe.

Almighty Voice: one-act play for children 10 to 14; written in 1973; first published by Book Society of Canada in 1974; first produced by Young People's Theatre of Toronto in 1970; re-mounted in 1975 under the direction of Alex Dimitriev and Greg F. Rogers; subsequently produced by Giant's Head Theatre, British Columbia, in 1977 under the direction of Ken Smedley.

Billy Bishop and the Red Baron: one-act children's play; written in 1974; first published by Simon and Pierre, Toronto, in 1975 in *A Collection of Canadian Plays,*

Volume IV; first produced by Young People's Theatre in 1975 under the direction of Greg F. Rogers.

Etienne Brule: one-act children's play; written in 1975; unpublished; first produced by Young People's Theatre in 1977 under the direction of Greg. F. Rogers.

Your World on a Plastic Platter: a musical; book and lyrics written in 1976; music by M. Surdin; unpublished; unproduced.

Radio Scripts

Over 1,200 original scripts and adaptations. A complete list of CBC scripts is available at Concordia University, Montreal.

Television Scripts

Over 40 original scripts and adaptations. Complete listing unavailable.

Miscellaneous Writing

Numerous film scripts written for and produced by the National Film Board. Complete listing available from the NFB.

Chipmunk: a novel.

Sharon Pollock

Born April 19, 1936, in Fredericton, New Brunswick, the daughter of a doctor. Growing up in Quebec's Eastern Townships, she returns to the Maritimes for two years as a student at the University of New Brunswick. Here she becomes involved in amateur theatre and in 1966 wins a Best Actress Award at the Dominion Drama Festival. Throughout this period, she works as both actress and director in theatres across Canada.

After marrying actor Michael Ball, she moves to Alberta and writes her first play, *A Compulsory Option,* in 1971. Winner of that year's Alberta Playwriting Competition, the play is premiered by Vancouver's New Play Centre two years later. At the same time she begins to sell radio and television scripts to the CBC.

Walsh, her next major stage play, is completed in 1973 and is premiered by Theatre Calgary the same year. It is produced by Stratford Festival's Third Stage in 1974. In 1976, *The Komagata Maru Incident,* dealing with Canadian racism, is premiered by the Vancouver Playhouse.

Canadian Press Photo

She tells an interviewer before the play opens, "The theatre is not a classroom, the playwright is not a teacher. But a good play should provoke intelligent discussion about an issue or theme pertinent to our lives."

The same year, she begins teaching at the University of Alberta. The following summer, she serves as head of the Playwrights' Colony at the Banff School of Fine Arts, a position she still holds. In 1977, she works with Edmonton's Theatre Network on a collective creation entitled *Tracings — The Fraser Story.* As playwright-in-residence at Alberta Theatre Projects between 1977 and 1979, she runs a bi-weekly workshop for aspiring drama- tists. By 1978, she has also written nine children's plays, mostly for Vancouver's Playhouse Holiday. A member of the Canada Council, she is the mother of six children, and currently makes her home in Calgary.

Stage Writing

A Compulsory Option: two-act comedy; written in 1971; unpublished; first produced by New Play Centre, Vancouver, 1972, under the direction of Pamela Hawthorn; produced by Citadel Theatre, Edmonton, 1975, under the direction of Keith Digby; subsequently produced by Festival Lennoxville, Quebec, 1977, under the direction of Bill Davis; produced by Theatre Passe Muraille, Toronto, 1977, as *No! No! No!* under the direction of Hrant Alianak, winner of the 1971 Alberta Playwriting Competition.

Walsh: two-act historical drama; written between 1972 and 1973; first published by Talonbooks, Vancouver, 1973; revised edition published by Talonbooks in 1974; first produced by Theatre Calgary, 1973, under the direction of Harold Baldridge; subsequently produced by Stratford Festival's Third Stage, Ontario, in 1974 under the direction of John Wood; produced by Manitoba Summer Festival of the Arts under the direction of Frank Adamson; subsequently adapted as a 60- minute script; first produced by CBC, Winnipeg, for national broadcast.

New Canadians: children's play; written in 1973; unpublished; first produced by Playhouse Holiday, Vancouver, 1973, as part of theatre-in-education program for elementary schools under the direction of Don Shipley.

Superstition Throu' the Ages: children's play; written in 1973; unpublished; first produced by Playhouse Holiday, 1973, as part of theatre-in-education program for junior high schools under the direction of David Barnet.

Wudjesay?: children's play; written in 1974; unpublished; first produced by Playhouse Holiday as part of theatre-in-education program for elementary schools, 1974, under the direction of Don Shipley.

The Happy Prince: children's play (adaptation of the Oscar Wilde story); written in 1974; unpublished; first produced by Playhouse Theatre School, Vancouver, 1974, under the direction of Don Shipley.

The Rose and the Nightingale (adaptation of the Oscar Wilde story): children's play; written in 1974; unpublished; first produced by Playhouse Theatre School, 1974 under the direction of Don Shipley.

Star-child: children's play (adaptation of the Oscar Wilde story); written in 1974; unpublished; first produced by Playhouse Theatre School, 1974, under the direction of Don Shipley.

The Great Drag Race or Smoked, Choked and Croaked: children's "mellerdramer"; written in 1974; unpublished; commissioned by the Christmas Seal Society of British Columbia for use in British Columbia secondary schools.

Lessons in Swizzlery: children's play; written in 1974; unpublished; first produced by Caravan Theatre, New Westminster, B.C. for tour under the direction of the author.

And Out Goes You?: two-act comedy; written from 1973 to 1975; unpublished; first produced by Vancouver Playhouse, 1975, under the direction of Christopher Newton; since re-written.

The Komagata Maru Incident: long one-act drama about Canadian racism; written between 1974 and 1975; first published by Playwrights Co-op, 1978; first produced by

Vancouver Playhouse, New Company, 1976 at the Vancouver East Cultural Centre under the direction of Larry Lillo; subsequently produced by Citadel Theatre, 1977, under the direction of James Defelice; produced by Toronto Workshop Productions at the Factory Theatre Lab, 1977, under the direction of Alex Dmitriev; produced by Western Canada Theatre, Kamloops, B.C., 1977, under the direction of Laurie Seligman; produced by Alberta Theatre Projects, Calgary, 1979, under the direction of Douglas Riske; adapted as 30-minute radio script; first produced by CBC, Vancouver, for regional broadcast.

Blood Relations: full-length; written in 1976; unpublished; first produced by Douglas College, New Westminster, B.C., in 1976, under the title *My Name is Lisabeth*, directed by Dorothy Jones; subsequently rewritten; produced by Theatre Three, Edmonton, in 1980, under the direction of Keith Digby and also by Theatre New Brunswick, Fredericton.

One Tiger to a Hill: full-length; written between 1976 and 1979; unpublished; first produced by Citadel Theatre in 1980 under the direction of Richard Ouzounian; subsequently produced by Festival Lennoxville in 1980 under the direction of Richard Ouzounian.

Tracings—The Fraser Story: a collective creation; written in 1977; unpublished; first produced by Theatre Network, Edmonton, 1977, under the direction of Mark Manson.

The Wreck of the National Line Car: children's play; written in 1978; unpublished; first produced by Alberta Theatre Projects in 1978 under the direction of Douglas Riske.

Generations: full-length; written between 1978 and 1980; unpublished; unproduced.

Passage: long one-act; written between 1979 and 1980; unpublished; unproduced.

Chautaqua Spelt E-N-E-R-G-Y: children's play written in 1979; unpublished; first produced by Alberta Theatre Projects in 1979 under the direction of Douglas Riske.

Mail vs. Female: one-act comedy; written in 1979; unpublished; first produced by Lunchbox Theatre, Calgary, in 1979 under the direction of Bartley Bard.

Mother Love: vignette for the stage; unpublished; unproduced.

Hon/Harold: vignette for the stage; unpublished; unproduced.

Radio Writing

Split Seconds in the Death Of: 30 minutes; written in 1971; unpublished; first produced by CBC, Calgary, 1971, for national broadcast.

We to the Gods: 30 minutes; unpublished; first produced by CBC, Calgary, for national broadcast.

31 for 2: 30 minutes; unpublished; first produced by CBC, Calgary, for national broadcast.

The B Triple P Plan: 60 minutes; unpublished; first produced by CBC, Calgary, for national broadcast.

Waiting: 20 minutes; unpublished; first produced by CBC, Vancouver, for national broadcast.

In Memory Of: 30 minutes; unpublished; first produced by CBC, Edmonton, for regional broadcast.

Generation: 60 minutes; unpublished; first produced by CBC, Calgary, for national broadcast.

The Komagata Maru Story: 30-minute adaptation of the stage play; first produced by CBC Vancouver for broadcast to schools in the Western Region.

Sweet Land of Liberty: 60 minutes; first produced by CBC Calgary for national broadcast.

Mrs. Yale and Jennifer: 30 minutes; first produced by CBC Calgary for regional broadcast.

Mary Beth Goes to Calgary: 30 minutes; first produced by CBC Calgary for regional broadcast.

In the Beginning Was: 60 minutes; first produced by CBC Calgary for national broadcast.

Miscellaneous

Portrait of a Pig: 60-minute television script; first produced by CBC, Winnipeg, for regional broadcast.

The Larsens: 60-minute television script; unpublished; first produced by CBC, Winnipeg, for broadcast in the Western region.

Ransom: 30-minute television script; first produced by CBC Edmonton for national broadcast.

Free Our Sisters, Free Ourselves: 60-minute television script; first produced by Access Television, Edmonton, for regional broadcast.

Country Joy: six 30-minute television scripts; first produced by CBC Edmonton for national broadcast.

Untitled Libretto: full-length; written between 1978 and 1980; unpublished; commissioned by the Banff Centre of the Arts.

Aviva Ravel

Born in Montreal in 1928, the eldest of four children. Parents work in a clothing factory. Raised in the heart of Montreal's Jewish ghetto, she attends the Bancroft School, Baron Byng High School and Commercial High School (". . . the latter to fulfil a parental dream: work in an office and marry the boss's son"). From age 12, she is an active member of the Zionist-Socialist movement. Her introduction to theatre comes through playing the part of Florrie in a production of Clifford Odets' *Waiting for Lefty*.

After graduating from high school, she enrols in a one-year teacher training program at the McDonald School for Teachers in Montreal, followed by a year of further study at New York's Bank Street School of Education. Returning to Montreal to work as an elementary school teacher, she marries Nahum Ravel, then serving in the Royal Canadian Air Force, in 1948.

The couple spend their first year of marriage in Ontario working as farm

labourers in preparation for life on a kibbutz in the new state of Israel. Illegal immigrants, they successfully elude the British blockade in a "dinky merchant ship" and settle on a kibbutz in the north where conditions are primitive. At first she joins her husband working in the fields but later she works as a nursemaid, nursery-school teacher and then as a teacher in both an elementary school and a high school. A driving force behind community theatricals, she acts in and organizes many productions; two of the Ravel's four children are born in Israel.

Returning to North America in 1959, she spends a year in New York during which time she studies playwriting at the Actors' Studio. Back in Montreal in 1960, the year that her third child is born, she begins 10 years as an elementary school teacher. In 1965, she tries her hand at playwriting for the first time. Two years later, she wins the Canadian Women's Press Club Award for Humour and the National Playwriting Seminar Award for her comedy, *Mendel Fish.*

Deciding to complete her academic studies, she receives a B.A. from Loyola College in 1967. During this period she and her husband adopt a fourth child. In 1973, during a four-year hiatus from playwriting, she earns her M.A. from the University of Montreal. A year later she returns to playwriting with a drama entitled *Soft Voices.* Between 1975 and 1978, she is guest lecturer at various universities teaching Canadian poetry and drama, as well as English as a Second Language at Collège Militaire Royal.

At present, she is a member of the National Council of the Guild of Canadian Playwrights, an executive of both the Association for Canadian Theatre History and the Montreal Playwrights' Workshop and a regional representative for the Playwrights Co-op. She is also in the process of completing her doctoral studies in Canadian Drama at McGill University (her dissertation topic is The Canadian Playwright). She tells *CTR* that the things she most enjoys today are "living, teaching, friends, family, travel, theatre, jazz, old films, my cat."

Stage Writing

Good-bye: one-act; written in 1965; unpublished; first produced by the Jewish Public Library, Montreal.

Arnold Had Two Wives: one-act comedy; written in 1966; unpublished; first produced by the Centennial Players, Montreal, 1967, under the direction of Pierre Lefebvre; the same production toured Canadian universities that year.

Mendel Fish: two-act comedy; written in 1966; unpublished; first produced at Hart House Theatre, Toronto, in 1967, under the direction of Ben Lennick; winner of 1967 Canadian Women's Press Club Award for Humour and the National Playwriting Seminar Award.

Shoulder Pads: one-act comedy; first published by the Book Society, Agincourt, Ontario, in 1967; first produced by Instant Theatre, Montreal, 1966, under the direction of Jacques Zouvi; subsequently translated into French by Luce Guilbault and performed at Instant Theatre as *Les Epaulettes.*

Soft Voices: two-act drama; written in 1965; first published by Simon and Pierre, Toronto, 1973, in *A Collection of Canadian Plays, Volume 3*; first produced at the Centre d'art Canadien, Montreal, 1966, under the direction of Paul Brennan; subsequently produced for the Quonta Festival, Sault Ste. Marie, 1967; by the St. John's Players, St. John's, 1974 under the direction of Roy Higgins, and by the Pendragon Players, Kingston, 1978.

No More Ketchup: one-act comedy; written in 1968; unpublished; first produced by Revue Theatre, Montreal, 1969, under the direction of Arleigh Peterson; winner of the 1968 Ottawa Little Theatre Competition.

Our Bed Is Green: two-act drama; written in 1968; unpublished; first produced at the Place des Arts, Montreal, in 1969 under the direction of Howard Ryshpan.

The Twisted Loaf: one-act drama; written in 1968; first published by Simon and Pierre, 1973 in *A Collection of Canadian Plays, Volume 3*; first produced at the Saidye Bronfman Centre, Montreal, 1974, under the direction of Roy Higgins.

Black Dreams: one-act drama; written in 1973; first published by Borealis Press in

Contemporary Canadian Drama, 1974; unproduced.

Horns: one-act drama; written in 1974; first published in *Callboard* (St. Mary's College), 1976; first produced at McGill University, Montreal, 1975; subsequently adapted and translated into Hebrew and broadcast by Israeli Radio, 1976.

King of the Mice: one-act; written in 1974; unpublished; first produced at Concordia University for the Quebec Drama Festival, Montreal, 1975, under the direction of Philip Coulter.

Dispossessed: two-act drama; written in 1976; first published by Playwrights Co-op, 1976, in *Women Write for the Theatre, Volume 3*; first produced at the Saidye Bronfman Centre, Montreal, 1977, under the direction of Sean Mulcahy; winner of the 1976 "Women Write for the Theatre Award" sponsored by Playwrights Co-op.

Listen, I'm Talking: one-act comedy; written in 1977; first published in *Quarry* magazine 1978; unproduced.

The Magic Transistor: full-length; written in 1975; unpublished; first produced by Herzlia High School, Montreal, 1975.

Playmates: one-act; written in 1978; unpublished; workshopped by Montreal Playwrights Workshop in 1978.

Miscellaneous

A biography of A. Zygielbaum, leader of the Jewish Trade Union Movement in Poland.

Several short stories, essays, and poetry for *Fiddlehead, Maclean's, Canadian Forum, The Journal of Canadian Fiction, Chatelaine,* and *Viewpoint.*

The Tuesday Games: 90-minute television play; written in 1966; produced by CBC Montreal in 1966; stage version unpublished; unproduced.

Zone: (translation of the drama by Marcel Dubé); written in 1976; to be published by Playwrights Canada in 1980; first produced at the Saidye Bronfman Centre, Montreal, under the direction of Daniel Simard.

Contemporary Quebecois Drama in Translation: translations of dramas by Françoise Loranger, Marcel Dubé, Jacques Languirand, Robert Gurik, André Simard, Felix Leclerc and Michel Garneau; written in 1976 for Master's thesis at Université de Montréal; unpublished.

La Petite Injustice: translation of drama by Raphael Levy; written in 1976; unpublished; first produced at the Saidye Bronfman Centre, Montreal in 1979 under the direction of Daniel Simard.

In Progress

Moving Along: a children's musical.

Doctoral dissertation on playwright Patricia Joudry at McGill University, Montreal.

James Reaney

Born September 1, 1926, on a farm near Stratford, Ontario. Is educated at a country school house and at Central Collegiate Vocational Institute, Stratford (1939-1944) where he begins to write poetry and short stories. He completes his first novel before he is 20. As an English major at the University of Toronto, he begins to publish poetry and short stories in various literary journals. He receives his B.A. in 1948, an M.A. the following year, and is then appointed to the Department of English at the University of Manitoba. In 1949, *The Red Heart*, his first published book of poetry, receives the Governor General's Award. In 1951 he marries Colleen Thibaudeau, a fellow poet and student from the University of Toronto. He later takes a two-year sabbatical to complete his doctorate at University of Toronto under the supervision of Northrop Frye. While an assistant professor at the University of Manitoba, he completes *A Suit of Nettles*, a second volume of poetry, and in 1958 receives a second Governor General's Award for it. He also finishes a less celebrated but equally significant work that year, his first play—*The Rules of Joy*, which is neither published nor produced.

Two years later, his next play, *The Killdeer*, receives the Massey and Governor General's Award. The same year, 1960, he takes up a teaching position at the University of Western Ontario and begins publishing/editing *Alphabet*, "a semi-annual devoted to the iconography of the imagination." In 1963, he writes *The Easter Egg*, as well as his first children's play, *Names and Nicknames*, the latter staged by John Hirsch at the Manitoba Theatre Centre. By 1965, he has written three more children's plays which he directs in non-professional productions in London, Ontario. Also in 1965, he begins an association with director Keith Turnbull who stages *The Sun and The Moon* in London, Ontario. In 1966, he founds the Listener's Workshop in London where he begins to work with a group of actors while his plays are still in an embryonic stage (either as a story line or as a series of

E. Hamilton

images). His search for a new approach to theatre also involves a desire to find a particular kind of performer. "I wanted to work with some other kind of actor; I had to find them since the kind of play I was beginning to write involved choral ensemble. Miniature Errol Flynns, Tallulah Bankheads and Greta Garbos are never going to get together in a play that demands the submerging of individual identity. But who does get together these days? The answer to this is: FAMILIES."

By using children as well as adult actors in his workshops, he strives to develop a company which will be able to express "the sense of fun" which he later describes as a "play box". In 1967, his play *Colours in the Dark* is premiered by the Stratford Festival under the direction of John Hirsch. In 1972, his collected poetry is published by New Press. The following year, after intensive workshops in Halifax, *Sticks and Stones*, the first part of a trilogy based on the "Black Donnelly" legend is premiered at Toronto's Tarragon Theatre in a production directed by Keith Turnbull. In 1974, *The St. Nicholas Hotel* and *Handcuffs*, parts two and three of the trilogy, are produced at Tarragon. *St. Nicholas Hotel* is named winner of the 1974 Chalmers

Outstanding Play Award. In 1975, he receives the Order of Canada as well as an honorary Doctor of Letters from Carleton University. He presently lives in London, Ontario, with his wife and two children and continues to teach various English courses at the University of Western Ontario.

Stage Writing

The Rules of Joy: written in 1958; unpublished; unproduced.

The Killdeer: originally written in 1960 as a three-act play; first published by Macmillan of Canada in *The Killdeer and Other Plays*, 1962; first produced by University College Alumnae, Toronto, in 1960, under the direction of Pamela Terry; subsequently produced at Glasgow Citizens Theatre, Scotland, for the Commonwealth Arts Festival in 1966 under the direction of David William; winner of the Massey Award, 1960; the collection, *The Killdeer and Other Plays*, receives the Governor General's Award for Drama in 1969; subsequently rewritten as a two-act play; first published by New Press, Toronto, in *Masks of Childhood*, 1972; revised version first produced by Stage Campus at the University of British Columbia, in 1970, under the direction of Jon Bankson.

Night-blooming Cereus: libretto for a chamber opera in one act; written in 1960 with music by John Beckwith; first published by Macmillan of Canada in *The Killdeer and Other Plays*, 1962; first produced at Hart House Theatre, Toronto, in 1960, under the direction of Pamela Terry.

One-Man Masque: one-act for one person; written in 1960; first published by Macmillan of Canada in *The Killdeer and Other Plays*, 1962; first produced, performed and directed by the author at Hart House Theatre, Toronto, in 1960.

The Easter Egg: three acts; written in 1962; first published by New Press, Toronto, in *Masks of Childhood*, 1972; workshopped by University of Western Ontario in 1962; first produced at Coach House Theatre in 1962 under the direction of Pamela Terry.

The Bacchae (translation of Euripides' tragedy): written in 1963; unpublished; unproduced.

Names and Nicknames: short play for children; written in 1963; first published by Longmans, Toronto, 1969, in *Nobody in the Cast*, edited by Robert Barton et al. and by New Plays for Children, New York, 1969; subsequently published by Talonbooks, Vancouver, in *Apple Butter and Other Plays for Children*, 1973; subsequently published by Equinox/Avon, New York, in *Contemporary Children's Theatre*, 1975, B.J. Lifton ed.; re-released by Talonbooks as a seaprate title in 1979; first produced by Manitoba Theatre Centre, Winnipeg, in 1963, under the direction of John Hirsch and Robert Sherrin.

Let's Make a Carol: play with music for children; book written in 1964; music by Alfred Kunz; first published by Waterloo Music, Waterloo in 1965; unproduced.
The Shivaree: libretto for an opera; written in 1964; unpublished; unproduced.
Aladdin and The Magic Lamp: marionette plays; written in 1965; unpublished; first produced and directed by the author at the Western Fall Fair, London, Ontario, in 1965.
Apple Butter: marionette play for children; written in 1965; first published by Talonbooks in *Apple Butter and Other Plays for Children*, 1973; re-released by Talonbooks as a single title in 1979; first produced and directed by James Reaney at the Western Fall Fair in 1965.
Little Red Riding Hood: marionette play for children; written in 1965; unpublished; first produced and directed by the author at the Western Fall Fair in 1965.

The Sun and the Moon: three acts; written in 1961; first published by Macmillan of Canada in *The Killdeer and Other Plays*, 1962; first produced at Summer Theatre, London, Ontario, in 1965, under the direction of Keith Turnbull.

Ignoramus: play for children; written in 1966; first published by Talonbooks in *Apple Butter and Other Plays for Children*, 1973; re-released by Talonbooks as a separate title, 1979; first produced by Second Theatre, London, Ontario, 1966.

Listen to the Wind: three acts; written in 1966; first published by Talonbooks in 1972; first produced by Summer Theatre, at Althouse College, London, in 1966, under the direction of the author.

The Canada Tree: written in 1967; unpublished; first produced by Girl Guide Heritage Camp, Morrison Island, Ontario, 1967.

Don't Sell Mr. Aesop: written in 1967; unpublished; first produced at Grand Theatre, London, Ontario, in 1968.

Colours in the Dark: full-length; written in 1967; first published by Talonbooks with Macmillan of Canada in 1969; revised edition published in 1971; subsequently published by Talonbooks in 1975; first produced at Avon Theatre, Stratford Festival, in 1967, under the direction of John Hirsch; subsequently produced by Vancouver Playhouse in 1969 under the direction of Timothy Bond.

Geography Match: short play for children; written in 1967; first published by Talonbooks in *Apple Butter and Other Plays for Children*, 1973; re-released by Talonbooks as a single title in 1979; first produced and directed by the author at Middlesex College Theatre, London, Ontario, in 1967, using a cast of children from Broughdale Public School.

Three Desks: two acts; written in 1967; first published by New Press in *Masks of Childhood*, 1972; first produced by London Little Theatre, London, Ontario, in 1967, under the direction of Peter Dearing.

Genesis: written in 1968; unpublished; first produced at Alpha Centre, London, Ontario, 1968, under the direction of the author.

The Donnellys: Part One (Sticks and Stones): full-length; first published by *Canadian Theatre Review*, Spring 1974 (*CTR* 2); subsequently published by Press Porcepic, Erin, Ontario in 1975; first produced by Tarragon Theatre, Toronto, in 1973, under the direction of Keith Turnbull; Chalmers Outstanding Play Award finalist in 1973.

The Donnellys: Part Two (The St. Nicholas Hotel): full-length; first published by Press Porcepic in 1976; first produced by Tarragon Theatre in 1974 under the direction of Keith Turnbull; winner of the Chalmers Outstanding Play Award, 1974.

The Donnellys: Part Three (Handcuffs): full-length; first published by Press Porcepic in 1977; first produced by Tarragon Theatre in 1975 under the direction of Keith Turnbull; Chalmers Outstanding Play Award finalist in 1975.

Baldoon (written with Marty Gervais): full-length; first published by *Porcupine's Quill*, Erin, Ontario, 1976; first produced by NDWT Company at the Bathurst Street Theatre, Toronto, in 1976, under the direction of Keith Turnbull; subsequently toured Ontario; re-mounted in 1977.

Wacousta: full-length; written in 1976; unpublished; workshopped at University Drama Workshop, University of Western Ontario in 1976; first produced by NDWT Company, Toronto, in 1977, under the direction of Keith Turnbull; subsequently toured Ontario.

The Dismissal: full-length; written in 1977; on commission by University College, University of Toronto; published by Press Porcepic in 1979; first produced by NDWT Company at Hart House Theatre, University of Toronto, 1977, in celebration of the University College's sesquicentennial, directed by Keith Turnbull.

At the Big Carwash: puppet play; written in 1978; unpublished; toured with the Caravan Stage Company, Armstrong, B.C., 1979.

Radio Writing

Poet and City—Winnipeg: music by John Beckwith; written in 1960; first published by Ryerson Press, Toronto, 1962, Eli Mandel, Jean-Guy Pilon, eds.; first produced on CBC's *Wednesday Night* series, 1960.

The Journals and Letters of William Blake: written in 1961; first broadcast by CBC on *Wednesday Night* series in 1961.

The Revenger's Tragedy (adaptation of Cyril Tourneur's work): written in 1961;

commissioned by CBC for *Wednesday Night* series; unproduced.

Wednesday's Child: music by John Beckwith; written in 1962; first broadcast by CBC on *Wednesday Night* series in 1962.

Canada Dash, Canada Dot: The Line Across (Part 1): music by John Beckwith; written in 1965; unpublished; first broadcast by CBC in 1965.

Canada Dash, Canada Dot: The Line Up and Down (Part 2): music by John Beckwith; written in 1966; unpublished; first broadcast by CBC in 1966.

Canada Dot (Part 3): music by John Beckwith; written in 1967; first broadcast by CBC in 1967.

Miscellaneous

Afternoon Moon: a novel; written between 1942 and 1945; revised portion in *Here and Now*, May 1948.

The Red Heart: poetry collection; written in 1949; first published by McClelland and Stewart, Toronto, in 1949; subsequently published by Press Porcepic in *Poems*, 1972; winner of Governor General's Award for Poetry in 1949.

A Suit of Nettles: poetry collection; written in 1958; first published by Macmillan of Canada in 1958; winner of Governor General's Award for Poetry in 1958.

Alphabet: "a semi-annual devoted to the iconography of the imagination"; edited from 1960 to 1971.

Twelve Letters to a Small Town: poetry collection; written in 1962; first published by Ryerson Press in 1962; subsequently published by Press Porcepic in *Poems*, 1972.

The Dance of Death at London, Ontario: poetry collection; written in 1962; first published by Alphabet Press, London, Ontario, in 1963.

The Boy with an R in His Hand: "a tale of the type of riot at William Lyon Mackenzie's printing office in 1866"; written in 1965; first published by Macmillan of Canada in 1965.

Poems: collected poetry; first published by New Press in 1972, G. Warkentin ed.

Myths in Some Nineteenth Century Ontario Newspapers: chapter in a collection.

Aspects of Nineteenth Century Ontario: written in 1973; first published by University of Toronto Press, 1974; F.H. Armstrong, ed.

Selected Shorter Poems: published by Press Porcepic in 1975, G. Warkentin ed.

Hallowe'en: "an occasional theatrical newsletter" in *Black Moss*; edited Nos. 1,2, 3, in 1976.

Fourteen Barrels from Sea to Sea: an account of the NDWT Company's national tour of the *Donnelly* trilogy; written in 1976; first published by Press Porcepic in 1977.

Numerous individual poems published in *Alphabet, Atlantic Monthly, Canadian Forum, Canadian Poetry Magazine, Contemporary Verse* and *Chicago Poetry*.

Numerous prose works and short stories published in *Canadian Forum, Queen's Quarterly, Here and Now, The Undergrad* and *Canadian Short Stories*.

Numerous critical articles in *Canadian Forum, Canadian Theatre Review, University of Toronto Quarterly, Canadian Art, The Globe Magazine*, and *Canadian Literature*.

In Progress

The Canadian Brothers: a stage play; in co-operation with the NDWT Company. Workshopped at University Of Western Ontario Drama Workshop, London, Ontario, in 1977.

A book on theatre; about "the polemics involved in founding a national theatre movement and the theory behind the kind of plays my theatre company has produced so far."

Book of Poetry: a series of illustrated poems.

An anthology of studies in Ontario regionalism.

A Donnellys sourcebook.

An anthology of material from *Alphabet*.

King Whistle! With Drama Club of Central Secondary School, Stratford, Ontario, for the school's centenary. Production by the

NDWT Company at Avon Theatre, Stratford, November, 1979.

Secondary Sources

Section on Reaney included in *Stage Voices* (Geraldine Anthony, ed.), Doubleday, 1978, pp. 140-164.

Study of Reaney's work in *James Reaney* by Ross G. Woodman, New Canadian Library, McClelland and Stewart, Toronto, 1974.

Reaney. J. Stewart. *James Reaney.* Agincourt, Ontario: Gage Educational Publishing, 1977.

Gwen Pharis Ringwood

Born on August 13, 1910 in Anatone, Washington. Mother a teacher; father, a farmer. In 1931, she leaves the States to study at the University of Alberta where she is introduced to the theatre by Elizabeth Sterling Haynes, a community theatre pioneer. She later writes that "we didn't have any CBC, any Little Theatre, university theatre departments, travelling companies or any money. We had seen very few plays. So we began a kind of Do-It-Yourself theatre." After graduation in 1934, she completes her first play, *The Dragons of Kent*. The play is produced at the Banff School of Fine Arts the following year. In 1936, she begins to write scripts for the radio, completing biographical plays on Beethoven, Cromwell, Florence Nightingale, Galileo and Socrates for a series produced by the University of Alberta radio station, CKUA. In 1937 she writes several episodes for an educational series broadcast by the CBC Western Regional Network. The same year, she moves back to the United States to work on a Master's degree at the University of North Carolina. It is there she meets Frederic Koch and begins working with his Carolina Playmakers on developing folk forms. She works for the Playmakers as both an actress and playwright, completing four plays by 1939 — *Still Stands the House, Chris Axelson, Blacksmith, Pasque Flower* and *One Man's House*, which are all produced by Koch's group. In 1939 she also writes *Dark Harvest*, her first full-length play, as her

M.A. thesis. She returns to the University of Alberta to teach playwriting, and several of her plays are later produced at the Banff School of Fine Arts. During this time, she is also commissioned to write three plays for the Alberta Folklore and Local History Project. The plays — *Hatfield, the Rainmaker, Stampede* and *The Jack and the Joker*, are all based on local historical incidents. Later she writes of playwriting in general during this war-time period: "Our belief in progress through democracy and free enterprise had not prepared us for the realities of our time. We escaped as writers towards myth, folklore, psychological drama ... We tried to recreate the past and often to celebrate the beauty of our countryside ... to cling to the belief that good will triumph and that the world can be saved by love. Few playwrights in Canada tried during those years to cope with the big problems in our plays." Her post-war plays begin to deal with more social and political issues. In 1953, she and her husband, a doctor, move to British Columbia. Her work continues to reflect local concerns such as the plight of the Indians, a theme which appears in several of her plays (*The Stranger, Lament for Harmonica*) and her novels *(Younger Brother, Pascal)*.

Her links with community theatre remain strong in B.C. and Alberta and in 1961 the town of Edson, Alberta commissions her to write a musical play celebrating their 50th anniversary — *Look Behind You, Neighbour.* The play uses a cast of 75 and is subsequently re-mounted for the Commonwealth Conference in Edmonton. Following a similar form, she writes *The Road Runs North* in 1967, this time as part of the centenary celebration of Williams Lake. In 1968, a civic theatre in the town is named in her honour. In 1971 she writes and directs one of her most experimental plays, *The Deep Has Many Voices,* which she describes as a "symphonic play using media and music." In 1976 she wins first prize in the Ontario Multi-Cultural Theatre Association's children's playwriting contest. She presently lives in Williams Lake where she continues her work as teacher, director, and writer for local theatre groups.

Stage Writing

The Dragons of Kent: one-act for young audiences; written in 1935; unpublished; first produced by Banff School of Fine Arts, Alberta, 1935.

Still Stands the House: one-act; written in 1937; first published by University of North Carolina, in *The Carolina Playbook,* June 1938; subsequently published by Samuel French, New York, in 1939 and by Appleton Century, New York, in *American Folk Plays,* 1939, F.H. Koch, ed.; Dent, Toronto in *Eight One-Act Plays,* 1966; *Canadian Books of Prose and Verse,* No. 5,

Toronto; Metheun Publications, Toronto in *Encounter, Drama in Four Media,* 1973, Eugene Benson, ed.; published in *Transitions 1: Short Plays* by Commcept, Vancouver, 1978; first produced by Carolina Playmakers, University of North Carolina in 1938; later adapted for radio and produced by CBC, Winnipeg, 1951.

One Man's House: one-act; written in 1938; unpublished; first produced by Carolina Playmakers, University of North Carolina, 1938.

Chris Axelson, Blacksmith: one-act; written in 1938; unpublished; first produced by Carolina Playmakers, University of North Carolina, 1938.

Pasque Flower: one-act; written in 1939; published by University of North Carolina in *The Carolina Playbook,* March 1939; subsequently published in *Canada's Lost Plays: Women Pioneers,* CTR Publications, Downsview, 1979; first produced by Carolina Playmakers, University of North Carolina, in 1939.

Dark Harvest: three acts; written in 1939; first published in 1945 by Thomas Nelson and Sons Ltd., Toronto; revised and subsequently published by *Canadian Theatre Review,* Winter 1975; first produced by University of Manitoba Dramatic Society, Winnipeg in 1945; adapted for radio and broadcast on CBC's *Wednesday Night* series in 1951.

The Days May Be Long: one-act play; written in 1940; unpublished; unproduced.

Red Flag at Evening: "playlet for stage"; written in 1940; unpublished; first produced by University of Alberta Extension Department, Edmonton in 1940.

Saturday Night: "playlet for stage"; written in 1940; unpublished; first produced by University of Alberta Extension Department in 1940.

The Courting of Marie Jenvrin: one-act; written in 1941; first published by University of North Carolina in *The Carolina Playbook,* 1944; subsequently published by Dodd, Mead, New York in

Best One Act Plays of 1942, 1943, M. Mayorga ed.; Ryerson, Toronto in *Canadian School Plays,* 1948, E.M. Jones, ed.; University of North Carolina Press, in *International Folk Plays,* 1949, S. Selden, Ed.; Samuel French, Toronto, 1951; Harcourt, Brace, New York, in *Adventure in Reading,* 1952, J.M. Ross and B.J. Thompson, eds.; Clarke Irwin and Co., Toronto in *Canada on Stage,* 1960; first produced by Banff School of Fine Arts, Alberta in 1941 under the direction of Sidney Risk; adapted for radio by Elsie Park Gowan and broadcast by CBC.

Christmas 1943: one-act; written in 1943; unpublished; first produced by University Women's Club, Edmonton in 1943.

The Jack and the Joker: one-act comedy; written in 1944; first published by University of Alberta Extension Department, Edmonton in 1944; commissioned by Alberta Folklore and Local History Project, Edmonton; first produced by Banff School of Fine Arts in 1944 under the direction of Sidney Risk.

Hatfield, the Rainmaker: one-act; written in 1945; first published by University of Alberta Extension Department in 1946; subsequently published by Playwrights Co-op, Toronto, 1975; commissioned by Alberta Folklore and Local History Project; first produced by Banff School of Fine Arts in 1945 under the direction of Sidney Risk; subsequently produced by Kamloops High School, Kamloops, B.C., under the direction of Thomas Kerr.

Stampede: three-acts; written in 1945; unpublished; commissioned and first produced by Alberta Folklore and Local History Project in 1945; subsequently produced by University of Alberta Drama Society, Edmonton in 1946; Banff School of Fine Arts in 1955.

The Drowning at Wasyl Nemitchuck (A Fine Coloured Easter Egg): one-act comedy; written in 1946; first published by Gage Educational Publishers, Toronto, 1946; first produced by Banff School of Fine Arts, 1946; adapted for radio and broadcast by CBC Radio, Edmonton.

Widger's Way: two-act melodrama-farce; written in 1952; first published by Playwrights Co-op in 1976; first produced by University of Alberta in 1952; subsequently produced by Williams Lake Players Club, Williams Lake, B.C. in 1959; Kawartha Summer Festival, Lindsay, Ontario in 1976 under the direction of Ronald Ulrich.

Lament for Harmonica (Maya): one-act tragedy; written in 1959; first published by Dell International, New York, in *Ten Canadian Short Plays,* 1975; first produced by Ottawa Little Theatre in 1959; subsequently adapted for television and broadcast by CBC Montreal on *Shoestring Theatre,* 1960; adapted for radio; produced by CBC, 1978.

Look Behind You, Neighbour: book for historical musical written in 1961; music by Chet Lambertson; unpublished; commissioned and first produced by the City of Edson, Alberta to celebrate its 50th anniversary in 1961; subsequently produced by Studio Theatre, Edson, Alberta in 1961 and at the Second Commonwealth Conference, Edmonton.

The Lion and the Mouse: one-act; written in 1964; unpublished; first produced by Cariboo Indian School, Williams Lake, B.C., 1964.

The Sleeping Beauty: one-act children's play; written in 1965; first published by Cariboo Indian School, in *My Heart is Glad,* Book II, 1965, Gwen P. Ringwood, ed.; first produced by Cariboo Indian School in 1965; subsequently produced at the Vancouver Drama Festival, 1966.

The Three Wishes: one-act children's play; written in 1965; unpublished; first produced by Williams Lake School in 1965.

The Road Runs North: book for an "historical musical" written in 1967; commissioned by the City of Williams Lake to celebrate its centenary; music by Art Rosoman; unpublished; first produced by Williams Lake Junior High School, Williams Lake in 1967.

The Deep Has Many Voices: one-act symphonic play using media and music; written in 1969; unpublished; first produced by CBC Montreal for broadcast on television series *Shoestring Theatre* in 1969; revised for stage and produced by Gwen Ringwood Theatre, Williams Lake in 1971.

Encounters: short sketches for production at coffee houses: written in 1970; unpublished; first produced by Gwen Ringwood Theatre in 1970.

The Stranger: one-act tragedy; written in 1971; unpublished; first produced by Gwen Ringwood Theatre in 1971 with Indian cast; also exists in radio version.

The Golden Goose: one-act children's play; written in 1973; unpublished; first produced by Cariboo Indian School, Williams Lake in 1973.

A Remembrance of Miracles: full-length; written in 1975; unpublished; first produced by Gwen Ringwood Theatre in 1975; adapted for radio and broadcast regionally by CBC Vancouver in 1978 for *Hornby* series.

The Magic Carpets of Antonio Angelini: one-act comedy for young audiences; written in 1975; unpublished; first produced by St. Boniface Theatre Company, Winnipeg, for the Multicultural Festival in 1976 under the direction of Jean Louis Hebert; subsequently toured Winnipeg parks and centres for six weeks in 1976; awarded first prize in Canadian Multicultural Theatre Competition, 1976.

The Lodge: three-act comedy about "greed and the threat it poses for life on earth"; written in 1977; unpublished; first produced by West Vancouver Little Theatre, 1976, under the direction of John Campbell; awarded second prize in New Play Centre play competition for women writers in 1975; play revised in 1978.

Mirage: historical revue with music; written in 1979; unpublished; first produced by the University of Saskatchewan for the annual meeting of the Association for Canadian Theatre History and the Learned Societies, 1979, under the direction of Tom Kerr.

Radio Writing

New Lamps for Old: 10 radio plays written for this series dramatizing lives of Beethoven, Cromwell, Socrates, Henry the Navigator, Florence Nightingale, Nansen of the North, Christopher Columbus, Prometheus; written in 1936; unpublished; first produced by CKUA Radio, University of Alberta Edmonton, 1936; later adapted and produced by CBC.

The Fight Against the Invisible: written in 1945; unpublished; first broadcast by CBC Edmonton, 1945.

Niobe House: written in 1945; unpublished; first broadcast by CBC Edmonton in 1945.

Books Alive: written in 1951; unpublished; first broadcast by CBC Edmonton in 1951.

Right On Our Own Doorstep: written in 1951; produced by CKUA Radio, Edmonton, 1951.

Frontier to Farmland: series written in 1952; unpublished; first broadcast by CBC Western School Network, Edmonton in 1952.

Health Highway Series: written in 1952; unpublished; first broadcast by CBC Vancouver in 1952.

Anchor to Westward: written between 1953 and 1954; unproduced.

The Bells of England: a play about the coronation of Elizabeth II; written in 1953; unpublished; first broadcast by CBC Edmonton, 1953.

So Gracious the Time: short Christmas play; written in 1953; first broadcast by CBC Edmonton, 1953.

The Wall: 30-minute comedy "about racial intolerance"; music by Bruce Haak; written in 1953; unpublished; first broadcast by CBC Edmonton and CBC Winnipeg in 1953.

Heidi: 13 episodes written in 1959; first broadcast by CBC Toronto, 1959.

Younger Brother: written in 1960; unpublished; first broadcast by CBC Edmonton, 1960.

Sammy Joe and the Mounties: short story; first published in *Family Herald;* later adapted for radio and broadcast by CBC.

Some People's Grandfathers: short story adapted for radio and broadcast by CBC.

Restez, Michelle, Don't Go: short story written in 1977; unpublished; adapted for radio and broadcast by CBC in 1977.

Miscellaneous

Oh Canada, My Country: "Edmonton pageant in late 40's or 1950 or 1951"; unpublished.

Younger Brother: novel written in 1957; first published by Longmans, New York, 1960.

Pascal: a novel written in 1970; unpublished.

Numerous short stories published in various magazines and anthologies.

In Progress

Ludmilla's Odyssey: third play of a trilogy about Indians.

You Walk a Narrow Bridge: a novel.

Secondary sources

Sections on Ringwood included in *Stage Voices,* (Anthony ed.), Doubleday, 1978, pp. 86-110 and *Transitions I: Short Plays*, Commcept, 1978, pp. 271-274.

Erika Ritter

Born in Regina, April 26, 1948. A distant relative of Buffalo Bill Cody, her father is a salesman; her mother a painter. While majoring in English at McGill University, she spends time acting with one of the university's two theatre companies. Graduating with her B.A. in 1968, she spends a year doing typing jobs, before enroling in the M.A. program at the University of Toronto's Graduate Centre for the Study of Drama. She marries while a student at the Centre and, in 1970, receives her degree.

Returning to Montreal a year later, she is hired to teach English and drama at Loyola College where her first play, *A Visitor From Charleston* is produced in 1974. That year she leaves the College to pursue a career as a full-time writer.

Articles by her on various subjects are published by *Saturday Night* and *Ms.*; her short stories appear in *Canadian Fiction Magazine* and *Chatelaine* among others. Her full-length comedy, *The Splits*, is produced to critical acclaim at Toronto Free Theatre in 1978 and later the same year by the Actor's Theatre of Louisville, Kentucky. The following year, her next play, *Winter 1671*, is premiered by Toronto Arts Productions. Separated from her husband, she currently makes her home in Toronto.

Stage Writing

A Visitor from Charleston: two acts; written in 1974; first published by Playwrights Co-op, Toronto, in 1975; first produced by Loyola College, Montreal, in 1974 under the direction of Harry Hill; subsequently produced by Manitoba Theatre Workshop, Winnipeg, in 1976 under the direction of Paula Sperdakos.

Moving Pictures: two acts; written in 1976; unpublished; first workshopped by Tarragon Theatre, Toronto, in 1976 under the direction of Patricia Carroll Brown.

The Girl I Left Behind Me: one act; written in 1976; unpublished; first produced by Walterdale Community Playhouse, Edmonton, in 1977 under the direction of Warren Graves; adapted for radio; broadcast as a 50-minute radio play for SJUS-FM, Saskatoon in 1977; broadcast by CBC Winnipeg in 1979.

The Splits: two-act comedy; written in 1977; first published by Playwrights Co-op in 1978; first produced by Toronto Free Theatre in 1978 under the direction of Paula Sperdakos; subsequently produced by Actor's Theatre, Louisville, Kentucky, in 1978.

Winter 1671: two-act historical drama; written between 1978 and 1979; first published by Playwrights Co-op in 1979; first produced by Toronto Arts Productions in 1979 under the direction of Leon Major.

Automatic Pilot: two-act comedy; written in 1979; first published by Playwrights Canada in 1980; first produced by New Theatre at the Adelaide Court, Toronto, in 1980 under the direction of William Lane.

Sheldon Rosen

Born August 26, 1943, in the Bronx, New York. Father a furniture salesman; mother an administrator for the Internal Revenue Service. He grows up in Rochester, New York, and receives a B.A. in Psychology from the University of Rochester in 1965. A year later, he earns an M.A. in Telecommunications from the University of Syracuse.

After graduation, he finds a job writing, producing and directing radio and television commercials for a large Minneapolis department store. Later, he becomes an Assistant Program Director at station KVCR-TV in San Bernadino, California. In the mid 60's, he is drafted into the US Army but after training for a job as a military policeman, he leaves because, as he tells the *Toronto Telegram* in 1970, "I didn't like what it was doing to me and I certainly didn't fancy the prospects of killing people in my country's name when I didn't believe my country was right." Moving to Canada, he supports himself in Toronto by delivering handbills door-to-door. At the Learning Resources Centre, run by the Toronto Public Libraries, he takes a course in theatre and studies acting, directing and writing. His first play, *The Love Mouse*, inspired by mice that come out of the walls of his apartment during renovations to the shoestore underneath, is produced in 1971 by the Forge, an experimental theatre group working out of the Learning Resources Centre. His second, also a surrealistic comedy, is called *Meyer's Room*. Both are later produced at Toronto's Poor Alex Theatre. In 1972, he obtains a $4,000 grant from the Canada Council, allowing him to start a career as a full-time writer. That same year, his third play, *The Wonderful World of William Bends Who Is Not Quite Himself Today* is produced by Toronto's Tarragon Theatre. In 1977, he moves to Vancouver where several of his plays are produced by the New Play Centre. Awarded a second Canada Council grant in 1976, he later becomes playwright-in-residence at Ottawa's National Arts Centre. During the summer of 1977, he holds the same position at the Stratford Festival

Glen E. Erickson

where his drama about the friendship between Edward Sheldon and John Barrymore, *Ned and Jack*, is produced. He calls this his first "real" play. "Previously, my work tended to live in the land of flippancy and fantasy with a dash of absurdity for superstition." Active in the Guild of Canadian Playwrights, he is single and continues to make his home in Vancouver.

Stage Writing

The Love Mouse: one-act comedy; written in 1971; first published by Playwrights Co-op, Toronto, 1972; subsequently published by Simon and Pierre, Toronto, 1972, in *A Collection of Canadian Plays, Volume 1*; first produced by the Forge at the Learning Resources Centre, Toronto, 1971, and at the Poor Alex Theatre, Toronto under the direction of Geoffrey Saville-Reed; subsequently adapted for radio; produced by CBC, 1972, for national broadcast.

Meyer's Room: one-act; written in 1971; first published by Playwrights Co-op, 1971; revised version published by Simon and

Pierre, 1972, in *A Collection of Canadian Plays, Volume 1*; first produced at the Poor Alex Theatre, Toronto, 1971, under the direction of Geoffrey Saville-Reed; subsequently adapted for radio; produced by CBC, 1972, for national broadcast.

The Wonderful World of William Bends Who Is Not Quite Himself Today: two-act comedy; written in 1972; first published by Playwrights Co-op, 1972; first produced by Tarragon Theatre, Toronto, 1972, under the direction of J.B. Douglas.

Alice in Wonderland: two-act musical; written in 1973; first produced by Theatre at the Fair and the PNE Coliseum, Vancouver, 1974, under the direction of Bill Millerd.

The Box: one-act; written in 1973; first published in *West Coast Plays*, Fineglow Books, Vancouver, 1974; first produced under the direction of Jace van der Veen by the New Play Centre, 1974; subsequently adapted for radio; produced by CBC Vancouver, 1975, for regional broadcast.

Molecules: one-act "poetic odyssey"; written in 1973; unpublished; first produced by Playhouse Holiday Workshop, Vancouver, 1974, under the direction of Stephen Katz.

Stag King: three-act adaptation of the play by Carlo Gozzi; written in 1973; unpublished; first produced by Tarragon Theatre, under the direction of Stephen Katz.

Frugal Repast: one-act; written in 1974; first published by Playwrights Co-op, 1978, in same volume as *The Grand Hysteric*; first produced by New Play Centre, at Vancouver East Cultural Centre, 1974, under the direction of Jace van der Veen.

Like Father, Like Son: one-act; written in 1975; first produced by New Play Centre, 1975, under the direction of Jace van der Veen; rewritten and redeveloped into *The Grand Hysteric*; first published by Playwrights Co-op in 1978 in the same volume as *Frugal Repast.*

Waiting to Go: one-act; written in 1976; unpublished; available in manuscript form from the New Play Centre.

Ned and Jack: two-act drama about the relationship between Edward Sheldon and John Barrymore; written in 1976-77; first published by Playwrights Co-op, 1978; first produced by New Play Centre, Vancouver, 1977, under the direction of Pamela Hawthorn; subsequently produced by the Stratford Festival, 1978, under the direction of Peter Moss; remounted at the Stratford Festival in 1979; adapted for radio; produced by CBC Vancouver, 1978, for regional broadcast; produced by CBC Toronto, 1979, for national broadcast.

Dwelling: one-act mime play; written in 1977; unpublished; first produced by Axis Mime, Vancouver, 1977, under the direction of Brian Richmond.

The Grand Hysteric (formerly titled *Like Father, Like Son*): one-act; written in 1977; first published by Playwrights Co-Op, 1978; unproduced.

Impact: full-length mime play; written in 1979; unpublished; to be produced by Axis Mime at Arts Club Theatre, Vancouver, 1980, under the direction of Peter Froehlich.

Miscellaneous

Glessun E. Goodhue Show: five 30-minute pilot episodes for a television series; written in 1972; only one of five aired; produced by CBC Toronto for national broadcast.

Portrait of Someone Else: 30-minute television show; written in 1972; first produced by CBC Toronto for national broadcast.

Oom Pa Pa: twelve 30-minute episodes; written in 1976; produced by CTV in Vancouver, for national broadcast.

Public Hearings: 30-minute radio script; written in 1978; first produced by CBC Vancouver, 1978, for regional broadcast.

Directs Tom Cone's *Herringbone* off-Broadway, New York, 1976.

Lawrence Russell

Born in 1941 in Northern Ireland. After moving to Canada, he enrols in the Creative Writing program at the University of Victoria. His first two plays, *There's a Hole In Your Floor, Good Woman of the House* and *A Blow For Freedom,* are published during this time in *The Centurion* magazine. Also while at the University, he wins the Benny Nicholas Award for Writing. Graduating in 1965, he moves to California to do an M.A. in Creative Writing at the University of California. After completing the M.A. in 1967, he returns to Canada to write and, for a time, tries his hand at acting. In 1968, he is named Best Actor at the Vancouver Festival of One-Act Plays.

Increasingly convinced of the potential inherent in oral rather than written literature, in 1971 he founds *DNA*, a "stereo" magazine which features tape recordings rather than printed pages and which deals with "sound, story and unlimited possibilities." In 1972, his play *Poodle* is staged by Toronto's experimental Factory Theatre Lab, the first of his scripts to be done professionally. That same year, the Stratford Festival commissions him to create a piece and the result—*Transmutation*—opens at Stratford's Third Stage that same summer. "I was told by a Festival dramaturge that it was a badly-written version of Star Trek."

Continuing to write for *DNA* (the initials stand for the chemical compound dioxyribonucleic acid), he argues during this time that "the time has come for us to re-evaluate our method of creating literature for, if literature has any value, it definitely needs regeneration in this era where electronic media have become the dominant form of communication...I recommend that writers scrap the typewriter and advance to the tape recorder...The symbolism of the DNA spiral is probably the most important reference point in our existence today."

Currently a professor of Creative Writing and Media at the University of Victoria, he considers himself "primarily an electronic dramatist." Now a Canadian citizen, he is married and lives in Victoria.

Stage Writing

There's A Hole in Your Floor, Good Woman of the House: one-act drama; written in 1961; first published by *The Centurion* magazine in 1962; unproduced.

A Blow for Freedom: one-act drama; written in 1962; first published by *The Centurian* magazine in 1963.

Penetration: one act drama; written in 1969; first published by Sono Nis in 1972 in an anthology entitled *Five Plays by Lawrence Russell* and subsequently by the Playwright's Co-op in 1971 and Alive Press in *Dialogue and Dialectic* in 1972; first produced by the University of Victoria (1969) directed by Mike Stephens.

Poodle: one-act drama; written in 1969; unpublished; first produced by the Factory Theatre Lab in Toronto (1972) directed by Tim Bond.

I Remember Dali When He Was Just a Little Kid and Couldn't Keep His Nose Clean: one-act drama; written in 1970; first published in 1973 by *The Malahat Review* and subsequently by the Angst World

Library (1975) in a four play anthology called *Mystery of the Pig Killer's Daughter and Other Plays*; first produced by Factory Theatre Lab in Toronto (1971) directed by Tim Bond and subsequently by the Stratford Festival, Ontario, and the Soho Poly, London, England.

Magic Juice; one-act drama; written in 1970; first published by *Canadian Fiction Magazine* in 1971 and subsequently as a part of the Sono Nis collection *Penetration* in 1972; first produced by stereophonic tape in 1971 at the Vancouver Art Gallery directed by the author.

Monster: one-act drama; written in 1970; first published in *A Collection of Four Plays* by Angst World in 1975 and subsequently as a part of the collection, *Mystery of the Pig Killer's Daughter and Other Plays*; first produced at the National Arts Centre, Ottawa in 1974 directed by Bill Lane and subsequently by the Toronto Free Theatre in 1975, also directed by Bill Lane.

Transmutation: two-act drama; written in 1972; unpublished; commissioned by the Stratford Festival, Ontario, for the Third Stage, unproduced.

The Beautiful Woman and the Bleeding Man: one-act drama; written in 1974; first published by *Canadian Fiction Magazine* in 1975; unproduced.

Mystery of the Pig Killer's Daughter: eleven-scene drama; written in 1974; first published by Angst World Library in 1975; first produced by Toronto Free Theatre in 1975 directed by Bill Lane.

The Dreaming Store: one-act drama; written in 1975; first published in *Quarry* magazine, 1979; unproduced.

Miscellaneous

A series of stereophonically-taped radio dramas—*Camouflage*(1972), *Geometry and Dream*(1973), *Blackout*(1974), *The Sleeper Awakes*(1975), and *Soyuz 954*(1978). These have been broadcast in the United States and Canada on many stations including: WBAI New York, KGNU Colorado, KCFR Denver, CFOR Vancouver plus others in Philadelphia, Memphis, San Francisco. *Camouflage* is also included on a CBC Radio International Transcription Disc E1057.

George Ryga

Born July 1932 in **Deep Creek, Alberta, a** recently-established community of Eastern European immigrants farming marginal land on the edge of the bush. Family of Ukrainian descent. "It was very primitive, in essence life hadn't changed from what it was in the 17th century in Europe. A lot of impressions of how people live when reduced to bare essentials still persist in my mind." A good student, he completes seven grades in the community's one-room school house. It is his only formal education.

Leaving school at the age of 12, he continues his studies through correspondence courses and the extensive use of a government-operated travelling library which, for a fee of 30 cents, lends him books on a wide variety of subjects. Of this period he says, "Coming into contact with literature and becoming aware of its dignity, beauty and severe discipline was probably the kind of challenge I needed at the time to begin to confront myself and to construct things on my own." As a teenager, he works periodically in lumbering, construction and farming jobs. At 17, he loses the three middle fingers of his right hand in an accident.

In 1949, encouraged by the instructor of his correspondence course in English, he enters the creative writing competition run by the Banff School of Fine Arts. The work he submits wins many prizes and he spends the summer at the School on a scholarship sponsored by the Imperial Order of Daughters of the Empire. Returning the next summer, having won even more prizes in the competition, his scholarship is that year revoked because of his refusal to apologize after one of his poems, critical of the Korean War, is circulated on a broadsheet, arousing the ire of the I.O.D.E. This is the first of many political incidents that are to mark his career, getting him into trouble with various powerful organizations and earning him the reputation of being a troublemaker.

He soon moves to Edmonton and begins three years as a copy writer with a commercial radio station. Within a year, he is made producer of a radio program

W. Smith

entitled *Reverie*. A year-and-a-half later, his political beliefs once again lead to a run-in with authority when he produces an Armistice Day program again critical of the war. Using lines from *Flanders Fields* and military music to counterpoint the writings of prominent pacificist poets, the show creates a storm of controversy. Since the program's sponsor, the Druggists' Association, supports Ryga, he is merely reprimanded by his employers. But later that year he is forced to resign after picketing and making speeches about the trial of Ethel and Julius Rosenberg. In poor health, he returns to Northern Alberta.

In 1955 he travels to Europe. As well as meeting various scholars, he spends several months in Scotland examining early manuscripts of Robert Burns, a poet whom he greatly admires, and tracing Burns' use of folklore and popular culture. While in Scotland, he is invited by the Canadian Peace Movement to serve on the Canadian delegation to the World Peace Assembly in Helsinki. Here he meets many of his literary heroes including Pablo Neruda and Nazim Hikmet and, through contacts with Third World artists, develops an interest in the role of folk dance in the literature and art of Black Africa. From Helsinki, he is invited to festivals in Warsaw and Bulgaria. Although a socialist, he is bothered by the lack of information and creeping bureaucracy in these countries. After the suppression of the Hungarian Revolution in 1956, he formally breaks with the Communist Party.

Returning to Edmonton that year, he spends six months as a copy writer in an advertising agency. The same year, his first collection of poetry, *Song of My Hands* is published. During the next years he works at various night jobs, including the running of a night-desk in a hotel, and carpentry. He writes during the day. Although frequently unemployed, he produces a steady stream of poetry, short stories and novels, six of which he writes before seeing a single one in print. During this period, he marries, legally adopts his wife Norma's two daughters and son, and eventually fathers two more children.

By 1962, having sold several short stories to CBC Radio, he is finally able to write full-time. That year he completes his first play, *Indian*, which is broadcast as part of CBC-TV's *Quest* series. This is followed by more than a dozen television scripts also produced by the network. His second play, *The Ecstasy of Rita Joe*, a passionate indictment of Canada's treatment of its native peoples, is commissioned and premiered by the Vancouver Playhouse as a Centennial Play in 1967 with Frances Hyland and Chief Dan George in the leading roles. A critical and popular success, *Rita Joe* helps bring the Playhouse to national prominence.

Because of his past political activities, he is not allowed to enter the United States when *Rita Joe* opens in Washington, D.C. Only through the intercession of the Canadian Department of External Affairs is he finally able to see the American production of his play.

In 1968, his new play *Grass and Wild Strawberries* premieres at the Vancouver Playhouse, and plays to capacity audiences. He is then commissioned to write another play for the theatre. The result is *Captives of the Faceless Drummer*, dealing with the imposition of the War Measures Act during the 1970 FLQ crisis. The play is refused production by the Playhouse and a political battle over censorship ensues.

The play is later produced by sympathetic members of the theatre community at the Vancouver Art Gallery in 1971. Ryga's work, from this point, is no longer produced by the Playhouse. In fact, his work is rarely produced thereafter on major Canadian stages. When it is produced, it is often by small professional companies or by non-professional and university groups. A ballet version of *Rita Joe* is, however, subsequently produced by the Royal Winnipeg Ballet.

By the mid-70s, he is earning most of his living by writing almost exclusively for radio and television. In 1974, he writes in the first issue of *Canadian Theatre Review* "Because I refuse to divorce theatre from the larger issues of life confronting us I get punished. My plays are produced less frequently in the regional theatres today than they were five years ago. Words written by me have been bastardized and rearranged beyond recognition, yet my name has been left on the playbills...the cause of a viable Canadian theatre has reeled under the counterrattack of a sqcial and political system that viciously defends itself against all criticism and examination. Certainly, I've been hurt. And because I've been hurt, so have you. Because I do no more than reflect your experiences, thoughts and possibilities through my art."

Teaching playwriting for a time at the University of British Columbia, Simon Fraser University and at the Banff School of Fine Arts, (while at Banff, he becomes involved in a controversy defending an Indian student in an alleged case of discrimination), he becomes interested in the People's Republic of China and makes two trips to China over the next four years. A novelized memoir of his travels in China is published by Doubleday under the title, *Beyond the Crimson Morning*. Married, he, his wife and their five children currently make their home in Summerland, British Columbia.

Stage Writing

Indian: originally written in 1962 as a television script; re-written in 1964 as a one-act stage play; first published by New Press, Toronto, in 1971 in the collection *The Ecstasy of Rita Joe and Other Plays*; also published by Dell, New York in 1975 in the volume *10 Canadian Short Plays*; first produced by CBC-TV in 1963 for the series *Quest* under the direction of George McGowan; subsequently produced by the Manitoba Theatre Centre in 1974 under the direction of Malcolm Black.

Nothing But a Man: originally written in 1966 as a television script; re-written as a full-length stage play; unpublished; stage version first produced by Metro Theatre, Vancouver.

The Ecstasy of Rita Joe: two-act drama; written in 1967; first published by Talonbooks, Vancouver, 1970; subsequently published in an anthology entitled *The Ecstasy of Rita Joe and Other Plays* by New Press, Toronto, in 1971; first produced by Vancouver Playhouse in 1967 under the direction of George Bloomfield; subsequently produced by National Arts Centre, Ottawa, in 1969; first produced in a French translation by Gratien Gélinas by Comédie Canadienne, Montreal, in 1970; by the Washington Theatre Club, Washington, in 1973; by Hampstead Theatre, London, England, in 1975; adapted as a ballet by Norbert Vesak and produced by the Royal Winnipeg Ballet in 1971.

Grass and Wild Strawberries: three-act drama about the 60s youth culture; written in 1968; first published by New Press, 1971, in the collection *The Ecstasy of Rita Joe and Other Plays*; first produced by Vancouver Playhouse in 1969 under the direction of Don Eccleston.

Captives of the Faceless Drummer: full-length political drama; written in 1971; first published by Talonbooks in 1971; commissioned by Vancouver Playhouse but unproduced; first produced as an Equity Showcase at the Vancouver Art Gallery; subsequently produced by Festival Lennoxville, Quebec in 1972 under the direction of John Hirsch.

Sunrise on Sarah: two-act drama; written in 1972; first published by Talonbooks in 1973; first produced at the Banff Centre in 1972 under the direction of Tom Peacocke; subsequently produced by Festival

Lennoxville in 1973 under the direction of William Davis.

Portrait of Angelica: full-length drama; written in 1973; unpublished; first produced at the Banff Centre in 1973.

Paracelsus: three-act drama about the medieval healer; written in 1974; first published by the *Canadian Theatre Review*, Summer 1974 (*CTR* 4); unproduced.

Ploughman of the Glacier: two acts; written in 1975 on commission from the Okanagan Mainline Regional Arts Council; first published by Talonbooks in 1978; first produced by Western Canada Theatre Company at Spratt's Ark Theatre, Vancouver, in 1976 under the direction of Tom Kerr.

Seven Hours to Sundown: two acts; written in 1976 on commission from Theatre Network and the University of Alberta; first published by Talonbooks in 1978; first produced by the University of Alberta in 1976 under the direction of Mark Manson.

Jeremiah's Place: full-length; written in 1978; unpublished; first produced by Kaleidoscope Theatre, Victoria in 1978 under the direction of Elizabeth Gorrie.

Prometheus Bound (adaptation): written in 1978; unpublished; unproduced.

Television Writing

The Storm: written in 1962; unpublished.

Gold in the Aspens: written in 1962; unpublished.

Bitter Grass: written in 1963; unpublished.

Chelkash: written in 1963; unpublished.

For Want of Something Better To Do: written in 1963; unpublished.

Two Soldiers: written in 1963; unpublished.

The Pear Tree: written in 1963; unpublished.

The Tulip Garden: written in 1963; unpublished.

Goodbye is Forever: written in 1963; unpublished.

Trouble in Mind: written in 1963; unpublished.

Erosions: written in 1964; unpublished.

Man Alive: written in 1965; unpublished.

Heritage: written in 1965; unpublished.

Moderate Cantabile (adaptation): written in 1965; unpublished.

A Feat of Thunder: written in 1966; unpublished.

Jingle-Jangle Children: written in 1966; unpublished.

In 1968, Ryga wrote two scripts for *The Manipulators* series and in 1969 one for *The Name of the Game.*

Newcomers 1927: written in 1978; produced by CBC for national broadcast in 1978; unpublished.

Film Writing

The Kamloops Incident: written in 1967; unpublished.

A Carpenter By Trade: written in 1967; unpublished.

Radio Writing

A Touch of Cruelty: written in 1961; unpublished.

Half Caste: written in 1962; unpublished.

Masks and Shadows: written in 1963; unpublished.

Ballad for Bill: written in 1963; unpublished.

Bread Route: written in 1963; unpublished.

Departures: written in 1963; unpublished.

The Stone Angel (adaptation of the Margaret Laurence novel); written in 1965; unpublished.

A complete list of radio scripts written since 1969 is unavailable at this time.

Novels

The Bridge: written in 1960; unpublished.

Wagoner Lad: written in 1961; unpublished.

Poor People: written in 1962; unpublished.

Hungry Hills: written in 1962; first published by Longmans Canada, Toronto, in 1963; subsequently published by Talonbooks, Vancouver in 1974.

Sawdust Temples: written in 1963; unpublished.

Old Sam: written in 1963; unpublished.

Ballad of a Stonepicker: written in 1965; first published by Macmillan of Canada, Toronto, in 1966; revised edition published by Talonbooks, Vancouver in 1966.

Nothing But A Man: written in 1967; unpublished.

Night Desk: written in 1975; first published by Talonbooks, Vancouver in 1976.

Beyond the Crimson Morning: novelized account of the author's trip to the People's Republic of China; written in 1978; first published by Doubleday, Toronto, in 1979.

Miscellaneous

Song of My Hands: a book of poetry; published in 1956.

Theatre in Canada: A Viewpoint on its Development and Future: essay; written in 1974; first published in *Canadian Theatre Review,* (*CTR* 1); Winter 1974.

Contemporary Theatre and its Language: essay; written in 1977; first published in *Canadian Theatre Review* (*CTR* 14), Spring 1977.

The Need for a Mythology: essay; written in 1977; first published in *Canadian Theatre Review* (*CTR* 16); Fall 1977.

Secondary Sources

Section on Ryga included in *Transactions I: Short Plays*, Commcept Publishers, Vancouver, 1978; pp. 279-280.

Excerpts from an uncompleted biography of Ryga by Peter Hay were published under the title *George Ryga: Beginnings of a Biography* in *Canadian Theatre Review* (*CTR* 23) Summer 1979.

Rick Salutin

Born August 30, 1942, in Toronto. Father a salesman; mother a secretary. After earning a B.A. in Near Eastern and Judaic Studies from Brandeis University, he moves to New York to do post-graduate work in religion at Columbia University and the New School of Social Research. While living in New York, he reads Harold Innis' book, *Fur Trade in Canada,* and for the first time becomes interested in the history of his own country. ("I liked history. I liked English and American history. I discovered how we as Canadians had been robbed of Canadian history.") After completing his M.A., he returns to Toronto in 1970, the day the War Measures Act is invoked. Becoming active in the trade union movement, he participates in the Artistic Woodwork strike during the early 1970s and winds up serving a short jail term for his activities. He supports himself in the years following as a journalist and freelance writer for a variety of magazines including *Harper's, Maclean's* and *Weekend* and also writes short satirical pieces for the CBC radio series *Inside from the Outside.*

As a reaction to the events in Quebec, he writes his first play in 1971, *Fanshen.* A dramatization of William Hinton's well-known account of the effects of the socialist revolution on a small Chinese village, the play is produced by Toronto Workshop Productions in 1972. That year he begins working with Paul Thompson and Theatre

Passe Muraille on *1837: The Farmers' Revolt,* a collective creation, about a 19th century "people's" uprising. The play is produced to great acclaim in various cities across Canada by Theatre Passe Muraille in 1973 and is the winner of the 1974 Chalmers Award for an Outstanding Canadian Play.

Speaking of collective work, he tells the *London Free Press,* "In a play in which no actor speaks unless he feels he really has something to say, there's a sense of commitment that can be overwhelming for someone seeing this kind of work for the first time." *The Adventures of an Immigrant,* his next collective creation, is also done with Passe Muraille. In 1975, he collaborates with Newfoundland's Mummers Troupe in a production of *I.W.A.,* a play about a strike of woodworkers in that province. His immensely popular *Les Canadiens,* winner of the 1977 Chalmers Award for an Outstanding New Canadian Play, is written "with an assist from Ken Dryden," goaltender for the Montreal Canadiens hockey team.

In 1978, after several months in Mozambique, he returns home and becomes chairman of the Guild of Canadian Playwrights, an organization he helps to found. As well as writing plays and continuing his involvement in the labour movement, he is an editor and a columnist for *This Magazine.* Unmarried, he currently makes his home in Toronto.

Stage Writing

Fanshen (adapted from the book by William Hinton): two-act drama focussing on "the Chinese revolution as it passes through a small village. The stage is the village. The cast are the inhabitants"; written between 1971 and 1972; unpublished; first produced by Toronto Workshop Productions, 1972, under the direction of George Luscombe.

1837: The Farmers' Revolt: a two-act collective creation about "the famous Canadian Revolution, complete with William Lyon Mackenzie and a cast of hundreds of thousands"; written in 1972 and rewritten in 1974; first published by *Canadian Theatre Review* in 1975; subsequently published as *1837: A History/A Play* by James Lorimer and Co., 1976; first produced by Theatre Passe Muraille, Toronto, 1973, under the direction of Paul Thompson; subsequently mounted by TPM at Festival Habitat (Vancouver 1976), the Cultural Olympics (Montreal) and at the National Arts Centre; also taken on tour through Scotland; adapted for television and broadcast nationally by CBC, Toronto, 1975.

The Adventures of an Immigrant: a full-length collective creation; written in 1974; unpublished; first produced by Theatre Passe Muraille, 1974, under the direction of Paul Thompson.

The False Messiah: full-length drama about a 17th century Jew who proclaims himself the messiah and challenges the Turkish Empire and the Sultan; written between 1974 and 1975; unpublished; first produced by Theatre Passe Muraille, 1975, under the direction of John Palmer.

I.W.A.: a collective creation in which "the great woodworkers' strike is crushed, live onstage, by Joey Smallwood"; written in 1975; produced by the Mummers' Troupe, St. John's, 1975, under the direction of Chris Brookes; subsequently taken on tour of Newfoundland, and presented at Centaur Theatre, Montreal, 1976.

Money: a one-act "musical anti-magic show, an economics treatise concerning money as the greatest of all mystifications"; written in 1976; unpublished; first performed by Young Peoples' Theatre, Toronto, 1976, directed by John Palmer.

Les Canadiens: full-length historical drama seeing "Hockey as history and history as hockey; from the Plains of Abraham to the PQ victory of '76"; written between 1976 and 1977; first published by Talonbooks, Vancouver, 1977; first produced by Centaur Theatre, Montreal, 1977, under the direction of Guy Sprung; subsequently produced by Toronto Workshop Productions, 1977, under the direction of George Luscombe; Arts Club, Vancouver, 1978, under the direction of Brian Richmond; Theatre Passe Muraille tour, 1978, under the direction of Miles Potter; Neptune Theatre, 1978, under the direction of John Neville; the Globe Theatre, 1978, under the direction of Ken Kramer; winner of the Chalmers Award in 1977 for an Outstanding Canadian Play.

Miscellaneous

Good Buy Canada (with Murray Soupcoff and Gary Dunford): written in 1974; first published by James Lorimer and Co., 1975.

Kent Rowley: The Organizer: biography of the Canadian union leader; written in 1979; published by James Lorimer and Co., Toronto in 1980.

Maria: 60-minute television drama; written in 1975; first produced by CBC Toronto for national broadcast, 1976.

Many articles in *This Magazine, Harpers, Maclean's, Weekend, Today.*

In Progress

Nathan Cohen: A Revue: a stage play.

Brian Shein

Born January 2, 1947, in Lindsay, Ontario. Father a Presbyterian minister who later becomes a professor of Russian at McMaster University. From 1964 to 1966, he studies languages and literature at the University of Toronto. He then moves to the University of British Columbia to do two years of graduate work in English literature and creative writing. In 1967, he writes his first play, a one-act drama entitled *Kafka*, which is produced at the University of British Columbia that same year. A year later, he wins the Macmillan Company of Canada's Short Story Award for *Will You Go Hunt My Lord*, published in *Prism International.* In 1969, he receives his first of three short-term writing grants from the Canada Council.

Beginning in 1971, he teaches creative writing at the University of British Columbia, a position he holds for two years. During this period he is also manager of Steady-State Productions, a Vancouver-based theatre company. At the same time, he works as a part-time editor at Vancouver's Pulp Press and does research on the native peoples for both the National Film Board and the U'Mista Cultural Society (cultural society of the Kwakiutl people, Alert Bay, B.C.). He also does research for CBC Radio, Vancouver, on the literature and politics of the Third World. His other work for radio includes plays, documentaries and comedy material including sketches for such shows as *Dr. Bundola* and *Inside from the Outside.*

Moving to Ontario in 1975, he begins

teaching creative writing, theatre history and script development at Canadore College in North Bay. At about the same time, he is named playwright-in-residence and member of the management committee of Playwrights Co-op. After two years in North Bay, he moves to Toronto. Later that year, he receives a playwriting grant from the Ontario Arts Council. An associate editor of the tabloid newspaper *Toronto Theatre Review* for a time, he is now an editor of the humour magazine, *National Lampoon.* He presently makes his home in Toronto with Robin Endres and their daughter, Ivanna.

Stage Writing

Kafka: one-act "ritual drama with a science fiction flavour"; written in 1967; first published by *Prism International* in 1968 and subsequently by Pulp Press, Vancouver, in *Theatrical Exhibitions* (1975); first produced by the University of British Columbia in Vancouver in 1967, directed by John Rapsey and subsequently by Vancouver Playhouse, Stage Two, in 1968.

Cowboy Island: one-act "Kabuki-style version of the Billy the Kid story"; written in 1971; first published in 1972 by Playwrights Co-op and subsequently in *Theatrical Exhibitions* (1975) and in *Five Canadian Plays* (1978) by the Playwrights Co-op; first produced by the Factory Theatre Lab in Toronto, in 1972, directed by Ken Gass and subsequently by the National Arts Centre Young Company in 1974.

Steady-State Doomsday: two-act science fiction dealing with an atomic holocaust; written in 1971; first produced by Steady-State Productions, Vancouver, 1972, under the direction of Norbert Ruebsaat; adapted for radio and published under the title *Ground Zero* by Pulp Press in *Theatrical Exhibitions*, 1975; produced by CBC Radio, Vancouver, 1975, for regional broadcast.

Rex Morgan, M.D.: one-act drama; written in 1972; first published in *Theatrical Exhibitions* by Pulp Press, Vancouver, 1975; unproduced.

Exhibitions: first produced at the Vancouver Art Gallery, 1973, under the direction of the author.

Glossolalia: one-act drama; written in 1972; unpublished; first produced at the Vancouver Art Gallery, 1972, under the direction of the author.

Trickster: two act "reworking of North American/African trickster myths"; written in 1976; unpublished; unproduced.

Boss Ubu: full-length adaptation of the Jarry play; written in 1977 in collaboration with Richard Payne; unpublished; first produced in 1977 by the University of Ottawa.

Radio Writing

An Entertainment at the Cafe Terminus: 60 minutes; written in 1974; first published by Pulp Press, 1975, in *Theatrical Exhibitions*; produced by CBC, Vancouver, 1975, for national broadcast.

Ground Zero: 30-minute radio adaptation of *Steady State Doomsday*; written in 1974; first published by Pulp Press, 1975, in *Theatrical Exhibitions*; produced by CBC Vancouver, 1975, for regional broadcast.

The Ways of the Shaman: 30 minutes; written in 1978; produced by CBC, Vancouver, 1979, for regional broadcast.

Miscellaneous

Will You Go Hunt My Lord: short story; written in 1968; published in *Prism International*; winner of the Macmillan Company of Canada's Short Story Award.

Potlatch: A Strict Law Bids Us Dance: 60-minute documentary on Northwest Coast native history and culture; written between 1973 and 1975; produced by the U'Mista Cultural Society, 1975, Alert Bay, British Columbia; a finalist in the Canadian Film Awards.

Theatrical Exhibitions: an autobiographical theatrical essay dealing with ritual and biological origins of theatre; included in the anthology of the same title; published by Pulp Press, Vancouver, 1975.

Beverley Simons

Born on March 31, 1938 in Flin Flon, Manitoba. Father in the lumber business. At the age of 12, she moves with her family to Vancouver for six months and then to Edmonton. Early background in music. Possibility of a career as a concert pianist. Begins performing publicly as well as teaching piano to adults and children at the age of 13. At the age of 16, she is offered a full scholarship to study further in Toronto, New York or Paris. Family urges her to remain at home. Begins writing at this time a verse drama entitled *Twisted Roots* (one act) which wins a national writing contest for high school students. The play is published two years later in a hardcover collection entitled *First Flowering* edited by Anthony Frisch. At the age of 18, she wins a scholarship to study Creative Writing at the Banff School of Fine Arts. While at Banff, she writes her first full-length play, *My Torah, My Tree*. In 1956, she enrols at McGill University in Montreal majoring in English. Is instrumental in forming an experimental theatre company at McGill to produce original plays. The group produces two of her one-acts — *A Play* and *The Birth*. She also acts, directs and helps administrate the company.

In 1958, she transfers to the University of British Columbia where she earns a B.A. in English and Theatre. The following year she is given a scholarship to study theatre during the summer at U.B.C. with Brian Way and Robert Gill. Between 1959 and 1961, she travels, works and studies in Europe. In 1961, the first of her three sons is born. In 1962, she completes *The Elephant and the Jewish Question* and *Green Lawn Rest Home* and over the next few years she writes several television and film scripts. In 1967 she receives a Canada Council grant to study theatre in the Far East, and describes this time as "a rich, dense two months, the equivalent of a year that I'm still unravelling." The following spring she completes the final draft of *Crabdance* which she had been working on for four years. In 1972, she completes a trilogy of

short plays, *Prologue, Crusader* and *Triangle* and the dramatic monologue, *Preparing*. She also receives a Canada Council Senior Arts Award and begins to work on *Leela Means to Play* which is completed in 1976. The same year, her trilogy of short plays is premiered by John Juliani's Savage God Company at York University on the occasion of an international critics' conference. In 1977 she puts out a videotape of *Crabdance* based on Malcolm Black's production at the Citadel Theatre. She describes the unorthodox move to produce her own work as "a necessary precedent." During the summer of 1978, *Leela Means to Play* is chosen for a workshop by the National Playwrights Conference at the Eugene O'Neill Theater Center in Connecticut. About this time, she decides to spend her energies in writing novels because "in prose I only have to find a publisher and the work will find its audience." She presently lives in Vancouver with her husband — an attorney — and her three children.

Stage Writing

Twisted Roots: a one-act verse drama; written in 1954; first published by Kingswood House, Toronto in *First Flowering*, 1956; Anthony Frisch, ed.; the play wins a prize in a national creative writing competition for high school students.

My Torah, My Tree: full-length; written in 1956; unpublished; unproduced.

The Birth: one-act; written in 1957; first produced by McGill University Players Club, Montreal, in 1957.

A Play: one-act; written in 1957; unpublished; first produced by McGill University Players Club in 1957.

The Elephant and the Jewish Question: three acts; written between 1960 and 1962; unpublished; first produced by the Vancouver Little Theatre Association under the direction of John Parker in 1968; commissioned for CBC Festival TV series in 1963; unproduced.

Green Lawn Rest Home: one-act; written in 1962; first published by the Playwright's Co-op, Toronto, in 1973 and subsequently by Talonbooks, Vancouver, as part of *Preparing* in 1975; first done as a public reading at the Arts Club, Vancouver, directed by Malcolm Black; first full production by Savage God at Simon Fraser University under the direction of John Juliani, 1969; produced by Manfrog Alive in 1978 and taken on a tour of British Columbia high schools.

Crabdance; three-act drama; written between 1964 and 1968; published by In Press, Vancouver, in 1969 and by Talonbooks in 1972; also included in *Stage One: A Canadian Scenebook* (Van Nostrand Reinhold) in 1974; first produced by A Contemporary Theatre, Seattle, under the direction of Malcolm Black in 1969; subsequently produced by the Playhouse Theatre Company in Vancouver under the direction of Frances Hyland with Jennifer Phipps as Sadie, 1972; at the Neptune Theatre's Second Stage in Halifax under the direction of Michael Mawson with Joan Orenstein as Sadie, 1972; at the Manitoba Theatre Centre's Warehouse under the direction of Jeremy Gibson with Helene Winston as Sadie, 1975; at the Citadel Theatre, Edmonton in 1977 under the direction of Malcolm Black; radio adaptation commissioned by CBC in 1974 for the Tuesday Night series; produced in 1976 with Patricia Hamilton as Sadie; videotape made from the 1977 Citadel Theatre production co-produced by Access Alberta and Beverley Simons under the direction of John Wright.

Preparing: a monologue in one act; written in 1972; first published in *Capilano Review* in January 1975 and subsequently as part of *Preparing* by Talonbooks in 1975; first produced at Simon Fraser University under the direction of Hagan Beggs in 1973 and subsequently by Vancouver's Tamahnous Theatre under the direction of Larry Lillo and John Gray, 1974.

Prologue: one-act; written in 1972 as part of a trilogy with *Crusader* and *Triangle*; first published as part of *Preparing* in 1975 by Talonbooks; subsequently published, by Commcept Publishers, Vancouver in *Transitions I: Short Plays,* 1978.

Crusader: one-act; written in 1972; first published as part of *Preparing* in 1975 by Talonbooks; first produced along with *Prologue* and *Triangle* by Savage God at York University in 1976 under the direction of John Juliani.

Triangle: one-act; written in 1972; first published as part of *Preparing* in 1975 by Talonbooks; first produced along with *Prologue* and *Crusader* by Savage God at York University in 1976 under the direction of John Juliani.

Leela Means to Play: two acts; written between 1970 and 1975; first published by the *Canadian Theatre Review,* winter 1976, (*CTR 9*); first produced in workshop at Eugene O'Neill Theater Center, Waterford, Connecticut in 1978 under the direction of Robert Ackerman.

Miscellaneous

Encounter: 45-minute film script: written in 1965 on commission from CBC-TV as an adaptation of an earlier Simons short story; unproduced.

If I Turn Around Quick: 60-minute film script; commissioned in 1966 by CBC-TV; unproduced.

The Canary: 60-minute film script; written in 1967 on commission from CBC-TV; ultimately produced by CBUT in Vancouver as a 30-minute film.

Is Anybody Out There: feature film; written in 1968-1969 on commission from the National Film Board; unproduced.

A Question of Symmetry: feature film; written in 1969-1970 on commission from the National Film Board; unproduced.

Ezekiel Saw a Wheel: feature film; written in 1971-1972; unproduced; first published by *Capilano Review*, Vancouver, Summer 1976.

The Boy With a Piece of Dark: children's book; written between 1976 and 1977; unpublished.

In Progress

Encounter: a collection of short stories dating from 1962 to 1978.

The Victim: begun in late 1960's.

One Two Three: a short play to accompany *Green Lawn Rest Home*; begun in 1970.

Judith: three-act play; begun in 1975.

The Hero: begun in 1978.

A Novel: tentative title — *Tabernacles.*

Secondary Sources

Essay by Simons included in *Transitions I: Short Plays,* Commcept, 1978. pp. 281-287.

Casebook on Simons included in *Canadian Theatre Review*, Winter 1976, (*CTR* 9).

Bernard Slade

Born on May 2, 1930, in St. Catharines, Ontario. Father a mechanic. Educated in England, he returns to Canada to begin an acting career at the age of 18. In 1954, he and his actress wife, Jill Foster, found the Garden Centre Theatre in Vineland, Ontario, where they produce and act in a weekly stock season of 25 plays. Describing the gruelling pace of the Vineland summer, he says, "I lost 25 pounds, started to turn grey, and was forced into premature maturity." Continuing to work as an actor, he appears in over 100 plays on television and in various theatres across Ontario, including Toronto's Crest. After a brief stint as a producer, he writes his first play, *The Prize Winner,* which is broadcast by CBC-TV in 1958. Later that year, the play is shown on NBC's Matinee Theatre under a new title, *The Long, Long Laugh* and is also broadcast on the *U.S. Steel Hour* (CBS). He decides to leave acting at this point in order to write plays for a living. "I started writing my first teleplay with one main thought in mind — a good role for myself. When three networks bought the teleplay and none of them hired me to play the part...I figured they were trying to tell me something." Beginning in 1958, he writes numerous television plays for CBC including *Men Don't Make Passes, Innocent Deception, The Gimmick, Do Jerry Parker, The Most Beautiful Girl in the World, The Big Coin Sound, The Oddball, The Reluctant Angels* and *Blue is for Boys.* His first play for the legitimate stage, *Simon Says Get Married,* is produced at the Crest Theatre in 1960 and is followed two years later by *A Very Close Family* premiered by the Manitoba Theatre Centre, under the direction of George McGowan, with leading roles played by Bud Knapp, John Vernon, and Gordon Pinsent. The play is subsequently shown on CBC with Melvyn Douglas, Tom Bosley, Jill Foster, Charmion King and Gordon Pinsent.

In 1964 he moves to Los Angeles with his wife and two children where he is contracted by Columbia Pictures to work as story editor on the television series, *Bewitched.* Over the next years he writes

scripts for many television series, as well as the pilot films for the following series: *Love on a Rooftop, The Flying Nun, The Partridge Family, Bridget Loves Bernie, The Girl with Something Extra, Mr. Deeds Goes to Town, The Bobby Sherman Show* and *Mr. Angel.* He also writes the screenplay for *Stand Up and Be Counted,* a feature film starring Jacqueline Bisset and Stella Stevens. In 1975, his comedy, *Same Time, Next Year,* premieres on Broadway with Ellen Burstyn and Charles Grodin, under the direction of Gene Saks. The play is an immediate success, enjoying a Broadway run of three-and-a-half years and winning a Tony Award nomination and a Drama Desk Award. The play is subsequently produced in theatre capitals around the world. For the 1977 Citadel Theatre (Edmonton) production, Slade and his wife return to the stage to play the two roles. The following year, his play *Tribute* opens on Broadway with Jack Lemmon in the leading role. A film version of *Same Time Next Year* featuring Ellen Burstyn and Alan Alda is also released in 1978. His next play, *Romantic Comedy,* opens on Broadway in 1979. He, his wife, and their two children continue to make their home in Los Angeles.

Stage Writing

Simon Says Get Married: full-length comedy; written in 1960; unpublished; first produced by the Crest Theatre, Toronto, in 1960, under the direction of Murray Davis, with Austin Wills, Drew Thompson and Jill Foster.

A Very Close Family: full-length drama; written in 1962; unpublished; first produced by Manitoba Theatre Centre, Winnipeg, in 1962, under the direction of George McGowan; starring Bud Knapp, John Vernon, Gordon Pinsent; subsequently broadcast as a 90-minute television play by CBC in 1963 under the direction of Harvey Hart, starring Melvyn Douglas, Tom Bosley, Jill Foster, Charmion King and Gordon Pinsent.

Fling: full-length comedy; written in 1971; first published by Samuel French, New York, in 1979; unproduced.

Same Time, Next Year: full-length comedy; written in 1974; first published by **Dell**, New York, in 1975; subsequently published by Delacorte Press in 1975; subsequently published by Samuel French; first produced by Morton Gottlieb at the Brooks Atkinson Theater, New York, in 1975, under the direction of Gene Saks, starring Ellen Burstyn and Charles Grodin; subsequently produced in major cities around the world and taken on a national tour of the United States and Canada; produced by Citadel Theatre, Edmonton, in 1977, under the direction of Warren Crane, starring Bernard Slade and Jill Foster; subsequently produced as a feature film, 1978, under the direction of Robert Mulligan, starring Ellen Burstyn and Alan Alda; nominee for a Tony Award in 1975; winner of a Drama Desk Award in 1975.

Tribute: full-length comedy-drama; written in 1976; first published by Doubleday, New York (Fireside Theatre) in 1978; subsequently published by Samuel French in 1979; first produced by Morton Gottlieb at the Brooks Atkinson Theater, New York, in 1978, under the direction of Arthur Storch and starring Jack Lemmon; also produced in Paris, Rome and Sidney.

Romantic Comedy: full-length comedy; written in 1978; to be published by Samuel French in 1980; first produced by Morton Gottlieb at the Ethel Barrymore Theater, New York, in 1979, under the direction of Joe Hardy and starring Tony Perkins and Mia Farrow.

Miscellaneous

Of numerous scripts written for television, the following have been chosen for listing:

The Prize Winner: a 60-minute television play; written in 1957; unpublished; first produced by CBC in 1958, directed by Paul Almond and starring Tom Harvey and Bruno Gerussi; subsequently re-written as *The Long, Long Laugh*; unpublished; produced by NBC on *Matinee Theater* in 1958, starring Russell Armes, June Lockhart; produced by CBS on *U.S. Steel Hour*, starring Arthur Hill and Teresa Wright.

The following teleplays were written between 1958 and 1964 and were all produced by CBC: *Men Don't Make Passes, Innocent Deception, The Gimmick, Do Jerry Parker, The Most Beautiful Girl in the World, The Big Coin Sound, The Oddball, The Reluctant Angels, Blue is for Boys.*

Bewitched: sixteen 30-minute episodes for the series.

Pilot television films for the following series: *Love on a Rooftop, The Flying Nun, The Partridge Family, Bridget Loves Bernie, The Girl with Something Extra, Mr. Deeds Goes to Town, The Bobby Sherman Show, Mr. Angel.*

Over sixty 30-minute episodes for various television series.

Stand Up and Be Counted; feature film; directed by Jackie Cooper; starring Jacqueline Bissett, Steve Lawrence, Loretta Swit, Stella Stevens.

Same Time, Next Year: film script adapted from the stage play; directed by Robert Mulligan and starring Ellen Burstyn and Alan Alda; nominated for Academy Award for best screenplay.

Tribute: film script adapted from the stage play; directed by Bob Clark and starring Jack Lemmon, Robbie Benson, Lee Remick and Colleen Dewhurst.

Ben Tarver

Born August 15, 1927, in El Paso, Texas. After receiving his Bachelor of Fine Arts degree from the University of New Mexico in 1950, he spends two years as a graduate student at the University of Denver. His first play, *Shakespeare, New Mexico*, is also his M.A. thesis.

Moving to New York in 1956, he begins 13 years in the professional theatre as an actor, stage manager and writer, as well as producing and directing off-Broadway shows. His professional directing credits include Upton Sinclair's *Cicero* in 1959, Gene Feldman's *Go Show Me a Dragon*, one year later, and *David Show* by A.R. Gurney Jr. He also works as an actor in television. *Man With a Load of Mischief*, another of his plays, receives its first production at the Jan Hus Auditorium in New York in 1966.

In 1969, he moves to Canada to teach playwriting at the University of Alberta. *The Savage Dream*, the first of his "Canadian" plays, is produced by Edmonton's Theatre 3 in 1971. Married and still teaching at the University of Alberta, he continues to make his home in Edmonton.

Stage Writing

Shakespeare, New Mexico: full-length; written as an M.A. thesis; written between 1951 and 1952; unpublished; unproduced.

Zalamea: full-length musical; unpublished; unproduced.

Arriba: three acts; unpublished; unproduced.

How Dirty Can You Get?: a comedy in two parts; unpublished; unproduced.

One of Our Millionaires Is Missing: full-length; unpublished; produced in trial production by Donald Goldman, Edmonton, in 1970.

Man With a Load of Mischief: two-act musical; written between 1964 and 1965; first published by Samuel French, New York, 1967; first produced at the Jan Hus Auditorium, New York, 1966, under the direction of Tom Gruenwal; subsequently produced by New Watergate Presentations Ltd. at the Comedy Theatre, London, under the direction of Bernard Delfont and Tom Arnold.

167

The Savage Dream: two-act adaptation of Calderon's *Life is a Dream*; written in 1970; first published by Playwrights Co-op, Toronto, 1972; first produced by Theatre Three, Edmonton, 1971, under the direction of Mark Schoenberg.

The Perfect Mollusc: two acts; written between 1976 and 1977; unpublished; first produced by Donald Goldman at the Players Theater, New York City, 1977, under the direction of George Wojtozek.

The Murder of Auguste Dupin: two-act comic mystery; written between 1976 and 1977; unpublished; first produced at Lennoxville Festival, 1979; subsequently produced by Northern Light Theatre, Edmonton, and also by New Mexico State University in 1980.

Just Tell Them That You Saw Me: musical; "based on the music of Paul Dresser (*My Gal Sal, On the Banks of the Wabash*) and his younger brother Theodore Dreiser (*Sister Carrie, An American Tragedy*)"; written in 1979 with music by Frank Moher; unpublished; unproduced.

Radio Writing

The Journey North: 30 minutes; written in 1977; first produced by CBC Radio, Edmonton, 1977, for regional broadcast.

The Vidoco Society: three 30-minute episodes; written with Gordon Pengilly in 1978; first produced by CBC Radio, Winnipeg, in 1978.

Film Scripts

Mountain of Fear: unpublished; unproduced.

Black Ball: unpublished; unproduced.

Alamogordo: full-length; written in 1975.

Cross and Cockade: full-length; written in 1972.

Getting There is All the Fun: full-length; written in 1974.

Skam: 90 minutes; written in 1978 with Bill Meilen and Henry Wolfe.

Miscellaneous

Walking Small: 90 minutes; written in 1978 with Bill Meilen and Henry Wolfe.

The Perfect Mollusc: a television version of the play.

The Montgomery Project: two parts of a projected six-part mini-series for television; commissioned by ITV, Edmonton.

In Progress

The Wildly Well Affair: a stage play.

The Trouble Man: a film script.

Aforesaid Bates: a stage play.

Yves Thériault

Born November 28, 1915, in Quebec City. While still a young child, he and his family move to an English-speaking suburb of Montreal. He attends Ecole-Notre-Dame-de-Grace and later Ecole Mont-Saint-Louis, the only French schools in the district. Fluent in both languages, he completes his formal education in 1929, at the age of 16, and realizes a lifelong ambition by beating 298 other applicants for a job as an announcer at CHNC, New Carlisle, a small provincial radio station. This is followed by a string of announcing jobs, mostly at radio stations outside Montreal, including CHNT (Quebec City), CHLT (Trois Rivières) and CKCH (Hull). During this 12-year period, he works as well as a talent-scout, producer and, on occasion, script writer. As part of a gradual move away from announcing, he writes his first radio script for CKCH in 1940. His frequent contact with the people of rural Quebec, whose way of life is still by-and-large traditional, provides him with material for much of his writing.

During the early part of his career, he develops tuberculosis, due to "primitive living conditions" and "habitual overwork." While recovering in a sanatorium on Lake Edward, Quebec he becomes enamoured with nature and this too provides a source of inspiration for his work. In 1942 he marries Michelle-Germaine Blanchet.

From time to time, he leaves radio for short forays into the business world. On one occasion, he works successfully as a tractor salesman. He leaves a job as an advertising promoter, however, because he finds the work "too frustrating." During other absences from broadcasting, he spends a year as a reporter for a Toronto newspaper and from 1942 to 1945 is a publicist and script-writer for the National Film Board of Canada. By this time, he is writing in both English and French and has almost completed the slow transition from announcer to writer. From 1944 onwards, his scripts win wide acclaim. In the same year, *Contes d'un homme seul*, a collection of short stories, is the first of his works to

Kéro

be published. Under contract to Radio-Canada, he writes his first radio serial, *La flamme du feu* between 1945 and 1950. Over the years he writes more than 1,300 radio and television scripts of all types for French-language programs such as *Sur toutes les scenes du monde, Théâtre populaire, En première* as well as for English series such as *Vancouver Theatre* and *Winnipeg Theatre.*

At the same time, he continues a parallel career as a novelist and writer of short stories. In 1950 he makes his debut as a playwright when *Le marcheur*, his first stage play, is produced at Montreal's Théâtre Gésu. As a dramatist, he demonstrates a strong interest in the family, a subject common among Quebec artists. In 1952, during a further absence from broadcasting, he tours the world while working on an Italian cargo ship and spends several months in Italy. His contribution to radio drama is recognized when, in 1953, he receives a prize for dramatic art from Radio-Canada. In 1958, his dramatic writing is honoured once again, this time with the presentation of Radio-Canada's Fignon Trophy for his television script *Aaron*. In the same year he is made a member of the Royal Society of

Canada. His novel *Ashini* wins the Governor General's Award in 1961. *Ashini*, along with *Agaguk*, also a novel, is awarded the 1962 Prix France-Canada.

Between 1965 and 1967 he serves as director of cultural affairs for the Quebec Ministry of Indian and Northern Affairs. In 1970 he wins the Molson Prize. With his wife and two children, he currently makes his home in Montreal.

Stage Writing

Le marcheur: three-act drama; written in 1949; first published by Leméac, Montreal, 1968; first produced at Théâtre Gésu, Montreal, 1950 under the direction of Huguette Oligny; adapted for radio and television; produced by Radio-Canada, Montreal, 1953; televised by Radio-Canada, 1956.

Bérangère ou la chair en feu: three-act comedy; written in 1960; published by Leméac, 1970 in same volume as *Les terres neuves* and *Frédange*; first produced by Théâtre de la Fenière, Notre-Dame-de-Lorette, Quebec, 1965, on the same program as *Frédange* and *Les terres neuves* under the direction of Georges Delisle.

Frédange; two-act drama; written in 1964; first published by Leméac, 1970 in the same volume as *Bérangère ou la chair en feu* and *Les terres neuves*; first produced by Théâtre de la Fenière, 1965 on the same program as *Bérangère ou la chair en feu* and *Les terres neuves* under the direction of Georges Delisle.

Les terres neuves: two-act drama; written in 1964; first published by Lémeac, 1970 in the same volume as *Bérangère ou la chair en feu* and *Frédange*; first produced by Théâtre de la Fenière, 1965, on the same program as Bérangère ou la chair en feu and *Frédange* under the direction of Georges Delisle.

Radio Writing

A selection

N'Mangolole magnifique: 30-minute drama; written in 1945; produced by Radio-

Canada, 1952 for the series *Nouveautés dramatiques.*

Sarah-la-borgne: 60-minute drama; written in 1945; produced by Radio-Canada, 1945.

Printemps du trouble: 30-minute drama; written in 1945; produced by Radio-Canada, 1945 for the series *La voix du pays.*

La belle moisson: 30-minute drama; written in 1946; produced by Radio-Canada, 1946.

Conte des moissons: 30-minute drama; written in 1946; produced by Radio-Canada, 1946.

David: 30-minute drama; written in 1946; produced by Radio-Canada, 1946, for the series *Théâtre Populaire.*

Le samaritain: 60-minute drama; written in 1952; published in *Ecrits du Canada français*, Volume 4, 1952; produced by Radio-Canada, 1952; winner of the 1952 Radio-Canada Grand Prize.

La colère: 30-minute drama; written in 1953; produced by Radio Canada, 1953, for the series *Nouveautés dramatiques.*

M'Batilaya: 30-minute drama; written in 1954; produced by Radio-Canada, 1954 for the series *Nouveautés dramatiques.*

La grue: drama; written in 1955; produced by CBF, Montreal (part of the Radio-Canada network) 1955, for the series *Nouveautés dramatiques.*

Peintre-avant-garde: satire; produced by CBF Montreal, 1956, for the series *La ineffables.*

Atisokan: 30-minute drama; written in 1962; produced by CBF Montreal, 1962, for the series *Sur toutes les scènes du monde.*

Television Writing

A selection

Aaron: 120-minute drama; written in 1958; produced by Radio-Canada, 1958 for the series *Théâtre populaire*; winner of the 1958

Radio-Canada Fignon Trophy.

Déclin: 90-minute drama; written in 1958; produced by Radio-Canada, 1958 for the series *En première.*

Dieudonne et l'abus des biens: 90-minute comedy; written in 1958; produced by Radio-Canada, 1958 for the series *En première.*

Prose Fiction

A selection

Contes pour un homme seul: short stories; written in 1943; first published by Editions de l'Arbe, Montreal, 1944; subsequently published by Editions HMH, Montreal, 1965.

La fille laide: novel; written in 1949; first published by Editions Beauchemin, Montreal, 1950; subsequently published by Editions de l'Homme, Montreal, 1965.

Les vendeurs du temple: novel; written in 1950; first published by L'Institute littéraire du Québec, Quebec City, 1951; subsequently published by Editions de l'Homme, 1964.

Le compteur d'ours: novel; written in 1950; published by Cercle du Livre de France, Montreal, 1951; subsequently published by Editions de l'Homme, 1965.

Aaron: novel; written in 1957; first published by L'Institut littéraire du Québec, Quebec City, 1951; subsequently published by Editions de l'Homme, 1966; published in German by Herbig, Berlin; published in Japanese by Riron-Sha, Tokyo, 1960; published in Portuguese by Portugalia, Lisbon, 1960; published in Serbo-Croat by Znanje, Zagreb, 1961; published in Italian by Aldo Martello, Milan, 1962; published in English by Ryerson Press, Toronto, 1963; winner of Premier prix de la province de Québec, 1957.

Alerte au Compe 29: novel; written in 1958; published by Editions Beauchemin, 1959, as part of the collection *Les Ailes du Nord* (for teenagers).

La revanche du Nascopie: novel; written in 1958; published by Editions Beauchemin, 1959, as part of the collection *Les Ailes du Nord.*

Ashini: novel; written in 1959; first published by Editions Fides, Montreal, 1960; subsequently reprinted by Editions Fides, 1965, winner of the Governor General's Award, 1961, and the Prix France-Canada, 1962 (with Agaguk).

L'Homme de la Papinachois: novel; written in 1959; published by Editions Beauchemin, 1960, as part of the collection *Les Ailes du Nord.*

La loi de l'Apache: novel; written in 1959; published by Editions Beauchemin, 1960 as part of the collection *Les Ailes du Nord.*

Roi de la Coté Nord—La vie extraordinaire de Napoléon-Alexandre Comeau: narrative; written in 1959; published by Editions de l'Homme, 1960.

Amour au goût de mer: novel; written in 1960; published by Editions Beauchemin, 1961.

Cul-de-sac: novel; written in 1960; published by l'Institut littéraire du Québec, 1961.

Les commettants de Caridid: novel; written in 1960; first published by L'Institut littéraire du Québec, 1961; subsequently published by Editions de l'Homme, 1966.

Le vendeur d'étoiles et autres contes: short stories; written in 1960; published by Editions Fides, 1961; winner of 1961 Prix Msgr. Camille Roy.

Séjour à Moscou: novel; written in 1960; published by Editions Fides, 1961.

Si la bombe m'était contée: novel; written in 1961; published by Editions du Jour, 1962.

Le grand roman d'un petit homme: novel; written in 1962; published by Editions du Jour, 1963.

Le rue d'Ikoué: novel; written in 1962; published by Editions Fides, 1963.

La rose de pierre—histoires d'amour: short stories; written in 1963; published by Editions du Jour, 1964.

L'appelante: novel; written in 1966; published by Editions du Jour, 1967.

Kesten: novel; written in 1967; published by Editions du Jour, 1968.

La morte d'eau: novel; written in 1967; published by Editions de l'Homme, 1968.

L'ile introuvable: short stories; written in 1967; published by Editions du Jour, 1968.

Mahigan: novel; written in 1967; published by Leméac, 1968.

N'Tsuk: novel; written in 1967; published by Editions de l'Homme, 1968.

Antoine et sa montagne: novel; written in 1968; published by Editions du Jour, 1969.

Tayaout fils d'Agaguk: novel; written in 1968; published by Editions de l'Homme, 1969.

Textes et documents: essays; published by Leméac, 1969.

Valérie: novel; written in 1968; published by Editions du Jour, 1969.

Le dernier havre: novel; written in 1969; published by L'Actuelle, Montreal, 1970.

Le haut pays: novel; written in 1972; published by René Ferron, Editeur, Montreal, 1973.

Moi, Pierre Hunneau: narrative with illustrations by Louisa Nicol; written in 1975; published by Editions Hurtubise, Montreal, 1976.

Michel Tremblay

Born June 25, 1942 and grows up in a working-class neighbourhood in east-end Montreal. Son of Armand Tremblay, a linotype operator, and his wife Rheauna. The family share a seven-room house occupied by a total of 13 people. The introduction of television in 1952 sparks his interest in theatre and he quickly becomes a devoted viewer of the bi-weekly dramas offered by CBC-TV (Radio-Canada). In 1955, he is awarded a scholarship to a Montreal school for gifted children. Finding its exclusive atmosphere distasteful, however, he soon returns to public school. At the age of 14, he sees his first live theatrical performance and at the same time begins to write plays in the style of the television dramas he is so used to.

Leaving school at the age of 17, he finds work as a linotype operator. During this

Jean-Pierre Karsenty

period he writes *Le Train*, a television play which wins first prize in the 1964 Radio-Canada Contest for Young Authors and which is produced by the network that same year. In 1964, he also meets director André Brassard who through the years becomes one of his closest friends and collaborators. Two years later, a volume of short stories, *Contes pour buveurs attardés* is published and *Cinq*, a one-act play, is produced by Mouvement contemporain. The same year, his full-length play, *Les Belles-Soeurs* is turned down by the jury of the Dominion Drama Festival. The first Quebec play to be written entirely in *joual*, the language of the working class, *Les Belles-Soeurs* later receives a public reading at Montreal's Centre d'Essai des auteurs dramatiques in 1968, followed soon after by a successful production at Théâtre du Rideau Vert. He spends two months in Mexico during that year on a Canada Council grant where he writes *La cité dans l'oeuf*, his first novel, and the dramatic monologue, *La Duchesse de Langeais*.

A fervent Quebec nationalist, his plays reflect both his political and social concerns. As he writes later, "If I choose to talk about the fringes of society it is because my people are a fringe society. We are six million French people in a North America of 300 million people. And in this fringe society in which I was raised I decided to make my point." Commenting on *Hosanna*, one of his most successful plays in both French and English and which subsequently plays on Broadway, he points out that the title character "is a man who always wanted to be a woman. This woman always wanted to be Elizabeth Taylor in *Cleopatra*. In other words, this Quebecois always wanted to be a woman who always wanted to be an English actress in an American movie about an Egyptian myth in a movie shot in Spain. In a way, that is a typically Quebecois problem. For the past 300 years we were not taught that we were a people, so we were dreaming about being somebody else instead of ourselves." Among his many adaptations are works by Aristophanes, Paul Zindel and Tennessee Williams.

Until 1977, he refuses to allow his plays to be done in English in Quebec. That year, however, he gives permission to Festival Lennoxville to stage *Forever Yours Marie-Lou*. Later that year, he completes *Damnée Manon, Sacrée Sandra*, the eleventh in the cycle of plays begun with *Les Belles Soeurs*. Shortly thereafter, he announces his intention to take a rest from the theatre and devotes himself to *La Grosse Femme d'à côté est enceinte*, a novel which is published in 1978. He returns to the theatre with a satire, *L'Impromptu d'Outremont*, which is produced in both French and English in 1980.

Single, he continues to make his home in Montreal.

Stage Writing

Le Train: one act; written in 1960; unpublished; unproduced; winner of the 1964 CBC competition for young writers.

Messe noire: adaptation for the stage of selections from Tremblay's short story collection, *Contes pour buveurs attardés;* written in 1965; unpublished; first produced by "Mouvement contemporain" troupe at Théâtre du Gésu, Montreal, 1965, under the direction of André Brassard.

Cinq: six one-act plays; written in 1966; they include *Berthe, Johnny Mangano and his Astonishing Dogs* and *Gloria Star* which are later published by Leméac, Montreal, 1971; the same three plays along with *La Duchesse de Langeais* are subsequently published in English by Talonbooks, Vancouver, 1976, in a translation by John Van Burek; first produced by Mouvement contemporain, 1966, under the direction of André Brassard; *Berthe, Johnny Mangano and his Astonishing Dogs, Gloria Star* televised by Radio-Canada, 1969, under the title *Trois Petits Tours* for the series *Les Beaux Dimanches*; re-broadcast, 1971; *Les Socles (The Pedestals)* is published in both French and English in *CTR 23* (Fall 1979) (English translation by Renate Usmiane).

Les Belles-Soeurs: full-length; written in 1965; first published by Holt, Rinehart and Winston, Montreal, 1968; subsequently published by Leméac, 1972; first published in English by Talonbooks, 1974 in a translation by John Van Burek and Bill Glassco; first produced by Théâtre du Rideau Vert, Montreal, 1968, under the direction of André Brassard; subsequently produced at Place des Arts, Montreal and in Paris, 1973, under the direction of Brassard; first produced in English, under the same title by St. Lawrence Centre, Toronto, 1973, under the direction of Brassard; judged best foreign play of the year, Paris, 1973; adapted for television; produced in English by CBC, 1978.

En pièces détachées: full-length; revised version of *Cinq* including two new sketches; written in 1968; first published by Leméac, 1970, in same volume as *La Duchesse de Langeais;* first published in English, under the title *Like Death Warmed Over*, by Playwrights Co-op, Toronto, 1973, with translation by Allan Van Meer; subsequently published under the title *Montreal Smoked Meat*, by Talonbooks, 1975, with translation by Allan Van Meer; first produced by Mouvement contemporain, 1969, under the direction of André Brassard; adapted for television, 1971; produced by CBC Montreal, 1971, as part of series *Les Beaux Dimanches*; first produced in English, under the title *Like Death Warmed Over* by Manitoba Theatre Centre, Winnipeg, 1973, under the direction of Brassard; subsequently produced under the title *Montreal Smoked Meat*, by New Theatre, Toronto, 1974, under the direction of Jonathan Stanley; produced under the title *Broken Pieces* by Arts Club Theatre, Vancouver, 1974, under the direction of Bill Millerd.

La Duchesse de Langeais: monologue; written in 1968; first published by Leméac, 1970, in same volume as *En pièces détachées*; subsequently published by Leméac, 1973, in same volume as *Hosanna*; first published in English in *La Duchesse de Langeais and Other Plays* by Talonbooks, 1976; first produced by Les Insolents, Val d'Or, 1969, under the direction of Hélène Bélanger; subsequently produced by Théâtre du Nouveau Monde at the Théâtre de Quat'Sous, Montreal, 1970, under the direction of André Brassard.

Lysistrata: adaptation of the play by Aristophanes; written in 1968; first published by Leméac, 1969; first produced by Théâtre du Nouveau Monde at the

National Arts Centre, Ottawa, 1969, under the direction of André Brassard.

L' Effet des rayons gamma sur les vieux garçons: translation of Paul Zindel's *The Effect of Gamma Rays on Man-in-the-Moon Marigolds*; written in 1969; first published by Leméac, 1970; first produced by Théâtre de Quat'Sous, 1970, under the direction of André Brassard.

Demain matin, Montreal, m'attend: musical-comedy with music by François Dompierre; written in 1969; revised version published by Leméac, 1972; first produced by Jardin des Etoiles à la Ronde, 1970, under the direction of André Brassard; revised version produced at Place des Arts, 1972, under the direction of Brassard.

A toi pour toujours ta, Marie-Lou: full-length; written in 1970; first published by Leméac, 1971; published in English under the title *Forever Yours, Marie-Lou*, by Talonbooks, 1975, with translation by John Van Burek and Bill Glassco; first produced by Théâtre de Quat'Sous, 1971, under the direction of André Brassard; first produced in English under the title *Forever Yours, Marie-Lou*, by Tarragon Theatre, Toronto, 1972, under the direction of Bill Glassco.

Les Paons: one-act fantasy; written in 1970; unpublished; first produced by l'Atelier d'Ottawa, 1971.

Et Mademoiselle Roberge boit un peu: translation and adaptation of Paul Zindel's *And Miss Reardon Drinks a Little*; written in 1970; first produced by Leméac, 1971; first produced at Place des Arts, 1972, under the direction of André Brassard.

Au pays du dragon: four one-act plays translated and adapted from Tennessee Williams; written in 1971; unpublished; first produced by Théâtre de Quat'Sous, 1972, under the direction of André Brassard.

Hosanna: full-length; written in 1972; first published by Leméac, 1973, in same volume as *La Duchesse de Langeais*; published in English under the same title by Talonbooks, 1974 in a translation by John Van Burek and Bill Glassco; first produced by Théâtre de Quat'Sous, 1973, under the direction of André Brassard; first produced in English by Tarragon Theatre, 1974, starring Richard Monette and under the direction of Bill Glassco; subsequently taken on a national tour and produced on Broadway under the direction of Bill Glassco (30 performances).

Mistero Bufo: translation and adaptation of the play by Dario Fo; written in 1972; unpublished; first produced by Théâtre du Nouveau Monde, 1973, under the direction of André Brassard.

Bonjour, là, bonjour: full-length; written in 1973; first published by Leméac, 1974; first published in English, under same title, by Talonbooks, 1975; first produced by National Arts Centre in Montreal, 1974, under the direction of André Brassard; first produced in English by Tarragon Theatre, Toronto, 1975, under the direction of Bill Glassco.

Surprise! Surprise: one act; written in 1974; first published by Leméac, 1977, in same volume as *Damnée Manon, Sacrée Sandra*; first published in English by Talonbooks, 1976, in the same volume as *La Duchesse de Langeais, Berthe, Johnny Mangano and his Astonishing Dogs* and *Gloria Star* in a translation by John Van Burek; first produced by Théâtre du Nouveau Monde, 1975, under the direction of André Brassard; first produced in English by Toronto Arts Productions (St. Lawrence Centre), 1975, under the direction of Eric Steiner.

Les héros de mon enfance: musical-comedy with music by Sylvain Lelière; first published by Leméac, 1976, first produced by Théâtre de Marjolaine, Eastman, Quebec, 1976, under the direction of Gaàtan Labrèche.
Toronto, 1976.

Mademoiselle Marguerite: translation and adaptation of Roberto Athayde's *Aparaceu a Margarida*; written in 1974; first published by Leméac, 1975; first produced at National Arts Centre, 1976, under the direction of Jean Dalmain; subsequently produced by Théâtre de P'tit Bonheur, Toronto, 1976.

Sainte Carmen de la Main: full-length; written in 1975; first published by Leméac, 1976; first published in English, under the title *Saint Carmen of the Main*, by Talonbooks, 1978, in a translation by John Van Burek; first produced during the Olympics at Place des Arts, Montreal, 1976, under the direction of André Brassard; subsequently produced by Théâtre du Nouveau Monde, 1978, under the direction of Brassard; first produced in English, by Tarragon Theatre, Toronto, 1978, under the direction of Brassard.

Damnée Manon, Sacrée Sandra: long one-act; written in 1977; first published by Leméac, 1977, in same volume as *Surprise! Surprise!*; first produced by Théâtre de Quat'Sous, 1977, under the direction of André Brassard; first produced in English by Mount St. Vincent University, Halifax, 1978; subsequently produced by Tarragon Theatre, 1979, under the direction of Bill Glassco.

L'impromptu d'Outremont: full-length; written in 1979; unpublished, first produced by Théâtre du Nouveau Monde, 1980, under the direction of André Brassard; first produced in English at Tarragon Theatre, Toronto, 1980.

Film Scripts

Françoise Durocher, Waitress: 29 minutes; written in 1971; produced by National Film Board of Canada, 1972, under the direction of André Brassard; televised by Radio-Canada, 1972; winner of the 1975 Canadian Film Festival Award for best scenario.

Backyard Theatre: film on Tremblay and Brassard with characters from *Les Belles-Soeurs* and *Demain matin, Montréal m'attend*; produced by National Film Board of Canada, 1972.

Il etait une fois dans l'est: 100 minutes; written in 1973 in collaboration with André Brassard; published by L'Aurore, Montreal, 1974; distributed by Cine/Art, Montreal; official Canadian entry to the 1974 Cannes Film Festival.

Le Soleil se lève en retard: 112minutes; written in 1974; directed by André Brassard; distributed by Films 16, Montreal; televised by Radio-Canada, 1979.

Parlez-vous d'amour: written in 1974; directed by Jean-Claude Lord; distributed by Films 16.

Miscellaneous

Contes pour buveurs attardés: short stories; written in 1965; first published by Editions du Jour, Montreal, 1966.

Manous: short story; written in 1965; first published in *La Barre de Jour*, January-February 1966.

La Cité dans l'oeuf: novel; written in 1968; first published by Editions du Jour, 1969.

C't'a tontour, Laura Cadieux: novel; written in 1972; first published by Editions du Jour, 1973.

Bonheur d'occasion: television script adapted from the novel of the same name by Gabriel Roy; written in 1977; unproduced.

La Grosse Femme d'à coté est enceinte: novel; written in 1977; first published by Leméac, 1978.

Secondary Sources

In English:

Casebook on Tremblay included in *Canadian Theatre Review*, Fall 1979 (*CTR* 24).

Section on Tremblay included in *Stage Voices*, (Geraldine Anthony ed.) Doubleday, 1978, pp.

In French:

Michel Belair, *Michel Tremblay*, Montreal: Presses de l'Université du Québec, 1972.

Jean-Cleo Goden and Laurent mailhot, *Le Théâtre Québécois*, Montreal, Editions HMH, 1970, pp. 191-202.

Herman Voaden

Born on January 19, 1903, in London, Ontario. Son of Dr. Arthur Voaden, principal of the St. Thomas Collegiate Institute and the Arthur Voaden Vocational School in St. Thomas. Upon graduation from the St. Thomas Collegiate Institute in 1920, he enters Queen's University in Kingston. It is here that his life-long enthusiasm for theatre begins with comprehensive courses in modern drama. He is greatly attracted to the revolt then being made against realism in theatre.

V. Tony Hauser

Graduating in 1923, he moves to Toronto to take teacher training courses at the College of Education. This begins a period of intensive playgoing which continues during two years of teaching at Glebe Collegiate Institute in Ottawa (1924-1926) and as head of the English Department of the Windsor-Walkerville Technical School, Windsor (1926-1928). He travels to theatres in Toronto and Detroit and makes frequent trips to New York City.

As well as pursuing his theatre interest by attending avant-garde performances over these years, he completes his Master's degree at Queen's University in 1926 with a thesis on Eugene O'Neill. At about this same time, he begins his practical theatre work as an actor playing the young gangster in O'Neill's *The Dreamy Kid* at Hart House Theatre. He continues acting at the Detroit Repertory Theater.

While in Sarnia, he becomes the first director of the city's Drama League and seeks to strengthen the community theatre movement by showing how a small centre could have a vital theatre with the highest artistic standards. By 1928, after a summer of theatre-going in Europe, he is again in Toronto where he takes up an appointment as director of English at the Central High School of Commerce. In addition to his day-time teaching, where theatre forms an integral part of his work, he directs an evening adult play-production course and produces such writers as Shaw, Barrie, Synge, Yeats and O'Neill at the school's newly-constructed theatre space. He has also begun writing articles for the *Globe and Mail* and these are used in his crusade to develop a strong national theatre. Also in

1929, he sends a letter to Vincent Massey suggesting a National Drama Festival modelled on the British Drama League and his ideas are later incorporated in the founding of the Dominion Drama Festival in 1933. A festival of one-act plays that he conducts at Central Commerce at this time stipulates that the plays entered must "have an exterior setting and in character and atmosphere reflect phases of Canadian life in Northern Ontario". From the plays entered in this 1929 festival, he selects six for publication in 1930 in an anthology called *Six Canadian Plays*.

Through his University of Toronto Drama course, two performance groups emerge in 1930. One is directed by Glen Liston and the other by Dora Mavor Moore. These groups reflect his interest and collaboration with the Group of Seven who have already inspired much of his thinking on Canadian art in general and the theatre in particular. During the summer of this year, he travels across Canada with Lowrie Warrener and together they write "a painter's ballet" called *The Symphony*. That fall he begins a year at Yale University where, in addition to other drama courses, he studies playwriting with O'Neill's former teacher, George Pierce Baker.

While at Yale, he writes an essentially

realistic piece entitled *Wilderness* but, after a workshop of the play at Yale and a production by the Faculty Players at Queen's, he returns to Toronto in 1932 and rewrites it, stripping it of all realistic detail. Retitling it *Rocks*, he presents it on the Commerce Stage and it is the first example of the new theatre he endeavors to establish—"symphonic expressionism". It attracts great interest and he restages it that fall and includes the reading of seven poems with the production. He describes these as "theatral poems" and tries to enhance the reading by using single and multiple voices, changing multi-coloured lights and sculpturally posed figures.

In 1967, he organizes the St. Adèle Seminar to examine Centennial initiatives and future directions for the performing arts in Canada. As President of the Canadian Guild of Crafts (1968-1970) he helps establish a single multi-media craft organization. He is elected a Fellow of the Royal Society of Arts in 1970 and 1974 sees him appointed a member of the Order of Canada.

An exhibition by Hart House Theatre in 1974 honours his work. That year he also completes another anthology, *Look Both Ways: Theatre Experiences*, and begins working on his genealogy and biography, *The Book of the Voadens*. He presently lives in Toronto, continuing his work on *The Book of the Voadens* and a memoir of his theatre experiences.

Earth Song, is produced by the Sarnia Drama League in 1932 and further develops his concept. Following this production he travels extensively through Europe and the Orient for most of 1933. While in Germany, he experiences some of the results of Hitler's takeover. His next play, *Hill-Land*, is written during this period and is produced as part of a Play Workshop which he initiates in Toronto in 1934.

He marries in 1935, the year that he writes *Murder Pattern* which is produced in 1936 by The Play Workshop and later entered in that year's Dominion Drama Festival. As this is a further step toward "symphonic expressionism", the adjudicator sees fit to place it outside the realm of "dramatic art", though its striking effect is given due credit.

Play Workshop members at this time include such people as Jamieson Field, Dora Smith Conover, A. Bertram Green, J.E. Middleton and T.M. Morrow. He has two major successes in 1936. One, a mimed production of *Romeo and Juliet* to the music of Tchaikowsky's *Overture*,

is staged at the Varsity Arena as part of the Promenade Concert Series sponsored by the University of Toronto and viewed by an audience of over 5,000 people. The other is the first Canadian production of T.S.Eliot's *Murder in the Cathedral*, first shown at Queen's University and later at Toronto's Massey Hall.

He continues to write and produce his own work and, in 1938, scenes from his adaptation of Louis Hémon's novel, *Maria Chapdelaine,* are presented for the Dominion Drama Festival at Hart House Theatre. After *Maria Chapdelaine*, he begins work on what he hopes will be a full cycle of plays and the result is *Ascend as the Sun*. It is produced at Hart House Theatre with the Boris Volkoff Dancers and music by Godfrey Ridout in 1942.

His next work is a dance drama based on Poe's *The Masque of the Red Door* presented on the Commerce Stage in 1943 with music by Godfrey Ridout. That year he begins a collaboration with American composer Frederick Jacobi to write the libretto for an opera, *The Prodigal Son*. Also in 1943, he joins the Co-operative Commonwealth Federation, now known as the New Democratic Party.

He begins a long career at this time of lobbying for the arts by being part of a committee which prepares a brief for presentation to the Turgeon Committee of the House of Commons. He writes the summary of the group's proposals and is part of the delegation which presents it on June 21, 1944, during a march on Parliament Hill. Shortly thereafter, the lobby group formalizes itself into the Canadian Arts Council (now the Canadian Conference of the Arts) and he becomes its first president (1945-1948). As president, he plays a leading role in arranging for Canada's participation in the 1948 Cultural Olympics. In 1949 and 1950, he is a member of a committee to prepare and present a brief to the Massey Commission.

His time for writing is severely diminished by his continued teaching and cultural/political activities. He completes only three theatre pieces over the next 10 years — *Coronation Ode* presented by CBC in 1953; *Emily Carr* written for the 1958 play competition sponsored by the Stratford Festival and the Toronto *Globe and Mail*; and *Esther*, a libretto for a dramatic symphony composed by Godfrey Ridout and produced in 1952. Much of his writing time is taken up with the preparation of briefs: one for the Royal Commission on Broadcasting (1956); two (1965-1966) presented to the Royal

Commission on Bilingualism and Bi-culturalism; and a report, *The Arts and Education*, written under the auspices of the Canadian Conference of the Arts while he is Associate and then National Director of that organization (1966-1968).

Stage Writing

Wilderness: one-act realistic drama; written at the Yale School of Drama between 1930 and 1931; first published in *Boreal*, 10-11, Hearst College, Ontario, in 1978; subsequently published by Canadian Theatre Review Publications, Toronto, in 1980 in *Canada's Lost Plays: The Developing Mosaic*, Vol. III; first produced as a workshop by Yale University; subsequently produced by the Faculty Players, Queen's University, Kingston, in 1931.

Rocks: one-act symphonic drama; a revised, non-realistic, stylized version of *Wilderness*; written in 1932; first produced by the Play Workshop at Central High School of Commerce, Toronto, in 1932, under the direction of the author; production repeated in the fall of 1932, also under the direction of the author; subsequently produced at the regional finals of the Dominion Drama Festival, Hart House Theatre, Toronto, in 1933, under the direction of Gordon Alderson; produced at Queen's University, Kingston, in 1934, under the direction of the author.

Earth Song: five-cycle symphonic drama; written in 1932; first published by Playwrights Co-op, Toronto, in 1976; first produced by the Sarnia Drama League, Sarnia, in 1932, under the direction of the author.

Hill-Land: two-act symphonic drama; written in 1933; unpublished; first produced by the Play Workshop, Toronto, in 1944, under the direction of the author; scene five of this play was subsequently produced for the regional finals of the Dominion Drama Festival at Hart House Theatre, Toronto, in 1935, under the direction of the author.

Murder Pattern: one-act symphonic drama; written in 1935; first published in *Canadian Theatre Review*, Winter 1975 (*CTR* 5); subsequently published by Canadian Theatre Review Publications in 1980 in *Canada's Lost Plays: The Developing Mosaic*; first produced by

the Play Workshop, Toronto, in 1936, under the direction of the author; subsequently produced for the Dominion Drama Festival Regional Competition at Hart House Theatre, Toronto, in 1936, under the direction of the author.

Maria Chapdelaine: a drama in 16 scenes; based on the book by Louis Hémon; written in 1937 and 1938; unpublished; first produced in part by the Play Workshop, Toronto, in 1938, and repeated for the Dominion Drama Festival Regional Finals at Hart House Theatre, Toronto, in 1938, under the direction of the author; a reading performance of the full-length play was given at the Canadian Literature Club, Toronto, in 1947, under the direction of the author and starring Lorne Greene and Charmion King.

Ascend as the Sun: two-act symphonic drama; written between 1938 and 1941; unpublished; first produced at Hart House Theatre, Toronto, with Boris Volkoff Dancers and with music by Godfrey Ridout in 1942, under the direction of the author.

Brébeuf and His Brethren: a libretto for a pageant in 13 scenes with music by Healey Willan; based on a poem by E.J. Pratt; written in 1941 for production at the site of historic Fort Ste. Marie; project not completed; unpublished; unproduced.

The Prodigal Son: libretto for an opera composed by Frederick Jacobi; written between 1943 and 1945; unpublished; first produced for the Forest Hill Concert and Theatre Series in 1954, under the direction of Jack McAllister with choreography by Gweneth Lloyd.

Esther: libretto for a dramatic symphony composed by Godfrey Ridout; written in 1952; first produced by the Royal Conservatory Symphony Orchestra at Massey Hall, Toronto, in 1952; the text was printed in the program; subsequently produced for the opening ceremonies of the Edward Johnson Building at the MacMillan Theatre, Toronto, in 1964.

Emily Carr: written in 1958; unpublished; first produced by the Department of Drama, Queen's University, Kingston, in 1960, under the direction of William Angus, starring Amelia Hall; subsequently produced by the Greater Victoria Centennial Society at McPherson Playhouse, Victoria, in 1966.

Stage Directing

The Iron Door (based on *The Ode* written by E.J. Pratt): produced by the Play Workshop, Toronto, in 1935.

Within (Bertram Brooker): Produced by the Play Workshop, Toronto, in 1935.

Cabana (Alan Field): produced by the Play Workshop, Toronto, in 1936.

The Dragon (Bertram Brooker): produced by the Play Workshop, Toronto, in 1936.

Romeo and Juliet (Shakespeare): dance-drama produced as part of the Promenade Concert Series sponsored by the University of Toronto at the University of Toronto Varsity Arena in 1936.

Murder in the Cathedral (T.S. Eliot): first produced at Queen's University in 1936; subsequently produced at Massey Hall in 1936.

Plays and Drama Collections Edited

Six Canadian Plays: published by Copp Clark Publishing Company, Toronto, in 1930.

A Book of Plays: published by Macmillan Company of Canada Limited, Toronto, in 1935.

Four Good Plays: published by Longman Canada Limited, Toronto, in 1944.

On Stage: published by Macmillan Company of Canada Limited, Toronto, in 1945.

Murder in the Cathedral: published by Kingswood House and Faber and Faber, Toronto, in 1959.

Four Plays of Our Time: published by Macmillan Company of Canada Limited, Toronto, in 1960.

Drama IV: published by Macmillan Company of Canada Limited, Toronto, in 1965.

Human Values in Drama: published by Macmillan Company of Canada Limited, Toronto, in 1966.

Julius Caesar: published by Macmillan Company of Canada Limited, Toronto, in 1966.

Nobody Waved Goodbye and Other Plays: published by Macmillan Company of Canada Limited, Toronto, in 1966.

Look Both Ways: Theatre Experiences: published by Macmillan Company of Canada Limited, Toronto, in 1975.

Miscellaneous

Numerous articles published in *The Globe, The Dancing Times, Food for Thought, Canada Overseas Reference Book*, and *The Humanities in Canada* (a publication of the Humanities Research Council of Canada).

Secondary Sources

A chapter on Voaden is included in *Stage Voices*, ed. Geraldine Anthony, Doubleday.

An extended taped interview with Voaden was done in 1976 for the Ontario Historical Studies Series and a transcript is on deposit with the Ontario Public Archives.

In Progress

The Book of the Voadens: family history.

Memoirs of his theatre experiences.

Bryan Wade

Born May 29, 1950 in Sarnia, Ontario. During the early 1960's he travels across Canada, supporting himself by a variety of outdoor jobs including logging, tree-planting, and gardening. In 1971, he travels extensively throughout the Middle East and then spends several months in England before returning home.

His first play, *Nightshift*, written during his travels, is produced by Ottawa's Space Tool Company in 1973. In 1974, he completes his Bachelor of Fine Arts degree in creative writing at the University of Victoria. Two years later, he directs *Tanned*, one of his owns plays, at Factory Theatre Lab. He also directs a full-length workshop production of the play in Montreal a year later. Throughout the middle and late 70's, his work is produced by many of Toronto's alternate theatres. A permanent resident of Toronto, he is currently living in Los Angeles where he is completing an M.F.A. in Film and Television at U.C.L.A.

Stage Writing

Nightshift: one act; written in 1971; first published by Playwrights Co-op in 1976 in an anthology along with *Electric Gunfighters* and *Lifeguard*; first produced by the Space Tool Company, Ottawa, in 1973 under the direction of William Lane.

Electric Gunfighters: one act; written in 1972; first published by Playwrights Co-op in 1975 in an anthology along with *Nightshift* and *Lifeguard*; first produced by the Tarragon Theatre, Toronto, in 1973 under the direction of Candace O'Connor; subsequently produced by the Space Tool Company, Ottawa, in 1973 under the direction of William Lane.

Lifeguard: one act; written in 1972; first published by Playwrights Co-op in 1975 in an anthology along with *Nightshift* and *Electric Gunfighters*; first produced by the New Play Centre at the Vancouver Art Gallery, Vancouver, in 1973 under the direction of Pamela Hawthorn.

Aliens: one act; written in 1973; first published by Playwrights Co-op in 1975; first produced by Factory Theatre Lab, Toronto, in 1975 under the direction of David McIlwraith.

Blitzkrieg: "a day in the life of Adolf Hitler and Eva Braun"; one act; written in 1973; first published by Playwrights Co-op in 1974; first produced by the Tarragon Theatre, Toronto, in 1974 under the direction of Eric Steiner.

Alias: one-act comedy "with the Lone Ranger and Tonto"; written in 1974; first published by Playwrights Co-op in 1974; first produced by the University of Guelph in 1975 under the direction of Sidney H. Bryun.

Underground: three acts; written in 1974; first published by Playwrights Co-op in 1975; first produced by Factory Theatre Lab, Toronto, in 1975 under the direction of Eric Steiner; subsequently produced by Penguin Productions, Ottawa, in 1976.

Anti-Gravitational Menopause: one act; written in 1974; first published by Playwrights Co-op in 1974; unproduced.

This Side of the Rockies: two acts; written between 1974 and 1975; first published by Playwrights Co-op in 1977; first produced by Factory Theatre Lab, Toronto, in 1977 under the direction of Eric Steiner.

Breakthrough: a fictional romance dealing with the painter, Tom Thompson; two acts; written between between 1975 and 1976; first produced in a closed workshop at the Stratford Festival in 1976 under the direction of John Van Burek and Eric Steiner; subsequently produced by the NDWT Company, Toronto, in 1978, under the direction of Alan Richardson.

Tanned: one act; written in 1976; first published by Playwrights Co-op in 1976; first produced by Factory Theatre Lab, Toronto, in 1976 under the direction of the author; subsequently produced by City Stage, Vancouver, in 1977 under the direction of Ray Michal.

Tanned: full-length version of the one act play of the same name; three acts; written in 1977; first published by Playwrights Co-op in 1977; first produced as a workshop in Montreal in 1977 under the direction of the author.

Television Plays

A Brief History of the Subject: 30 minutes; written in 1974-75; first produced by CBC-TV Toronto for the national broadcast in 1975.

One of the Beautiful People: 60 minutes; written in 1975 for CBC-TV, Toronto; unproduced.

Something for the Soul: 60 minutes; written in 1976-77 for CBC-TV, Toronto; unproduced.

Marooned: 30 minutes; written in 1977; unproduced.

Film Script

Offside: eight minutes; directed by the author and filmed in black and white on Super-8.

In Progress

Tourists: full-length stage play; suspense thriller set in Toronto.

Outlaws: a television feature set in British Columbia.

Self-Defense: 30-minute film shot and directed by the author.

George F. Walker

Born August 23, 1947, in Toronto. Having graduated from high school, he made his debut as a playwright at the age of 23 after seeing an announcement that a new theatre—The Factory Theatre Lab—was looking for Canadian plays. He writes a two-character piece, *Prince of Naples*, and submits it. From this point on, he is closely associated with Factory Theatre which produces all of his early plays. In 1971 he receives the first of five Canada Council grants which allow him some measure of financial security while pursuing a career as a full-time playwright. A painfully shy and private individual, he says that he has always had "a love-hate" relationship with theatre and feels it has "to be changed a lot." As a playwright, he says his work—if it has a common theme—is obsession, "obsession almost as a way of coping with life and surviving."

In 1973, the Factory brings his play *Bagdad Saloon*, written in London during his first trip abroad in 1972, to the Bush Theatre in London, England. Becoming "removed and introspective" because of the generally weak critical response to his work, he toys with the idea of writing novels and later writes a draft of a naturalistic play called *Decades*. He and Stephanie Staton, his lady during this period, buy a truck and travel to Las Vegas, to California and ultimately to Vancouver. Returning to Toronto in 1975, he writes his next play, *Ramona and the White Slaves*, which is premiered at the Factory in 1976 under Walker's own direction, the first time he has tried his hand at staging a play. He later becomes an associate director at the Factory. The following year, the Factory revives *Beyond Mozambique*. That year also sees the premiere of *Gossip*, the first of his plays to be produced by Toronto Free Theatre. *Zastrozzi*, a gothic comedy, is produced by the same theatre a few months later, winding up as a finalist for the 1977 Chalmers Award for an outstanding play.

In 1978, productions of *Gossip* are seen in Chicago, Seattle and Williamstown, Massachusetts, followed a year later by stagings in Minneapolis and New York. As well, the play enjoys a run at Seattle's Empty Space Theatre and is optioned for production by Joseph Papp of New York's Public Theatre. Also in 1978, he takes over as artistic director of the Factory Theatre when Ken Gass leaves for a sabbatical.

As he tells the *Globe and Mail* in 1977, "Like many of my generation, my mind is like sort of a media garbage bag sometimes. We're all so influenced by television and movies that you don't have to be very perceptive to see it coming out in new plays. The dilemma for me was not to rebel against the problem—it is, after all, a fairly central reality—but to assimilate it and make something of it." In 1978, he tells the Ontario theatre magazine *Scene Changes*, "I'm trying in all my work to walk that fine line between the serious and the comic...we live in chaos and it's difficult to differentiate between the two." He continues to write for the stage and occasionally for radio and television from his home in Toronto.

Stage Writing

Prince of Naples: one-act; written in 1970; first published by Playwrights Co-op,

Toronto, in 1972; subsequently published in *Now in Paperback: Six Canadian Plays of the 1970's* by Fineglow, Toronto, 1973; first produced by Factory Theatre Lab, Toronto, 1971, under the direction of Paul Bettis; later adapted for radio and broadcast by CBC Vancouver in 1973.

Ambush at Tethers' End: two-act; written in 1971; first published by Playwrights Co-op in 1972; subsequently published in *The Factory Lab Anthology* by Talonbooks, Vancouver, in 1974; first produced by Factory Theatre Lab, 1971, under the direction of Ken Gass; later adapted for radio and broadcast by CBC Vancouver, 1974.

Sacktown Rag: two-act; written in 1971; first published by Playwrights Co-op, Toronto, 1972; first produced by Factory Theatre Lab, 1972, under the direction of Ken Gass.

Bagdad Saloon: "a cartoon" in two acts; written in 1972; first published by Playwrights Co-op in 1973; subsequently published by Coach House Press, Toronto, in *Three Plays by George F. Walker*, 1978; first produced by Factory Theatre Lab, 1973, under the direction of Eric Steiner.

Demerit: full-length; written in 1973; unpublished; first produced by Factory Theatre Lab in 1974 under the direction of Ken Gass.

Beyond Mozambique: one act; written in 1974; first published by Playwrights Co-op, 1975; subsequently published by Coach House Press in *Three Plays*, 1978; first produced by Factory Theatre Lab, 1974, under the direction of Eric Steiner with Frances Hyland and Donald Davis starring; subsequently revived by Factory Theatre Lab, 1978, under the direction of the author.

Ramona and the White Slaves: full-length; written in 1976; first published by Coach House Press in *Three Plays*, 1978; first produced by Factory Theatre Lab, 1976, under the direction of the author.

Gossip: two acts; written in 1976; unpublished; first produced by Toronto Free Theatre, 1977, under the direction of John Palmer; subsequently produced at the

Goodman Theatre, Chicago, 1977; produced at the Empty Space Theatre, Seattle, 1978, under the direction of Jeff Steitzer; produced at Williamstown Festival, Massachussetts, 1978, under the direction of David Rotenberg; produced at PAF Playhouse, New York, 1979, under the direction of Peter M. Schifter; produced at the Arts Club Theatre, Vancouver, 1979, under the direction of Brian Richmond.

Zastrozzi: full-length; written in 1976; first published by Playwrights Co-op, 1977; first produced by Toronto Free Theatre, 1977, under the direction of William Lane; subsequently produced by Centre Stage, London, Ontario, 1978; produced by Wakefield Tricycle Theatre at King's Head Theatre, London, England, 1978, under the direction of Ken Schulf; produced at Empty Space Theatre, Seattle, 1979, under the direction of Jeff Steitzer; produced by the Australian Performing Group, 1979.

Filthy Rich: full-length; written in 1978, unpublished; first produced by Toronto Free Theatre, 1979, under the direction of William Lane.

Rumours of Our Death: full-length; written in 1979; first published in Winter 1980 issue of *Canadian Theatre Review*; first produced (as a musical) in 1980 at the Factory Theatre.

Radio Writing

The Private Man: 30 minutes; written in 1972, unpublished; first produced by CBC Halifax in 1973.

Miscellaneous Writing

Sam, Grace, Doug and the Dog: 30-minute television script; written in 1975; first produced by CBC in 1976.

Capital Punishment: a television microdrama; written in 1976; first produced by CBC in 1977.

Overlap: a television microdrama; written in 1976; first produced by CBC in 1977.

In Progress

Curious: a radio play.

Jack Winter

Born April 19, 1936, in Moose Jaw, Saskatchewan. Grows up in Montreal. Enrols in the English Department at McGill University in 1953, graduating with a B.A. in 1957 and an M.A. in 1958. He spends one year teaching English at Collège Militaire Royal de St. Jean in Quebec. He then moves to Ontario to begin his Ph.D. studies at the University of Toronto in English literature. He also teaches at U. of T. for three years and subsequently at York University (1962-1968). From 1963 to 1967 he is resident playwright at Toronto Workshop Productions where his first play, *Before Compiegne*, is produced in 1963. It subsequently wins the *Toronto Telegram* Award for best new Canadian play of the season. Over the next few years he writes *The Mechanic, The Death of Woyzeck, Hey Rube!* (based on T.W.P.'s 1961 production) and *The Golem of Venice*, all for T.W.P. From the mid-60's onward, he writes radio and television scripts for the CBC and in 1968 is hired as a writer for *The Bruno Gerussi Show.* He completes numerous poems and monologues for the radio series over the next four years.

In 1969, the National Arts Centre commissions him to write a play for the Centre's official opening. Entitling the play *Party Day*, he both writes and directs it. An article he writes in Montreal that year receives the Man and his World Award for best newspaper feature of 1969. He writes two plays, *The Centre* and *Waiting*, for government agencies — the first for the Ontario Housing Corporation and the second for the Department of Manpower and Immigration. In 1971, he writes two film scripts, *Selling Out* and *Search for Solutions. Selling Out* is produced by CBC-TV and later released as a short film. In 1972, the film receives a Canadian Film Award as Best Documentary and the following year receives an Academy Award nomination in the Best Short Subject category. Continuing his connection with T.W.P. into the 70's, he completes *Mr. Pickwick* in 1972, *Letters from the Earth* in 1973, and *Ten Lost Years* in 1974. The latter play, based on Barry Broadfoot's book, is

Craft

highly successful, touring the country twice and, under the sponsorship of the Department of External Affairs, is produced at the Holland Festival and at theatres across England and Wales. A Chalmers Award finalist in 1974, *Ten Lost Years* is re-mounted by T.W.P. in 1975 and 1976, and is also produced by CBC-TV. Along with *Ten Lost Years*, two of his other works are produced by T.W.P. in the 1975 season: *You Can't Get Here from There* and *Summer '76.*

In 1977, he moves to England and in 1978 receives a C. Day Lewis Fellowship. A published poet, he gives public readings of his work in universities and concert halls across Great Britain under the sponsorship of the London Poetry Secretariat and the National Poetry Secretariat. He also teaches literature and creative writing in various secondary schools in and around London where he now makes his home. Married and the father of two children, he is a member of the Writers Guild of Great Britain and International PEN. His papers have been collected by McMaster University in Hamilton.

Before Compiegne: full-length drama; written in 1963; unpublished; first produced by Toronto Workshop Productions in 1963 under the direction of George Luscombe; adapted as a 60-minute radio script; first produced by CBC in 1965; winner of the *Toronto Telegram* Theatre Award for Best New Canadian Play of the 1963-64 season.

The Mechanic: full-length drama; written in 1964; unpublished; first produced by Toronto Workshop Productions in 1964 under the direction of George Luscombe.

The Death of Woyzeck (based on the play by George Buchner): full-length drama; written in 1965; unpublished; first produced by Toronto Workshop Productions in 1965 under the direction of George Luscombe.

Hey Rube! (based on T.W.P.'s original 1961 production): full-length circus drama; written in 1966; unpublished; revival first produced by Toronto Workshop Productions in 1966.

The Golem of Venice: full-length drama; written in 1967; unpublished; first produced by Toronto Workshop Productions in 1967 under the direction of George Luscombe; rewritten in 1976; revised version produced by Toronto Workshop Productions in 1972 under the direction of George Luscombe.

Party Day: long one-act; written in 1969; first published by Playwrights Co-op, Toronto, in 1972; commissioned and first produced by the National Arts Centre to celebrate its opening in 1969; directed by the author.

The Wrecked Blackship: one act; written in 1970; first published in *Performing Arts in Canada*, Vol. 7, No. 2, (Summer 1970); rewritten for television and produced by CBC-TV in 1970 under the title *Blackship*.

Who Am I?: one-act play about playwriting written in response to a request by *Performing Arts in Canada* for an article on playwriting; written in 1970; first published in *Performing Arts in Canada*, Vol. 7, No. 4, (Winter 1970).

The Centre: full-length; written in 1971; unpublished; commissioned and first produced by the Ontario Housing Corporation in Sudbury, Ontario, in 1971, under the direction of the author; subsequently produced at Regent Park Theatre, Toronto, in 1972, under the direction of the author.

Waiting: full-length; written in 1972; unpublished; first produced for the Department of Manpower and Immigration, Toronto, 1972, under the direction of the author; subsequently taken on a tour of Ontario; adapted for radio; first produced by CBC in 1973.

Mr. Pickwick (full-length adaptation of Charles Dickens' novel, *Pickwick Papers*): written in 1972; unpublished; first produced by Toronto Workshop Productions in 1972 under the direction of George Luscombe.

Letters from the Earth (full-length adaptation of Mark Twain): written in 1973; unpublished; first produced by Toronto Workshop Productions in 1973 under the direction of George Luscombe; subsequently produced at National Arts Centre, Ottawa.

Ten Lost Years (with Cedric Smith): full-length musical adaptation of the book by Barry Broadfoot; written in 1974; unpublished; first produced by Toronto Workshop Productions in 1974 under the direction of George Luscombe; subsequently taken on a tour of Canada and, under the sponsorship of the Department of External Affairs, taken on a tour of England and Wales and to the Holland Festival; subsequently re-mounted by Toronto Workshop Productions in 1975 and 1976; adapted into a 60-minute television play; first produced by CBC-TV in 1975; Chalmers Award Finalist in 1974.

You Can't Get Here from There: full-length; written in 1975; unpublished; first produced by Toronto Workshop Productions in 1975 under the direction of George Luscombe.

Summer '76: full-length Olympics play; written in 1975; unpublished; first produced by Toronto Workshop Productions in 1975 under the direction of George Luscombe; subsequently taken on a tour of England and Wales under the sponsorship of the Department of External Affairs; re-mounted by Toronto Workshop Productions in 1976.

Radio Writing

Happy Birthday Death!: 30 minutes; written in 1967; first produced by CBC in 1967.

A Saltykov-Shchedrin Sketchbook: 60 minutes; written in 1968; first produced by CBC in 1968.

The Prudent Minnow: 30 minutes; written in 1968; first produced by CBC in 1968.

The Wrecked Blackship: 30 minutes; written in 1969; first produced by CBC in 1969.

The Speaker: 30 minutes; written in 1971; first produced by CBC in 1971.

My Bathurst: 60 minutes; written in 1972; first produced by CBC in 1972.

An Acadian Party: 60 minutes; written in 1973; first produced by CBC in 1973.

The Island: 60 minutes; written in 1973; first produced by CBC in 1973.

Arts and Letters in the G.D.R.: 60 minutes; written in 1974; first produced by CBC in 1974.

Women in the G.D.R.: 60 minutes; written in 1974; first produced by CBC in 1974.

Five Great Days: 60 minutes; written in 1975; first produced by CBC in 1975.

Vern: 30 minutes; written in 1976; first produced by CBC in 1976 under the title *Untimely Death.*

Many poems and monologues written between 1968 and 1972 for the CBC series, *The Bruno Gerussi Show* and *This Country in the Morning.*

Television Writing

Blackship: 30 minutes; written in 1970; first produced by CBC in 1970.

Selling Out: 30-minute film for television; written in 1971; first produced by CBC in 1971; subsequently produced as a 16mm and 35mm educational film; distributed by Encyclopedia Britannica; winner of Canadian Film Award for best documentary in 1972; Academy Award nominee for Best Short Subject in 1973.

Italo: 30 minutes; written in 1974; first produced by CBC in 1974.

The Fifth Sun: 30 minutes; written in 1975; first produced by CBC in 1975.

Tamara's Tapestry World: 30 minutes; written in 1975; first produced by CBC in 1975.

Wild: 30 minutes; written in 1975; first produced by CBC in 1975.

Miscellaneous

Cabaret Canada: writer/performer from 1972 to 1973; wrote three episodes per week for CITY-TV (Toronto) series; also made two single-play recordings as part of the group and performed in live concerts in Vancouver, Montreal, Toronto and Berlin.

Selling Out: 30-minute film; written in 1971; produced by CBC-TV; later released in both 16mm and 35mm, distributed by Encyclopedia Britannica; winner of the award for best documentary film at the 1972 Canadian Film Awards; nominated for an Academy Award in 1973.

Search for Solutions: 30-minute film; written in 1971; produced as a 16mm film and distributed by Ontario Housing Corporation.

Scales: book of poetry; written in 1956; privately published in 1957.

The Island: book of poetry; written in 1972; first published by Fiddlehead Press, Fredericton, in 1973.

Numerous articles and poems published in *Modern Language Quarterly*, *The Canadian Annual Review*, *The Canadian Forum*, *Exchange*, *Toronto Star*, *Toronto Telegram*, *Performing Arts in Canada*, *Earth and You*, *Canadian Jewish Outlook*, *The City: Attacking Modern Myths* (McClelland and Stewart, 1972), *The Second Century Anthologies of Verse: Book Three* (Oxford University Press, 1975), *New Poetry 5* (The Arts Council of Great Britain, 1979), *Country Life Magazine*, *The Times Educational Supplement*.

A collection of Winter's manuscripts, correspondence and personal papers is located in the Mills Memorial Library, McMaster University, Hamilton, Ontario.

Betty Jane Wylie

Born February 21, 1931, in Winnipeg, Manitoba. Her father is a doctor; her mother, a school teacher. In 1951, she graduates from the University of Manitoba with a Bachelor of Arts in French and English. The following year she completes her Master's degree at the same university, majoring in Twentieth Century Poetry and minoring in Anglo-Saxon and Old Norse. In 1962, her first stage work, an adaptation of Ibsen's *An Enemy of the People*, is produced by the Manitoba Theatre Centre. She also writes several puppet plays which are performed under her direction and later shown on television. During this same period she marries William Wylie who later becomes the General Manager of the Manitoba Theatre Centre and eventually General Manager of the Stratford Festival. While in his Stratford position, he dies suddenly at the age of 45.

In 1972, William Hutt directs her play *Mark* at the Stratford Festival. Later, she works in collaboration with Toronto's Theatre Passe-Muraille on a documentary piece — *The Horsburgh Scandal*, produced in 1976. That same year she obtains a grant from the Iowa State Arts Council to assist The Waterloo Iowa Playhouse in their production of her comedy, *Size Ten*. In 1977, her rock opera adaptation of *Beowulf* is produced by the AMAS Repertory Theater Company in New York. She presently lives in Toronto where she does free-lance journalism and continues her theatre writing.

Stage Writing

An Enemy of the People: a three-act Canadian adaptation (set in Saskatchewan) of the play by Henrik Ibsen; written in 1962; unpublished; first produced by the Manitoba Theatre Centre, Winnipeg, 1962, under the direction of John Hirsch; subsequently rewritten and produced at the St. Lawrence Centre, Toronto, in 1970, under the direction of Leonard White.

George Dandin: three-act translation and musical adaptation (set in Manitoba) of the play by Molière with lyrics set to French Canadian folk songs; written in 1962; unpublished; first produced by Manitoba Theatre Centre, Winnipeg, in 1964, under the direction of Robert Sherrin.

Kingsayer: a one-act play for children; written in 1967; first published by Playwrights Co-op, Toronto, in 1978 in the same volume as *The Old Woman and the Pedlar*; first produced by Manitoba Theatre Centre, Winnipeg, in 1967, under the direction of Edward Gilbert; subsequently rewritten and produced by the University of Calgary, Calgary, in 1969, under the direction of Joyce Doolittle.

I See You, I See You: one act; written in 1969; unpublished; first produced by the Stratford Festival Workshop, Stratford, in 1970, under the direction of Clark Rogers; subsequently produced by CBC Radio, Toronto, for the "Stage 70" program for national broadcast.

Mark: two-act drama about a man dying of cancer; written in 1971; first published by Playwrights Canada, Toronto, in 1979; first produced by Stratford Festival on the Third Stage in 1972, under the direction of William Hutt.

The Horsburgh Scandal: two-act musical-drama based on the life of Russell Horsburgh, the United Church minister; written in 1976 in collaboration with Theatre Passe Muraille with music by John Gray; unpublished; first produced by Theatre Passe Muraille, 1976, under the direction of Paul Thompson.

Size Ten: three-act comedy; written in 1975; unpublished; first produced by Waterloo Playhouse, Waterloo, Iowa, in 1976, under the direction of Charles Stilwill.

Beowulf: a rock opera with music by Victor Davies; written in 1975; recorded by Daffodil Records, Toronto, 1975; first produced by AMAS Repertory Theatre Company, New York, 1977, under the direction of Voigt Kempson.

The Old Woman and the Pedlar: a one-act play for children; written in 1976; first published by Playwrights Co-op, Toronto, 1978 in the same volume as *Kingsayer*; first produced by Young People's Theatre, Toronto, 1977, under the direction of Joyce Doolittle.

Double Swap: two acts; written between 1978 and 1979; unpublished; workshopped by Gravenhurst Opera House, Gravenhurst, in 1979, under the direction of the author.

Blind Spot: one-act drama "about four people in an eye doctor's waiting room"; written in 1978; unpublished; workshopped by New Play Centre, Vancouver in 1979 under the direction of Pamela Hawthorn.

Puppet Plays

Don't Just Stand There—Jiggle: seven puppet plays; written in 1979; first published by Black Moss Press in 1980; all first produced by Junior League of Winnipeg.

Miscellaneous

Play With a Tiger: a stage adaptation of the work by Doris Lessing; written in 1970; first produced by CBC Radio, Toronto, 1970, for national broadcast.

Beginnings — A Book for Widows: written between 1976 and 1977; first published by McClelland and Stewart, Toronto, 1977; reprinted in softcover by Canadian Life Insurance Association, 1978.

The Encore Cookbook: first published by McClelland and Stewart, Toronto, 1979.

Betty Jane's Diary: a radio series.

Summer Soap: newspaper serial appearing in *Toronto Star* Monday through Friday in July and August 1979; "about an actress who cleans for a living and falls in love with her Thursday client".

Regular publication of articles and criticism in major Canadian magazines.

In Progress

Androgyne: a stage play "about a girl who disguises herself as a boy in order to try out for the girl's parts in Shakespearean plays"; commissioned by Ontario Arts Council in 1978 for Red Light Theatre, Toronto.

A rewrite of **Size Ten.**

Soap Bubbles: a musical (with composer Victor Davies) for the 1979 summer season of Muskoka Theatre.

The Second Shepherd's Play: a musical adaptation of the Wakefield Mystery play with music by Quentin Doolittle; commissioned by Ontario Arts Council on behalf of Berkeley Studio, in 1980.

A Very Special Person: two-act play with music based on the life of Emily Murphy; (in collaboration with Beth Palmer).

A Place on Earth: one-act play about an old woman living alone in a room, based on the experience recorded in a series of five articles which appeared in the *Toronto Star*, "Old and Alone", December 1979.
A book based on the radio series *Betty Jane's Diary.*

Larry Zacharko

Born July 25, 1950, in Edmonton, Alberta. In 1969, having decided to pursue a career as a writer, he enrols in the University of Alberta's playwriting program. When the program is cancelled, he switches to acting. A folk dancer since his teens, he performs with both Alberta Contemporary Dance Theatre and Orchesis while still at U. of A. In 1973, after completing his B.F.A. in Theatre, he works as an actor at both the Barter and the Studio Theatres in Alberta.

His search for acting jobs takes him to Toronto where he lands the role of Owen in the Actors' Theatre production of James Reaney's *Listen to the Wind.* To supplement his acting income, he works as a supply teacher. This provides the impetus behind his first attempts at playwriting. In order to hold the attention of a class, he begins to write plays to read to them.

His first play, *The Land of Magic Spell*, finds an audience beyond the classroom when produced by Toronto's Young People's Theatre in both 1974 and 1975. He then joins a Tarragon Theatre playwriting workshop which stages his second play, *Maximillian Beetle*, in 1975. The following year the play is given a full-scale

production in Toronto by Young People's Theatre and subsequently taken to Montreal as part of the Arts and Culture Program at the Olympic Games. His third play, *A Knight in Kilometre Country*, is produced in 1975 and re-mounted a year later.

The same year, he collaborates on *I Wanna Die in Ruby-Red Tap Shoes*, a collective creation spoofing Toronto theatre, produced by the NDWT Company. The same company workshops his next play, *Bells, Lockers N' Cans*, the following year. Described by its author as "a high school musical comedy," it is given a full production by North Toronto Collegiate in 1978. This play is published by NDWP, the collective publishing branch of NDWT, the theatre company with which he remains associated. He continues today to write from his home in Toronto. A current play about "how the Calgary Stampede was started" he says, is part of his attempt to "try and educate the East that history didn't stop at the Ontario border."

Stage Writing

Land of Magic Spell: one-act children's play; written in 1973; first published by Simon and Pierre, Toronto, in *A Collection of Canadian Plays*, Vol. 4 in 1975; first produced by Young People's Theatre, Toronto in 1974 under the direction of Arif Hasnain; re-mounted by the same theatre in 1975 under the direction of Alex Dimitriev and Greg F. Rogers.

Maximillian Beetle: one-act children's play; written between 1974 and 1975; first published by Playwrights Co-op, Toronto, in 1977; first workshopped by Tarragon Theatre, Toronto, in 1975, as part of its Writers-in-Residence program; first produced by Young Peoples' Theatre, in 1976, under the direction of Keith Turnbull in Montreal for the Arts and Culture program of the 1976 Olympics.

A Knight in Kilometre Country: one-act children's play; written in 1975; unpublished; first produced by Young Peoples' Theatre in 1975 and 1976 under the direction of Jon Redfern.

I Wanna Die in Ruby-Red Tap Shoes: a collective creation; written 1976; unpublished; first produced by the NDWT Company, Toronto, in 1976.

Bells, Lockers, N' Cans: "a high school musical comedy"; written in 1977; first published by NDWP, a publishing branch of the NDWT theatre company, Toronto, 1979; first workshopped by NDWT in 1977; first produced by North Toronto Collegiate Institute in 1978 under the direction of Paul Robert.

In Progress

TS: a stage play about "how the Calgary Stampede was started."

Yeah, Me Too: a children's play for grades three and four.